PSYCHOTHERAPY WITH CHILDREN
The Living Relationship

Clark E. Moustakas
Center for Humanistic Studies, Detroit

CARRON PUBLISHERS
A Division of Mentor Enterprises, Inc.
826 Ninth Street
Greeley, Colorado 80631

First CARRON PUBLISHERS edition published 1992

ISBN: 0-9634031-0-9

Contents

To Betty Herrington Moustakas, my wife,
who lives within these pages,
particularly in "The Ma"

FOREWORD
Byron E. and Carol Crowell Norton

When a book is written, its purpose is to influence the reader. Dr. Moustakas has influenced a generation of play therapists. This book has meaning that relates to the human presence of a caring individual and how that caring can create empowerment for another through the countenance of the relationship. That acceptance, which is implicit in the relationship, can allow children to experience their own uniqueness and give new meaning to their value of self. Whether we relate to children as parents, teachers or therapists, the basic meaning of engaging the dignity of another is consistent over time. This book is a classic example of how our quality of humanness is our gift to our children. The important aspects of a therapeutic relationship do not change with time. Dr. Moustakas has shared the basic human element of the therapeutic alliance in his work with children. Through this book and the process of play therapy, Dr. Moustakas has shared that which we believe should be shared with child therapists for generations to come. This book is truly a classic in the field of child therapy and especially for children in play therapy.

The work represented in this text is a model of honoring a child through a relationship and that honoring giving identity to the child. A child may not always remember what is said but will never forget how s/he is treated by another. The relationship is the "honoring process" that gives freedom to the individual to experience the conditions of her/his existence. For the child, truth is in the experience. The process of reaching children is honoring the presence of the child as the child chooses to present her/himself. Through Dr. Moustakas' book, we see how caring and honoring children in psychotherapy remains the heart of the change process. One sees how children emerge within the strength of this relationship to share the experiences of their lives. Simply stated, children care about the way they are respected. A therapist may have knowledge of the clinical skills necessary for work with children, but Dr. Moustakas engages the therapist on the "how" of using clinical knowledge. This book exemplifies the validity of children's experiences and the importance of respecting their perceptions. This respect creates an ability in the child to personally confront the pressing experiences that consume the child's potential for perceiving their environment as a place to explore with reassurance that their well-being will remain intact and respected.

Dr. Moustakas has been a guiding example of how to understand children in the context of honoring another's state of being. That respect, in turn, allows the person to move her/his experience toward a more authentic "presence in existence." The person working with children will receive from this book the meaning of the relationship which gives integrity to the child. It is not for us to decide how the human spirit will move but to move toward the rights of the child to express her/his humanness in the unique ways that children express their presence.

Childhood is the creation of the next generation and future generations. By Dr. Moustakas' very sensitive accounts of children we feel the connections between acceptance of children's dignity and the freedom that children gain to risk in their state of being. Now the child can journey toward her/his sense of well-being and eventually the well-being of others.

This classic should be part of every play therapist's evolution. There are few works written on the basic value of children's perceptions in the human experience. Play therapy is a journey through the meaning of a human experience toward the worth and dignity of the child. This book will make that journey more meaningful to the child who enters your playroom seeking a sense of worth and respect that feels so distant and unattainable.

August 1992
Family Psychological Consultants
Greeley, Colorado

Preface

This book grew out of my own necessity to express the nature of my experiences in psychotherapy with children and the related encounters with parents, teachers, and students. As significant episodes occurred in my immediate life as a therapist, an inner sense or desire for expanded self-awareness and understanding brought me to a place of quietude where my thoughts could take form. I began to write and, in writing, to create for myself the basic dimensions of the therapeutic process. Only after searching my own experience and resolving personal resistance to the idea did I come to see that growth within a genuine and fundamental relatedness constitutes the heart of therapy. The alive relationship between the therapist and the child is the essential dimension, perhaps the only significant reality, in the therapeutic process and in all interhuman growth.

I saw that I must stop playing the role of the professional therapist and allow my potentials, talents, and skills, my total experiences as a human being, to blend naturally into the relationship with the child and whenever humanly possible, to meet him as a whole person. Thus I came to realize that one person, a direct, human-loving person, a unified personal and professional self, meets another person, a loving or potentially loving child and through a series of deep human encounters, waits for and enables the child to come to his own self-fulfillment.

Much later I thought of bringing my explorations of significant experiences in therapy into book form. At first, I organized the material to include professional review and statistical research, but Ross Mooney helped me to see that I could cut out the formal talk and aim directly to show the inside of a psychotherapist at work and more importantly, the inside being of the gifted, the handicapped, the frustrated, and the normal child. I chose to present the relationship in therapy in its authentic form through verbatim recordings and to let the reader learn the heart of the matter in his own way.

A theory is developed, but it is not a theory for manipulating others or a map of strategy for outfoxing some child or teacher or parent. It is a theory which requires that the reader open himself to himself and bring

ix

an alive self to his reading. It is a theory which has relevant implications for creative mental health in the guidance clinic, the home, and the school, but which can be understood only if the person can relate himself to it.

The theory presented is associated with one of the basic orientations in work with children—that of relationship therapy, which presents certain contrasts to psychoanalytic therapy. Although in both approaches a relationship between the therapist and child is essential, the nature of the relationship differs and its value is viewed differently. In relationship therapy, the relationship is both means and end. The relationship is the significant growth experience. In psychoanalytic approaches, the relationship is the means through which other goals of therapy are achieved. Client-centered therapy, a significant approach in its own right, comes close to relationship therapy, but here the focus is not on the relationship itself but on the therapist and child as separate individuals, with the therapist making reflections and clarifications, conveying empathic understanding, and having unconditional regard for the client.

A general theoretical background to relationship therapy is available in the works of both Otto Rank and Alfred Adler. The beginning of relationship therapy as a specific philosophy and practice in psychotherapy with children was, however, first introduced and illustrated by Jessie Taft and Frederick Allen. Virginia Axline, following a client-centered approach, provided details of the process and suggested eight basic principles to guide the therapist. More recently, the author presented examples of play therapy with normal children and children faced with temporary anxieties and problems. He made further elaboration of the theory and process.

The present book is a continuation of an examination of the living relationship in psychotherapy with children. There is special emphasis on growth and creativity in psychotherapy, parent counseling, relations with schools, implications of therapy for the home and the school, therapy with the gifted and the handicapped child, and supervision of students who plan to become child therapists. Although the book is primarily the result of my own deliberations and struggles to understand the genuine meanings inherent in my experiences as a psychotherapist with children, parents and teachers, others faced with the same task of understanding the inner life of the child and relating on a fundamental basis may find within these pages the necessary impetus for self-study and self-growth.

January 1959   CLARK MOUSTAKAS

Acknowledgments

A number of persons have participated in bringing this publication into existence. The opportunity to explore my experiences with my colleagues, David Smillie and Dorothy Lee, and with each of my graduate students during the past ten years enabled me to understand more fully the nature of child therapy; suggestions from Ross Mooney helped me to see the way to maintain the essential focus and themes of the book; resources made available by The Merrill-Palmer School and the encouragement and support of Pauline Park Wilson Knapp, director of the school, made it possible for me to experiment and to think through the essential conditions in the therapeutic process and to remain with a child long after others had given up; expert transcription of tape recordings by Deno Moustakas, Elsie Rosak Perry, Ann Hunt, and Doris Anderson provided the basic raw data.

I wish to express my appreciation to the respective publishers for permission to reprint portions of the following references:

Natalie P. Fuchs, "Play Therapy at Home," *Merrill-Palmer Quarterly,* Vol. 3, 1957, portions of text from pages 89-95.

Karen Horney, "Finding the Real Self," *American Journal of Psychoanalysis,* Vol 9, 1949, excerpts from pages 5-6.

Clark Moustakas, "Situational Play Therapy with Normal Children," *Journal of Consulting Psychology,* Vol. 15, 1951, portions of the text from pages 227-230.

Clark Moustakas, *Children in Play Therapy,* McGraw-Hill Book Company, l953, case illustrations from pages 80-100, and pages 208-211.

Clark Moustakas, and Greta Makowsky, "Client centered therapy with parents," *Journal of Consulting Psychology,* Vol. 16, 1952, illustrations and portions of text appearing on pages 339-341.

Clark Moustakas, "Emotional Adjustment and the Play Therapy Process," *Journal of Genetic Psychology,* Vol. 86, l955, case illustrations from pages 79-100.

Martin Buber, *I and Thou,* Translated by Ronald Gregor Smith, Charles Scribner's Sons, 1937, portions of text from pages 4-11.

I
Essential Conditions in Child Therapy

RELATIONSHIP therapy is a unique growth experience created by one person seeking and needing help and another person who accepts the responsibility of offering it. In everyday life we observe what happens naturally to people as they grow and live together. The intensified, consciously structured, growth experience which is therapy can be understood by the same principle and seen as not essentially different from any other life experience in which two people participate in a genuine and fundamental way (14).

A sense of relatedness of one person to another is an essential requirement of individual growth. The relationship must be one in which the person is regarded as an individual with resources for his own self-development rather than as the helpless victim of a neurosis which can be cured only through a dependency relationship. The process of self-growth sometimes involves an internal struggle between dependency needs and strivings for autonomy, but the individual eventually feels free to face himself if he is in a relationship where his human capacity is recognized and cherished and where he is accepted and loved. Then he is able to develop his own quantum in life, to become more and more individualized, self-determining, and spontaneous (46).

In an important exploratory study, Jessie Taft made the first detailed presentation of the process and procedure of relationship therapy with children. She explained the meaning of therapy in the following way: "The word 'therapy' has no verb in English, for which I am grateful; it cannot do anything to anybody, hence . . . [it] represents a process going on, observed perhaps, assisted perhaps but not applied. Therapy comes from the Greek noun servant. The verb is to wait."

The therapist waits for the child to come to terms with himself, to express his difficulties, and to find new ways of relating and living. He waits for the child to be willing to face himself and to develop in accordance with his own individual nature. Waiting is a positive force, a commitment of faith actively expressed by the therapist. This is in direct contrast to the psychoanalytic approach in which the therapist establishes himself as a powerful person as quickly as possible in order to

1

direct the therapeutic process and to involve the child in a dependency relationship.(26) .

In relationship therapy there is a respect for the unique nature of the child. He is never considered or talked about as an "it," as an object for study, but always regarded as a person with individual integrity. The therapist does not view the child in abstractions or from external judgments. He relates with the child in alive, growth experiences. It is this heightened and deepened experience in living which constitutes the heart of therapy (4).

In contrast to analytic therapy where there is a continual examination of the past (32), in relationship therapy the focus is always on the present, living experience. The therapist begins where the child actually is and deals directly and immediately with his feelings rather than with the problems or symptoms and their causes. This gives an immediate impetus and meaning to the therapeutic process. Taft states: "He does not want a father or a mother but he does want someone who will permit him ultimately to find himself apart from parent identifications, without interference or domination; someone who will not be fooled, someone strong enough not to retaliate."

The child may have to regress before he can go on to a creative use of his mature self, but the therapist assists this growth when he is firmly oriented to the growth-inducing values of the immediate experience. The child comes to see the therapist as a symbol of a new reality in the present world. Through this relationship he restores the powers of his individual nature and affirms his real self.

When the therapist holds the focus on the past, he confuses the unique influence he can represent to a child who is trying to use the relationship to become free of the past (4). As Allen explains, "Therapy is an awakening process, but if the waking up is not in the world of immediate reality, of people and events, it is not a waking up but a new medium to continue a dream existence."

In this approach, the therapist listens in order to understand and empathize with the emotionalized expressions of the child. He does not see predetermined sexual symbolism in the child's play nor does he interpret the meaning of the child's play constructions and the content of play. He regards every situation as a unique, living experience which contains its own requirements and its own method or techniques. The only thing the therapist can do for the child is help him gradually to be himself and make creative, responsible use of his capacities and abilities. Although interpretation and explanation are sometimes used in this therapy, it is the child's new experiencing of himself with a person who accepts him as he is that gives clarifying value to these methods. Free verbal expression of the child is encouraged by the therapist, but the value of talking lies less in the particular content and more in the freedom to talk. The child who gains the freedom to talk has gained the freedom to share himself (4).

The Child

At the root of the child's difficulty is the submission and denial of his self. Somewhere along the line of his growth and development, he has given up the essence of his being and the unique patterns that distinguish him from every other person. The growth of the self has been impaired because of his rejection in important personal relationships. He has been severely rejected by others and he has come to reject himself. He is cut off from vital self-resources which would enable him to develop in accordance with his own particular talents.

In every aspect of therapy, the child is encouraged to face himself, to regain touch with his real feelings. The freedom to talk, to express himself, to make decisions, the constant recognition of his self, and the process involved in these experiences enable the child to recover a sense of self-esteem and to restore his powers as a unique individual.

The child will fight any direct attempt to change him because such a plan is a rejection of him as he is. He will resist individuals who try to take away or minimize his world, who tell him his feelings are unreal or inappropriate or distorted. However inadequate or destructive his behavior may seem to others, only if he is accepted as he is and cherished as a lovable, whole person, only if he is free to do what he feels he must do, can the relationship have a significance which enables him to come to be a real self. As paradoxical as it may seem, if he can express his hostility, he may become inwardly tranquil; if he can utter his fears, he may come to feel safe and unafraid; if he tells of his cowardice or inadequacy, he can gain confidence and courage; if he is free to attack and destroy, he is also free to love and cherish and honor. The child comes to realize that he is free to make choices and that valid meanings are attained through his own perceptions of what is real.

Through the relationship the child feels a sense of self and self-value. He feels the warm, human empathy of the adult, and knows that the adult trusts him and believes in him. He comes to regard himself as an important person and to honor his own expressions of self because they belong to him and are congruent with others and with life.

In therapy the child feels the complete, undivided attention of the adult. He senses the concern and the tender, caring attitudes of the therapist. He knows that however severe his feelings are, he will not be depreciated or criticized. He knows that even his deepest fears do not frighten the therapist but provide a basis for a continuing relationship.

When the child regards himself as worthwhile, when he values his contribution to others, he is on the road to the recovery of a self in control, a self which is growing and not involved only in defending and maintaining itself.

The child, through the stimulation and value of the therapeutic relationship, comes to cherish his own way of expressing himself, his own way of living, his own interests and peculiarities.

In therapy, the child expresses convictions and ideas which he recognizes as an integral aspect of his personality, expressions that make him a unique person and differentiate him from every other individual. He no longer doubts himself. He does not fear that he will be criticized, condemned or rejected if he expresses his real feelings and beliefs. He faces himself, grows within, and acts in terms of the person he really is. He knows what he wants and what he wants to do. He is able to initiate projects and to see them through to some conclusion. His own wishes, thoughts, and feelings are healthy expressions and not the product of whim or fancy or a reaction to some real or imagined attack. Value lies within the child and he can use this value in effecting his own growth. Through the process of self-expression and exploration within a significant relationship and through realization of the value within, the child comes to be a positive, self-determining, and self-actualizing individual.

THE THERAPIST

The therapist begins where the child actually is and deals directly and immediately with the child's feelings rather than with his symptoms or problems. The therapist conveys his unqualified acceptance, respect, and faith in the child and the child's potentialities. He conveys these attitudes in many different ways. He encourages the child to make his own decisions, accepting and valuing everything the child does. He listens with complete attentiveness to every expression of the child. He urges the child to explore his thoughts and feelings further. He concentrates with his whole being on what the child is saying or doing. He insists that the child lead the way. He participates in the child's plans, sometimes by playing with him, but more often by following his cues, listening with tenderness and concern, or by watching with a desire to understand. He attempts to see the child as he is and he respects all that he sees. In effect he conveys to the child by his words and feelings: "These are your feelings. These are your ways. You have a right to cherish them because they belong to you. I hold your peculiarities, your loves and your hates, your mannerisms and your habits in esteem and honor as I do all aspects of your self." The therapist considers all the child's ways and values with respect because they are the child's. They have a unique worthiness the moment the child expresses them. In every aspect of the relationship the child is seen as an individual with an ever-present capacity for self-determination. He is regarded as a person who can work out his difficulties, make decisions which will contribute to self-fulfillment, and discover what is best in his own personal reality. The child is encouraged to express his feelings fully, to explore his interests, thoughts, and experiences and to come to a recognition of himself as a loving and lovable person and as a participant and observer in his own growth and development.

Step by step therapist and child share significant experiences and each in his own way comes to new self-insights.

Thus, in this approach to child therapy, the central focus is the emergence of a significant relationship in which the adult maintains a deep concern for the growth of the child, a special interest in his individuality, and an educated talent for sensing, feeling, understanding, examining, and exploring the child's experience with him.

THE SETTING

The setting for relationship therapy is usually a playroom. The toys and materials form a part of this setting and to some extent influence the nature and content of the child's play. A variety of play materials are used.

Sand, water, paints, and clay are among the most frequently used items. The unstructured nature of these materials makes it possible for the child to use them in a way that enables him to express and release tense, pent-up feelings. As Buhler (14) has indicated, it is possible for unstructured material to be deformed, amassed, spilled, spread, molded, combined, torn apart, brought into shape, or destroyed. It is also possible for the child to organize the material in such a way that significant interpersonal situations are recreated. The unstructured items seem particularly valuable in the early phases of therapy because they allow the child to express his attitudes in an indirect and diffused way when he is not ready to face his feelings openly.

Structured items such as guns, knives, swords, darts, and puncho the comeback toy are frequently used by children to express hostility. Children find these materials appropriate because they can use them to express strong aggression in socially acceptable ways. Children with disturbing problems, and particularly boys, eventually express their most severe feelings through shooting, stabbing, punching, cutting, and attacking and killing in other ways.

Family dolls, puppets, and other items representing human figures are essential because they provide a basis for direct expression of feelings. Frequently these are used by children who wish to play through family crises and conflicts in a direct way. Fears, anger, sibling rivalry, and other feelings can be directly expressed while the child manipulates in play dramas and play activities the various significant individuals in his life. Solomon (45) has suggested that a great deal of therapeutic movement can be realized when the therapist actively introduces into the play situation a doll representing himself.

Items such as cars, trucks, tractors, checkers, paper, pencils, and boats are important because the child uses them to play games and to participate in noncommittal activities until he is ready to express his feelings either indirectly and diffusely through the nonhuman items or directly through the family and other human figures.

By no means is the setting or atmosphere determined solely by the play materials and equipment or space. The atmosphere or emotional climate emerges from a combination of factors including the attitudes of the therapist and the personal interaction between therapist and child.

The emotional climate of the playroom holds a vital meaning for the child. The playroom becomes *his* place and because it is his place, it is where he belongs.

The materials and the attitudes of the therapist are consistent and stable aspects of the therapeutic process. The playthings are arranged in the same way each time the child enters the room. The therapist remains a constant source of strength and support for the child. Outside the playroom, the child lives in a changing world where others make the changes, but in the playroom, he is the guide. If any changes are made, he makes them.

In the playroom, the child eventually feels a sense of relatedness and harmony in all that he sees. He is at one with his environment. He feels the pure aspects of the setting, the absence of preconceived standards, expectations, and pressures, the lack of prejudice or bias. In the positive sense, he perceives the constant tenderness of feeling, the profound respect for him and the honoring of him by the therapist. There is a reverence for everything he says and does. A sense of tranquillity is felt by the child. Although he may be disturbed and agitated, an atmosphere of peacefulness and quietude surrounds him and gradually enters into his private world of perception. Outside the playroom there is a busy, moving, goal-directed world, but in the playroom there is a constant sense of peace. Even when the child is actively at play and noisily expressing himself he recognizes the calm atmosphere. He is often keenly aware of outside movements and sounds.

The atmosphere of harmony, tranquillity, and human relatedness makes the playroom a precious place to the child and enables him to feel a sense of fitting and belonging. He knows there is a pure valuing of him, that he has an intrinsic and inviolate claim to respect. These dimensions of tranquillity, harmony, and reverence are often verbalized by children. Not uncommon are such remarks as "It's always so quiet in here, not like outside"; "This playroom is mine—do other children come here too?"; "When I come here I do whatever I want"; "I have these things at home but it's here that I like to play with them"; "You always listen when I talk"; and "You're not like a doctor but like my family. This is my other home."

The child comes into a relationship with the play materials, a relationship which is not unlike the warmth, comfort and protectiveness he feels when he holds or sleeps with his blanket or some other precious possession. No person can give the child what he experiences in a relationship with a toy or play material. It is an inward warmth and safety which he feels, an inseparable relationship that makes him want to possess the item. Misako Miyamoto, a psychologist from Japan who spent several months observing many different children in play therapy at the Merrill-Palmer School, wrote, in a personal communication:

> Through the observations of the sessions, I have unexpectedly felt the same atmosphere between the tea room in the Japanese Tea Ceremony and the playroom. It has given me a great impression. When the atmosphere of the playroom is in a state of good, the therapist and child relate with harmony, reverence, purity and tranquillity. There is a continuing sense of relatedness and mutuality throughout the experience. The playroom becomes a sanctuary from the vexations of the outer world. This atmosphere is not only between therapist and child but also includes the room, toys, and everything. In such a state the child uses the toys with respect. He knows the real meaning and purpose of a thing and relates to it positively. The thing is no longer material but comes into contact with the child. He touches it and comes into a relationship with it. If he does not accept the thing, he does not use it with any real meaning. In this case he does not respect it. If a child destroys a doll, a doll is not re-

spected as a real meaning. If he uses a doll in its proper sense, truthfully, the sense of doll becomes alive in his mind, and "respect" exists between the child and the doll. So I think respect exists in the whole atmosphere if a situation is good.

It is because the playroom becomes that other world of constant peace and harmony free of external and extraneous elements where the child is revered as a precious person that the child treasures his experience, expresses himself, and develops his powers and skills as a human being.

STRUCTURING THE RELATIONSHIP

During the early phases of therapy, structuring is an important process. The child is introduced to the playroom and the permissive nature of the situation is conveyed to him. Through the structuring statements of the therapist, the child gains an understanding of the therapeutic relationship and the nature of his freedom and responsibility.

The therapist may use expressions such as the following: "In here you are free to do what you want"; "I would rather know what your opinion is"; "This is your time and place"; "What you say here is between us—not anyone else's affair"; "I can't decide for you; the only thing that matters is that you decide for yourself"; "You want me to tell you what to do and I say it's up to you to decide"; "You want me to do that for you but here you do things for yourself"; "This is your project. I cannot manage it for you"; "You must see it through"; "I understand. It's not so easy to work it. Perhaps I can help by giving you a start. Then I think you can finish on your own." The therapist may offer information, or point out possibilities the child has not seen, or even offer help when it is absolutely necessary, but his constant attitude is that the child can use his own capacities and skills and can take full responsibility for his actions and decisions. The structuring statements aid the child in becoming aware of himself, in facing his inner conflicts, and in working through painful, negative self-attitudes. They give recognition to the child's self and help him to come to terms with himself and to bring to expression his own real feelings, thoughts, choices, and wishes.

SETTING OF LIMITS

One of the most important aspects of relationship therapy is the setting of limits. Without limits there could be no therapy. Limits define the boundaries of the relationship and tie it to reality. They remind the child of his responsibility to himself, the therapist, and the playroom. They offer security and at the same time permit the child to move freely and safely in his play. They help to make the playroom experience a living reality.

A time limit is a dimension of child therapy. The therapist indicates this limit briefly at the end of each session. He lets the child know when he has only a few minutes left to play. Then at the end of the session, he says, "I see that our time is up for today. We'll have to stop now."

There are limits too in the use of materials. For example, they are ordinarily used only in the playroom. "I know you want to take that home but you have to use it here," is one way of setting the limit while at the same time recognizing the child's feelings. Certain expensive or irreplaceable items usually may not be destroyed.

Generally, the child is not permitted to abuse physically the therapist or his clothing. "You really want to smear me with paint, but that is one thing I cannot let you do here."

If the child decides to leave before a session has ended, he is usually not permitted to return to the playroom on that day. "You can go now if you want; it's up to you. If you go, though, I cannot let you come back today." There are also a few health and safety limits. The therapist might say, "It would be fun to smash that bottle against the wall, but I can't let you do that"; or "Billy and Jack, you may play with the sand in other ways, but you may not throw it in each other's faces."

Limits may be thought of as the requirement inherent in the realities of a therapeutic situation. Without them, the child would be forced to move in threatening and unfamiliar areas which might unnecessarily stimulate anxiety and arouse guilt. The therapist would feel unnecessary discomfort and anxiety. Externally induced feelings create a barrier and seriously threaten the relationship.

In most instances, children accept the limits but occasionally a child insists on breaking them. The therapist must then decide what to do to enforce a limit. He may place a toy or area of the room out of bounds, or stand by the child and repeat the limit, or hold the child a few minutes. Whatever the therapist does, he must continue to help the child feel accepted even though he cannot be permitted to do certain things.

It is partly through these processes of structuring and setting of limits that therapy becomes more than just a theoretical postulate. It becomes a warm, practical, living experience which enables the child to live freely and fully and enables a relationship between two persons to deepen and grow.

THE MEANING OF THE LIMIT IN THE RELATIONSHIP

Limits exist in every relationship. The human organism is free to grow and develop within the limits of its own potentialities, talents, and structure. In psychotherapy, there must be an integration of freedom and order if the individuals involved are to actualize their potentialities.

The limit is one aspect of an alive experience, the aspect which identifies, characterizes, and distinguishes the dimensions of a therapeutic relationship. The limit is the form or structure of an immediate relationship. It refers not only to a unique form but also to the possibility for life, growth and direction rather than merely to a limitation. Because a significant relationship in therapy always involves growth, as new experiences occur, patterns emerge which require that limits be established. When limits grow out of a unique reality, they represent, not limitations, but the positive presence of a substance which makes a particular relationship distinct from every other relationship. A relationship can only be what it emerges into in experience. A starfish cannot be a starfish without the particular limited form which identifies it as a starfish. It can develop as a starfish and use its capacities only within its own defined structure.

In a therapeutic relationship, limits provide the boundary or structure in which growth can occur. They are as existential and meaningful as the inherent requirements of a situation. The therapist does not know in advance which limits must be established. Every experience is unique. Every child is unique. Every therapist is unique each time he meets a child. The therapist, though a consistent person with substance and strength, is also a person coming to be. Who he is in a relationship depends to a significant degree on the unique dimensions of that specific, developing relationship. This means that a limit set with one child may not be set with another. Every limit depends upon the given nature of the two individuals involved. Restrictions set by individuals outside the situation or out of obligations, "shoulds," or preconceived standards, expectations, or goals or by anything external or extraneous are not limits at all but limitations, blocks, and deterrents to growth. Such limitations are not living realities but ideas, abstractions, and rationalities which get in the way of seeing, understanding, accepting, and growing within the organic limits of life.

I can be free to live as a growing, human being if I can accept my own being with its limited form which identifies me as a unique person and is the basis for my own growth and development. In psychotherapy with children, I must usually limit the child when he tries to attack or punish me physically not only because he suffers inwardly when he hurts another human being, not only because he often attacks me most severely when he is afraid of loving me, but also because of who I am at any given moment in life. I cannot continue to be if I do not accept the fact that I hurt when I am severely attacked, that I can bear only so much pain without losing myself. Unless I recognize and accept this as a fact of my being, I cannot continue to relate as a person.

THE BROKEN LIMIT

Frequently limits arise which create a struggle between the therapist and child, limits which toss the relationship into the depths of hostility or despair and create issues and controversies. Some final limit must emerge and be maintained or the relationship is seriously impaired. The therapist must continue to be there living through the experience with the child. He must share the experience with him, perhaps even suffer with him, while at the same time express a fundamental valuing and love. Even when the child wishes to kill him, he must stand by with the same degree of respect for the child, with the same determination to help him develop in a positive sense. It may be necessary to face him with all his destructiveness, to face his accumulated fury and murderous impulses with understanding, to comfort and support him while at the same time hold to the requirement which has been set. It is easier to remove the child or give in to him than to plunge into an unknown journey. It is safer to respond with old patterns than to explore uncertain feelings and an untested process. It is more comfortable to remain on the edge of a real relationship than to enter it fully. It is sometimes an extremely complex and painful process to live with an enraged child in the full human sense long enough to help him discover within himself the talents and possessions which are really his, the possibilities for positive relatedness, for love and tenderness, for self-examination and self growth.

From the experiences of a shared life (however turbulent these may be), the deepest roots of a relationship are established giving structure and substance to the growing selves of child and adult. In a sense, the child's rejection of a painful limit is an ultimate point in his experience. From here there is only one way to go. He can only move in a forward direction.

When I set a limit in psychotherapy it is an aspect of my being, an expression of who I am at a particular moment in time. It is my limit, a boundary of me. When the child accepts the limit, a bond is formed between us. The limit is then a structure or boundary of our relationship. It is a reality held in a relationship, not an isolated expression of the individual personalities of therapist or child. The child confirms me and together we accept a structure through which our relationship can develop.

When the child rejects or breaks the limit it is not a reality of a relationship. It is a boundary held by the therapist alone which no longer has an alive meaning in a particular relationship. It is a pattern the therapist has established which is not confirmed, not completed. No bond is formed. No structure exists. The therapist literally does not know who he is in the relationship. He can withdraw, end the contact, and refuse to participate in an unknown process. Or he can perceive the situation, the issue, the dispute, and the conflict as an opportunity to face the child freshly and to participate in a new dimension of experience.

When the therapist decides to terminate the session because a limit has been broken, he will not discover what it means to live with a child who refuses to be denied. He will not know what it is to enter fully as a human being into an emotional dispute or controversy and to see it through to some positive solution.

The therapist who ends the session and removes the child loses touch with a vital aspect of himself and denies his own possibility for learning and growth. He is unable to continue to face the child, to live with him in this moment of great suffering. He sends him away and thus loses him in his greatest need, when love, support, and understanding count the most. He is unable to work through the issue or controversy to a creative solution. He rejects the child and expects him to return to face the therapist. He requires the child to take the first step to restore the relationship.

There is another way. The limit has been broken but the child remains. The therapist can set a new limit, and another if necessary, until bedrock is reached, until an ultimate limit, a true dimension of an unfolding relationship is established and held. Only this final limit is a reality. It becomes the boundary through which a relationship can grow and from which the child can face his fear and anger. Thus the child's breaking of the limit can be regarded as a source of strength, as the possibility for the discovery of a new reality and for the positive development of a personal relationship.

The broken limit in two relationships in psychotherapy is illustrated in the following examples.

TIM

When I first saw Tim, age 5, I immediately noticed the way he was dressed. He wore short jersey pants considerably above the knees and high white shoes. He buried his face in his mother's coat and refused to face me. I remarked that the playroom was ready and we could go downstairs if he wished to play. He pulled at his mother's coat. I explained that his mother could accompany him but would return upstairs to wait until we were finished playing. Tim held his mother's hand tightly all the way down but as soon as we entered, he rushed to the easel, saying, "I wanta paint." His mother cautioned him, "The doctor wants you to put an apron on." Trying to maintain a positive approach, while at the same time feeling caught in the middle, I said to Tim, "I think, Tim, that what your mommy means is that she wants you to have the apron on because she's afraid you'll get paint on your clothes." In this first session, Tim's mother stayed twenty-five minutes, following Tim in every activity and cautioning him each step of the way. When he showed the slightest anger or tendency to rebel, she got him interested in something else or told him he was a big boy and should act like one. Finally, she said to Tim, "Timmy, Mommy has to go make a telephone call; is it all right?" Tim responded immediately, "Yes." His mother continued, "I won't be gone long. You won't worry about me, will you?" "No." "You won't miss me, will you?" "No." "You won't cry while I'm away, will you?" "No." Five minutes later, his mother left.

Tim returned to an activity his mother had directed him away from. He began to squeeze finger paints out of plastic tubes. The paint streamed out all over several scraps of wood. When he got some paint on his hand, he seemed utterly repelled. He moved away quickly, throwing down the tube. He rushed out the door to wash his hands. As he did so he bumped into his mother, who had not gone to make a phone call but had been listening outside the door. She was shocked suddenly meeting Tim face to face. She shouted, "What are you doing out here?" Tim did not answer. He washed his hands and returned to the playroom. The time was about up. I set my first limit with him, saying, "In a short while, we'll have to leave." The following conversation took place:

TIM: No, I'm going to stay.

MR. MOUSTAKAS: I can see you're not ready to stop but we have only so much time to be here, and when that time is up, we must leave.

TIM: My mommy can play with me.

MR. M.: I know your mommy can play with you, but I must close the room.

TIM: I'm not going.

MR. M.: You are determined to stay, but I must ask you to leave soon.

TIM: I'm going to tell my mommy; she'll come and play with me.
MR. M.: I guess she would, but not here. When you walk out the door I'm turning off the lights and closing the room.

Tim left to get his mother. He shouted to her, "Come down and play with me." This time she did not evade the issue or make excuses to him. "It is not my room, Tim. If the doctor says we must go, then we'll have to leave." I remarked to Tim that I'd see him again the following week. He seemed about to protest but left, somewhat reluctantly, with his mother.

For the second session, he was willing to come alone, but his mother was unable to separate from him. She followed us down to the playroom. This time she remained in the room about ten minutes. Tim repeated the activities of the previous week. He was extremely orderly and carried out certain rituals repeatedly. He was particularly anxious about getting sand or paint on himself. Toward the end of the session, I again mentioned that there were only a few minutes left to play. The following conversation occurred:

TIM: I'm going to play longer today.
MR. M.: You'd like to stay, but in a while we'll both have to leave.
TIM: Mommy can play with me.
MR. M.: Yes, she can. Upstairs, at home, in many places but not here in the playroom.
TIM: This isn't your house. I'm not going.
MR. M.: You say you're not, but I say you are.
TIM: You're a bad boy. My daddy will come and beat you up. (*Tim's father left the family when he was a baby.*)
MR. M.: I won't let you stay, so you want to hurt me.
TIM: My mommy will smash your face. Then my mommy and I will stay here all night. This will be our home. We'll never leave.
MR. M.: I see.
TIM: I hate you. I'm going to kill you.
MR. M.: I understand.
TIM: You're mean. You're a nasty man. (*Tim's body begins to shake. Tears fall slowly down his face.*) I'm going to hit you.
MR. M.: If you feel you must hit me, then I guess you must. (*Tim raises his arm to slap me but he stops in midair. There is terror in his face, and his arm freezes. He stands in this position crying for several minutes. He wants to strike me but seems paralyzed.*)
MR. M.: It's all right, Tim. I know. (*His hand barely touches my face. He draws away.*)
TIM: Shame on you. You do messes in your pants. You're a nasty boy.
MR. M.: You think everything about me is nasty and good-for-nothing.
TIM: My mommy will come and play with me and stay here and we'll never leave. I'm going to tell her now you're bad. You'll see, she'll come. This will be our home.
MR. M.: I understand how much you want to have her here, but when you walk out the door I'll close the room and you won't be able to come back until next week.

Tim left. He screamed for his mother, telling her that I was bad and nasty and asking her to kill me. She told him he ought to be ashamed, that I'm a gentle man. He protested, saying, "He does messes in his pants. Shame on him." His mother told him to stop, "Everyone is laughing at you." Tim looked out the window, crying harder, "I don't see anyone." His mother laughed shrilly, "They're looking all right, from their office windows and from cars. They're all laughing at you even though you can't see them." Tim covered his face with his hands. His mother repeated, "Shame on you." He went to a corner wall, raised his hands in the air. His body seemed racked in pain. He sobbed uncontrollably. I approached him, "Tim, as far as I'm concerned there's nothing to be ashamed of. You have every right to say what you are saying to me. I must leave now but I'll see you next week." Tim stopped crying. He took his mother's hand and they walked out of the building.

COMMENTS

As difficult as it was to see Tim suffer so, to see the sickness in his relationship with his mother unfold before me, to see Tim's mother trapped, ashamed, and humiliated, it was the first time we had really met as one person with another person. I had to hold fast in the face of his disorganization, to stand by maintaining my position, not only because significant roots of our relationship were being formed and a consistency and strength were being established but also because it gave him an opportunity to bare his "wicked shameful" self before me, to project onto me his "badness" and "shame," and to express his feeling that, as far as others were concerned, he was better off dead.

BRIAN

Brian had been coming for weekly therapy sessions for almost a year when his intense feeling of love and hate reached a peak. For three months, each experience had begun with a sword and gun battle between us. He screamed with delight each time he "pierced or cut" me, each time he shot and killed me. When these battles were first initiated we had agreed to keep them within a ten-minute time limit. Following the battle with me, he would proceed to shoot and kill all human and animal figures in the room. He would take a rifle and scrape to the floor all items on tables and the tops of cabinets. Often he would open the plastic paint containers and place them at the edge of a shelf. He would shoot at the containers until the paint sprayed against the walls and onto the floors. This barrage and hostile attack had been repeated in similar pattern for thirteen weeks. Then one day we faced each other on a different interpersonal level.

The usual ten-minute battle had been completed but Brian refused to stop. He decided to use me as a target for what he called "bow and arrow" practice. I explained that there were items in the room that he could use but that I would rather not be his target. The following conversation took place:

MR. M.:   Brian, I have already explained I do not want to be used as a target. (As *I express my feeling, Brian shoots again, this time hitting my arm.*)

MR. M.:   Brian, that hurt. Perhaps that's what you want—to hurt me. *(Brian is about to shoot again.)*

MR. M.:   No, Brian. I will not permit it again. I'm going to have to insist that you give me the bow and arrows. I do not intend to let you shoot me again. *(Brian laughs nervously with a sadistic glee in his voice. He tries to pull away but I hold the bow firmly. He drops the arrows.)*

MR. M.:   I'll just put these out of reach for the rest of this hour. You can play with them again next time you come. *(Brian throws the bow at me. I pick it up and remove it. He picks up a pistol, gun belt, and knife and throws them at me with much force. I go over to him and hold his arms.)*

MR. M.:   I can see nothing will satisfy you until you've hurt me. You're determined to have it your way, but I'm just as determined not to be a target for your attacks. If you persist I'm going to have to make all these things out of bounds for the rest of the time. *(Brian laughs in my face as I talk to him. He pulls away.)*

BRIAN: You never let me do anything. All you ever think of is No! No! No!

MR. M.:   Yes, I know. You think I stop you at every turn.

BRIAN: *(Throws a container of paint at me.)* I hate you.

MR. M.:   You have every right to hate me but I will not permit you to throw things at me. For the rest of this time this entire section of the playroom is out of bounds. *(Brian is infuriated. He glares angrily at me. His eyes focus on the blackboard, a cunning look crosses his face, and a sneering smile.)*

BRIAN: Will you play tic-tac-toe with me?

MR. M.:   Yes, if you'd like me to, but I saw your thought. I know what you intend doing. If you throw one more item at me I'm going to have to do something drastic. *(The game begins. Suddenly Brian begins laughing wildly. He throws the chalk and eraser at me. He tries to run to the "out-of-bounds" area. I block his path. He picks up a pile of books and throws them.)*

MR. M.:   All right, Brian. Everything in the room is out of bounds for the rest of this time. You may have only this small space here. We can sit and talk or just sit.

BRIAN: You can't make me stay in this part.

MR. M.:   Oh, yes, I can. We've reached a point now where this is the only place we have. *(Pause.)*

BRIAN: I hate you. *(Pause.)* I could kill you.

MR. M.:   Yes, you really want to hurt me the way you feel I have hurt you. *(Brian slaps me.)*

MR. M.:   I now must hold your arms. *(Suddenly Brian completely relaxes. He lays his head on my shoulder.)*

BRIAN: You never let the baby have his bottle.

MR. M.:   You always had to cry and throw things before you were fed.

BRIAN: I want my bottle.

MR. M.:   Would you like me to rock you? *(Sitting together quietly on the floor, the therapist rocks Brian a few minutes. Brian becomes tense again.)*

BRIAN: I hate you. I could kill you. *(Brian begins spitting. I turn him around.)*

MR. M.:   It's as hard for me to have to hold you as it is for you to be held. I know you are doing what you feel you must, but we have reached a point now where I am also doing what I feel I must. *(Brian screams and laughs shrilly.)*

MR. M.:   It's time to leave now, Brian. Do you want to walk out by yourself or do you want me to take you out?

BRIAN: I'll go myself. *(Brian walks toward the door. As he reaches it, he picks up several items and throws them at me. He comes toward me and pushes and punches at me. I take him and pull him out the door.)*

MR. M.:   I realize, Brian, you couldn't hold to your decision. It's all right. *(Brian begins to cry silently.)*

BRIAN: I hate you and I never want to see you again.

MR. M.:   But I want to see you again. I'll be here at the same time next week. *(Brian leaves.)*

COMMENTS

This was a full, vital, complete experience of two persons, involving much struggle, suffering, and pain, but also a definite growth experience. The limits were important not only because they provided a structure or form in which self-exploration could occur but also because they emerged within a situation where child and therapist faced each other as whole beings and lived through a significant controversy, forming deep ties between them and the roots of a healthy relationship.

Tim and Brian both returned. Each child greeted me with a new feeling of intimacy and relatedness. The dispute over the broken limit had affected the nature of their experiences in psychotherapy. Each child plunged into new areas of conflict and emotionalized expression. For the first time in his life, Tim learned to live with another person, to accept himself, and to regard the limits inherent in the situation as facilitating and enhancing rather than as impeding and denying. Having lived through a significant controversy with his therapist and having met his therapist as a person, Brian was able to verbalize his feelings of self-doubt, to say that his parents considered him a "bad," destructive child, and to relate directly a number of crucial experiences in which he had been severely denied as a self. Thus, in spite of the apparent breach, child and therapist formed deep ties between them which enabled the child to develop a sense of self and the freedom of real self-expression.

REFERENCES

1. Adler, Alfred. *The Case of Miss R.* New York: Greenberg, 1929.

2. ————. *The Neurotic Constitution.* New York: Dodd, Mead, 1930.

3. ———. *Understanding Human Nature*. New York: Greenberg, 1927.
4. Allen, Frederick H. *Psychotherapy With Children*. New York: Norton, 1942.
5. Alpert, Augusta. The Treatment of Emotionally Disturbed Children in a Therapeutic Nursery. *Amer. J. Orthopsychiat.*, 25, 826-832, 1955.
6. Amster, Fanny. Differential Uses of Play in Treatment of Young Children. *Amer. J. Orthopsychiat.*, 13, 62-68, 1943.
7. Ansbacher, Heinz, and Rowena Ansbacher. *The Individual Psychology of Alfred Adler*. New York: Basic Books, 1956.
8. Axline, Virginia M. Entering the Child's World Via Play Experiences. *Progr. Educ.*, 27, 68-75, 1950.
9. ———. *Play Therapy*. Boston: Houghton Mifflin, 1947.
10. ———. Play Therapy Procedures and Results. *Amer. J. Orthopsychiat.*, 25, 618-626, 1955.
11. Baruch, D. W. Doll Play in Pre-School as an Aid in Understanding the Child. *Ment. Hyg.*, 24, 566-577, 1940.
12. Bettelheim, Bruno. *Love Is Not Enough*. Glencoe, Illinois: Free Press, 1950.
13. ———. *Truants from Life*. Glencoe, Illinois: Free Press, 1955.
14. Buhler, Charlotte. Science Contributor: Play Therapy. *Child Study*, 4, 115-116, 1941.
15. Cohn, Hanna. A Field Theory Approach to Transference and Its Particular Application to Children. *Psychiat.*, 18, 339-352, 1955.
16. ———. Play as a Means of Communication Between Child and Adult in Three Cases. *J. Child Psychiat*, 2, 100-112, 1951.
17. Conn, J. H. The Child Reveals Himself Through Play. *Ment. Hyg.*, 58, 1199-1214, 1939.
18. ———. Play Interview Therapy of Castration Fears. *Amer. J. Orthopsychiat.*, 25, 747-754, 1955.
19. Davidson, Audrey, and Judith Fay. *Phantasy in Childhood*. New York: Philosophical Library, 1953.
20. Despert, J. Louise. Play Therapy—Remarks on Some of Its Aspects. *Nerv. Child*, 7, 287-295, 1948.
21. Dorfman, Elaine. Play Therapy. In Carl R. Rogers (Ed.), *Client-Centered Therapy*. Boston: Houghton Mifflin, 1951.
22. Eissler, Ruth S., Anna Freud, Heinz Hartmann, and Ernst Kris (Eds.). *The Psychoanalytic Study of the Child*. Vol. XI. New York: International Universities Press, 1956.
23. Erikson, Erik H. *Childhood and Society*. New York: Norton, 1950.
24. Fraiberg, Selma. Applications of Psychoanalytic Principles in Casework Practice with Children. *Quart. J. Child Behavior*, 3, 250-275, 1951.
25. Frank, Lawrence K. Play in Personality Development. *Amer. J. Orthopsychiat.*, 25, 576-590, 1955.
26. Freud, Anna. *The Psycho-Analytical Treatment of Children*. London: Imago, 1946.
27. Gillis, Emily P. Therapy Dramatics for the Public School Room. *Nerv. Child*, 7, 328-336, 1948.

28. Hambidge, Gove, Jr. Structured Play Therapy. *Amer. J. Orthopsychiat.*, 25, 601-617, 1955.
29. Jackson, Lydia, and Kathleen M. Todd. *Child Treatment and the Therapy of Play.* London: Methuen, 1946.
30. Karpf, Fay B. *The Psychology and Psychotherapy of Otto Rank.* New York: Philosophical Library, 1953.
31. Kimmel, Mary-Anne R. The Use of Play Techniques in a Medical Setting. *Soc. Casework,* 33, 30-34, 1952.
32. Klein, Melanie. *The Psycho-Analysis of Children.* London: Hogarth Press, 1932.
33. ————. The Psychoanalytic Play Technique. *Amer. J. Orthopsychiat.*, 25, 223-237, 1955.
34. ————. Paula Heinmann, and Roger Money-Kyrle (Eds.). *New Directions in Psychoanalysis.* New York: Basic Books, 1956.
35. Mann, Lester. Persuasive Doll Play: A Technique of Directive Psychotherapy for Use With Children. *J. Clin. Psychol.,* 13, 14-19, 1957.
36. Miller, Helen E. Play Therapy for the Institutional Child. *Nerv. Child,* 7, 311-317, 1948.
37. Moustakas, Clark E. *Children in Play Therapy.* New York: McGraw-Hill, 1953.
38. ————, (Ed.). *The Self.* New York: Harper, 1956.
39. Newell, H. Whitman. Principles and Practices Used in Child Psychiatric Clinics. *Quart. J. Child Behavior,* 4, 57-65, 1952.
40. Rank, Otto. *Truth and Reality and Will Therapy.* New York: Knopf, Inc., 1936.
41. Redl, Fritz, and David Wineman. *Controls From Within.* Glencoe, Illinois: Free Press, 1952.
42. Reymert, M. L. Play Therapy at Mooseheart. *J. Exceptional Children,* 13, 2-9, 1946.
43. Slavson, S. R. Play Group Therapy for Young Children. *Nerv. Child,* 7, 318-327, 1948.
44. Solomon, Joseph C. Play Technique and the Integrative Process. *Amer. J. Orthopsychiat.,* 25, 591-600, 1955.
45. ————. Play Technique as a Differential Therapeutic Medium. *Nerv. Child,* 7, 296-300, 1948.
46. Taft, Jessie. *The Dynamics of Therapy in a Controlled Relationship.* New York: Macmillan, 1933.
47. Walden, R. The Psychoanalytic Theory of Play. *Psychoanal. Quart.,* 2, 208-224, 1933.
48. Witmer, Helen. *Psychiatric Interviews With Children.* New York: Commonwealth Fund, 1946.
49. Woltmann, Adolf G. Concepts of Play Therapy Techniques. *Amer. J. Orthopsychiat.,* 25, 771-783, 1955.

2

The Therapeutic Process

IN the therapeutic situation, children, whether disturbed or "adjusted," tend to express similar types of negative attitudes in their play. They reflect fear and anger toward parents, siblings, and other significant individuals in their lives. They sometimes show anxiety in connection with cleanliness and orderliness, or regress in speech, thinking, eating, toileting, and motor behavior.

Children labeled as well adjusted and those considered disturbed differ in the frequency and intensity with which they express negative attitudes (9). In "well-adjusted" children, negative attitudes are expressed less often, with less intensity, and with more focus and direction. In disturbed children, negative attitudes are expressed frequently, and strongly, with less focus and direction. When feelings are expressed indirectly and diffusely, there is little release or satisfaction and the feelings continue to grow inside the person.

The disturbed child has been impaired in his growth of self. Somewhere along the line, he began to doubt his own powers for self-development. His faith in himself and his self-reliance have been shattered. He does not trust himself and he does not trust others. He is unable to utilize his potentiality to grow with experience.

The disturbed child is often motivated by undifferentiated and unfocused feelings of anger and fear (1). His behavior may manifest feelings of hostility toward almost everyone and everything (5, 7). Or his main expression may be an attitude of generalized fear (5). Wherever hostility is expressed in the child's overt behavior, anxiety is potentially a strong internal attitude and significantly affects the child's behavior. Wherever anxiety is the primary outer expression, hostility usually lies beneath it (5) and influences much of the child's behavior. These attitudes are an outgrowth of the child's personal relationships in the early years of his life (3). Parents gradually, often subtly and indirectly, convey to the child that they consider him a person of limited value and potentiality. The child will not at first show feelings of strong anger or fear, but as demands are made upon him and pressures increase, his feelings become generalized and diffused. Eventually he loses touch with the situations which aroused his deep feelings of self-inadequacy. He loses touch with his own real feelings, with himself.

If in his family he is permitted to express self-alienation only through anxious behavior, then his acts will show strong components of withdrawal and fear (5). The original feeling of being attacked as a self arouses hostility which grows and expands internally, just as his expressions of anxiety become more intense in his external behavior. If hostile expressions are permitted in his family, the child may freely express diffused angry feelings. As the disturbed child acts in a hostile manner, his feelings of guilt and anxiety are intensified. Expressions of anxiety and hostility never appear in isolation from each other, but one of these attitudes is usually expressed in the child's overt behavior.

Since the disturbed child can defend himself only as he appears to be, he is unable to develop his potentiality (10, 11). There is apparently no way he can grow though inward growth forces are always present and may find expression in a positive personal relationship.

The disturbed child has lost touch with his real self. He no longer knows who he is or what he can do. It is this loss of self which is his basic suffering. The loss of self and the significance of its restoration are expressed beautifully in the following paragraphs taken from a letter written by an adult in psychotherapy some time ago (4).

There is only one way out of chaos; and now that I knew all the other doors were locked, I made the tremendous discovery. The miracle that Dr. Y. had forced me to make on my own, not out of books this time at least not directly—but out of my own bowels. From ten thousand miles away I saw it as a blinding light: the importance, the necessity of a Self! One's own single self. My original life—*what had happened to it?* Chaos was here—all around and in me—that I understood in all my fragments. But was that all one could ever know? What about the perfect planets, this earth, people, objects? Didn't they exist and move? Couldn't they be known? Yes . . . but there has to be a knower, a *subject,* as well! (Meaning is a bridge between *two* things.) Beginnings, direction, movement had to be *from* a single point; and ours is where we stand, alone, our being *sui generis.*

Suddenly vistas spread out and out to the sky, and all came together at my feet. Was it possible that I had touched the key to the universe—the key which every man carries so nonchalantly in his pocket? Instantly I knew in my bones, and by grief itself, that I had discovered the very core and essence of neurosis—my neurosis and perhaps every neurosis. The secret of wretchedness was SELFLESSNESS! Deep and hidden, the fact and the fear of not having a self. Not being a self. Not-being. And at the end—actual chaos.

How is it possible to lose a self? The treachery, unknown and unthinkable, begins with our secret psychic death in childhood—if and when we are not loved and are cut off from our spontaneous wishes. (Think: What is left?) But wait—it is not just this simple murder of a psyche. That might be written off. The tiny victim might even "outgrow" it—but it is a perfect double crime in which he himself also gradually and unwittingly takes part. He has not been accepted for himself, *as he is.*

Oh, they "love" him, but they want him or force him or expect him to be different! Therefore he *must be unacceptable.* He himself learns to believe it and at last even takes it for granted. He has truly given himself up. No matter now whether he obeys them, whether he clings, rebels or with-draws—his behavior, his performance is all that matters. His center of gravity is in "them," not in himself—yet if he so much as noticed it, he'd think it natural enough. And the whole thing is entirely plausible, all invisible, automatic, and anonymous!

This is the perfect paradox. Everything looks normal; no crime was intended; there is no corpse, no guilt. All we can see is the sun rising and setting as usual. But what has happened? He has been rejected, not only by them, but by himself. (He is actually without a self). What has he lost? Just the one true and vital part of himself: His own yes-feeling, which is his very capacity for growth, his root system. But alas, he is not dead. "Life" goes on, and so must he. From the moment he gives himself up, and to the extent that he does so, all unknowingly he sets about to create and maintain a pseudo-self. But this is an expediency—a "self" without wishes. This one shall be loved (or feared) where he is despised, strong where he is weak; it shall go through the motions (Oh, but they are caricatures!) not for fun or joy but for survival; not simply because it wants to move but because it has to obey. This necessity is not life—not his life—it is a defense mechanism against death. It is also the machine of death. From now on he will be torn apart by compulsive (unconscious) *needs* or ground by (unconscious) conflicts into paralysis. Every motion and every instant canceling out his being, his integrity; and all the while he is disguised as a normal person and expected to behave like one!

In a word, I saw that we *become* neurotic seeking or defending a pseudo self, a self-system; and we *are* neurotic to the extent that we are self-less.

LEVELS OF FEELINGS

Through exploration of his feelings and attitudes in an extended personal relationship such as that which occurs in psychotherapy, the disturbed child realizes a sense of personal worthiness. In an accepting emotional climate he is freed from the damaging effects of his hostility and anxiety (2, 8) and recovers himself as a unique individual.

In the therapeutic relationship, the therapist conveys to the child a deep belief in him as a person and in his potentialities for growth. He respects the child's values, ways, peculiarities, and symbolisms and lets the child know these are worthy because they are part of him. The relationship enables the child to explore the full intensity, impact, and meaning of his generalized negative feelings. These attitudes were originally learned in his early experiences with parents and other significant adults. They may now be modified in a very different type of relationship where the child finds personal strength, experiences self-significance, and becomes able to express his capacities.

In the playroom, the disturbed child is left to face himself. In a sense, he is required to become aware of his real feelings. He often shows his fears, anger, or immaturity without definitely focusing these feelings on any particular person or situation. He may be utterly afraid or so angry he wants to destroy all people. He may prefer to be left completely alone or may wish to regress to simpler, less demanding levels of development. He may express his feelings in direct attacks on the toys, in smashing, pounding, breaking, in tearing and crushing and a variety of other actions.

As the relationship between the child and the therapist is clarified and strengthened, the child's deeper feelings of hostility become gradually sharpened and more specific. Anger is expressed more directly and often is related to particular persons or experiences. Pounding and smashing, even the desire to kill, may be expressed. If so, it is the parent or sibling or perhaps the entire family which is attacked either through play figures or in direct verbalization. The therapist or any other person may be attacked or denounced or threatened in the child's play. The child expresses and releases these negative feelings in direct ways and as these expressions are accepted by the therapist, the feelings become less intense and affect the child less in his total experience. The child begins to feel himself to be a worthy person.

A new level of the process now begins. The child is no longer so completely negative. He expresses ambivalence toward particular people in his life. For example, the child's anger toward his baby brother or sister may fluctuate; in his play, he may alternate between feeding and caring for the baby and spanking the baby or mistreating him in other ways. These ambivalent reactions may be severe in intensity at first, but as they are expressed again and again in the therapeutic relationship, they become less strong.

In the final stage of the process, positive feelings emerge. The child now sees himself and his relations with people more as they really are. He may still resent the baby at times, but he no longer consistently hates him merely because he is the baby. As a four-year-old once put it in one of her final sessions, "I'm going to have a big party and invite everybody, even my baby brother."

Similar changes in the expression of anxiety also occur. In the beginning of child therapy, anxiety may be diffuse. The child may be generally withdrawn and frightened, tense and garrulous, or over-anxious about being clean, neat, or orderly. The anxiety attitudes may be so pervasive that the child is immobilized and unable to start anything or complete anything, or even to think clearly or to resolve problems in his play. He does not seem to know how to go about doing what he really wants to do. Anxiety may take other forms, such as regular night terrors or bizarre fears of animals and things. In the first stage of the therapeutic process, anxiety seems to pervade the child's behavior. At the next level, it takes on more specific aspects. Fears of the father or the mother or some other particular person may be repeatedly expressed. Then it appears with diffuse hostility. Next, anxiety is largely replaced by feelings of confidence and courage, although the child vacillates between these feelings and attitudes of doubt and inadequacy. Finally, positive and negative fears toward particular people become separated and more in line with the actual situation. Negative feeling tones change from severe to moderate or mild.

The child's emotional problems and symptoms are reflections of his attitudes, and as the attitudes change, the problems and symptoms disappear. The levels of the therapeutic process and the changes in feeling tones are not distinct entities or even always definitely observable. They occur in the child's play and in his emotional behavior, not step by step, but in individually varying sequences.

The therapeutic process does not automatically occur in a play situation. It becomes possible in a therapeutic relationship where the therapist responds in constant sensitivity to the child's feelings, accepts the child's attitudes, and conveys a consistent and sincere belief in the child and a respect for him.

ILLUSTRATIONS OF THE THERAPEUTIC PROCESS

1. In the early interviews the disturbed child's negative attitudes often are diffused and pervasive. Anxiety, for example, may be expressed in the child's insistent, impelling need to keep perfectly clean, or in repetitive questions. In the following two examples, taken from verbatim recordings of first play sessions, Mary shows that a few grains of sand or spots of paint on her fingers or hands are threatening and frightening while Jane illustrates anxiety through her constant questioning.

EXCERPTS FROM MARY'S FIRST PLAY SESSION

M.:   *(Takes the shovel and gets into the sandbox.)* I don't want to get my suit dirty.

T.:   You're worried about getting your suit dirty, Mary?

M.:   Yes, 'cause I got to go back to nursery school. I don't want to get my shoes dirty. *(Brushes her dress with swinging motions of both arms.)* I don't want to get my dress dirty. *(Gets out of the sandbox and punches the Bobo.)*

M.:   *(Empties blue paint into a bathtub, dumps the paint from the bathtub into the pail of water.)* I'm going to poison this water. I can wash my hands in that water. *(Dips her hands in it.)* Look at this water. See how it's turning to a color. Now sit down. I'm making the water all goopy-gooey.

T.:   You're making the water all goopy and gooey and dirty.

M.:   No, I'm cleaning it. I'm cleaning it. I'm cleaning it. *(Goes over to water and washes her hands.)* What do you wipe your hands on?

T.:   *(Fetching a piece of paper.)* You can use this for wiping your hands if you want to.

M.:   *(Wipes her hands on the paper, then puts it aside. Returns to the house and dumps in more sand.)* Dirt into this room, and this room, and up here too. *(She puts sand into the upstairs rooms of the dollhouse.)*

T.:   Dirt upstairs too.

M.:   And dirt here too. *(She puts dirt on the stairs.)*

T.:   The stairs are full of dirt too.

M.:   Know why I'm doing this?

T.:   Why?

M.:   Why? I've got to do it.

T.:   You're doing it because you've got to.

M.:   I've got to put more dirt in the house. I've got to. Dirt on the rug too. Got to clean it. I've got to clean that dirt out.

T.: You have to clean it up?

M.: Yes. I've got to. Got any more bathtubs?

T.: I don't know if there are any more around, Mary.

M.: See this gooey water.

T.: Gooey water?

M.: It's not gooey.

T.: Now it's not gooey, you say.

M.: Come see the gooey water. *(T. comes over and looks at the water. M. dips the brush in the dirty water.)* Get the brush dirty.

T.: The brush is all dirty now too.

M.: No, I'm cleaning it. *(Dumps more paint into the water. Some of the paint splatters on the floor. She gets a sponge and starts wiping it up.)* Got to clean it up.

Excerpts from Jane's First Play Session, Showing Anxiety Through Repetitive Questions

J.: Where is it?

T.: Where is *it?*

J.: What?

T.: Whatever it was you were looking for.

J.: I'm not looking for anything.

T.: You're not looking for anything.

J.: Yes, now I am.

T.: You *are* looking for something.

J.: Yes. *(Laughs)* I know what this is. *(A car.)*

T.: You know what it is.

J.: What?

T.: What is it?

J.: A car. Do you know what this is? It's a tractor.

T.: Mm-hm.

J.: What's this?

T.: What could that be?

J.: It's a car. Look. What do you think this is?

T.: I wonder.

J.: What's this?

T.: That's up to you.

J.: It could be a gun.

T.: It could be.

J.: I know what this is. It could be a gun. *(Continues in the same vein throughout most of the session.)*

Frequently the anxiety attitude is even more intense. The child may, for instance, be so immobilized that he is unable to move. He remains motionless in the playroom, apparently without feeling. He is unable to decide what to do or even to decide if he wants to do anything. Or the child may react with such fear that he will remain in the therapy situation only if his mother is there beside him.

In contrast to such behavior, some children react to the therapy experience in a diffuse, hostile way. At the beginning of the third session Richard's hostility reached a climax as he screamed out at the therapist: "I'll drill the whole place full of lead! Do you hear me? I'm gonna dirty this place up so far that I don't think you'll be able to clean this stuff up with all the water in the world. I'm gonna really fix this stuff, I'm telling you. I'm gonna mess this room up like a coyote. And then I'll take this jackknife and cut everything up. Then I'll try it on you next."

2. At the second level the child often fluctuates between generalized anxiety and generalized hostility. In her second and third sessions Mary displayed this ambivalence.

M.:   Getting this all gooey-gooey. Now let's wash our hands. *(Runs quickly to the basin of water and washes her hands, then dries them on a scarf.)* I'm not making poison today. *(Gets her hands into the mud and rubs them together.)* Wash our hands! *(Runs to basin of water and dips her hands in the water.)* Look how I'm making this water all gooey.

T.:   *(Looking at water.)* Yes, it's different now, it's gooey.

M.:   I'm washing my hands.

T.:   Washing them in gooey water?

M.:   This isn't gooey water. I'm going to clean it.

T.:   You don't want it to be gooey, Mary?

M.:   No. I'm cleaning it. I'm cleaning it up. *(Washes a number of toys in the water, then scoops paint into the bowl with her fingers.)* I can do it with my fingers: I did it with my fingers. Now wash my hands. *(Runs to pan of water and washes her hands.)* Now it's gooey water.

M.:   Yeah. . . . *(Takes washing machine to the sandbox, dumps paint and mud into it.)* Got to wash my hands. This water is gooey. . . .

T.:   You want to get that goo in there real good.

M.:   Yeah. *(Runs to the water, washes out the washing machine and her hands.)* Gooey-gooey water. It's getting all gooey.

T.:   It's real gooey water.

M.:   I'm rubbin' it in. *(Returns to the sandbox, rubs more mud and paint on her hands.)*

T.:   Rubbing dirt on your hands, Mary?

M.:   It's only water.

T.:   You always want to be sure that I know it's just water, is that it, Mary?

M.:   *(Runs to water pail and washes hands.)* Got to get these all cleaned up.

M.:   *(Goes to shelves, looks at marionettes, picks them up one by one and pinches them, drops them with exclamations of disgust.)*

T.:   You don't like those, Mary?

M.:   I don't like any of them. But I like this one. *(Picks up clown puppet.)* No, I don't like him either. *(Squeezes clown and drops it, picking up the puppet she had characterized as "Joel" in a previous session.)* This is Joel. *(Looks at puppet with angry expression.)*

T.: You don't like him, do you, Mary?

M.: No, I don't. *(Drops Joel in a heap with the other puppets and picks up a gun.)* What can you do with this gun? Can you shoot it? *(Shoots at puppets.)*

M.: *(Starts carrying a boat full of water, sand, and paint to the sandbox, but there is a leak and the mixture drips to the floor.)* Oh, it's dripping, what should I do?

T.: You're worried because it's making a mess, hm?

M.: *(Taking the boat with its contents back to the table.)* I'm going to put it into the bottle and feed it to the baby.

T.: You want to feed that dirty water to the baby?

M.: Yeah. I'm gonna pour it in this bottle and then make the baby drink it. *(Empties all the dirty water into the bottle.)* Pour a little of this into the bottle, too. *(Goes over to the finger paints, tries to shake some out of a jar but is unsuccessful.)* It doesn't come out. *(Shakes harder and is still unsuccessful. Finally she dips a crayon into the bottle and gets some paint out and adds it to her mixture. Points to the floor.)* Gonna wipe this all up.

3. The third level is marked especially by focused hostile attitudes or strong fears more directly expressed. These attitudes are evident in the child's play in symbolic anger or fear reactions toward parents, siblings, and other persons. The initially generally anxious child may show specific fear or anger in later play sessions. In her fifth and sixth sessions Vera showed strong negative attitudes toward her parents and the new baby.

V.: *(Picks up group of family dolls.)* Bang! Bang-bang! What I'm thinking. There. I'm gonna shoot the baby. They're Indians. I'm an Indian.

T.: You're going to shoot them.

V.: Yeah. Bang! Shoot her. All of them. But I'm not gonna shoot the furniture 'cause I need those furnitures.

T.: You need those, but you're going to shoot all the family.

V.: *(Continues to shoot family dolls on floor.)* There. So I can get the furniture. I can.

T.: You'll shoot them and get the furniture.

V.: Yes. And I need it, and I need it. I need the furniture.

T.: You need it so much you'll shoot them to get it?

V.: Yes. Bang-bang! I'm gonna shoot her right in the butt.

T.: So angry you shot her right in the butt.

V.: Yes. I shooted them all. There, I got one. There, I got another. There, I got another.

T.: You're getting all of them.

V.: Yes, I'm getting all of them. Won't that be fun? Then you can have some and I'll have some.

T.: You'll give me some and you'll keep some.

V.: Yeah. We need the house too. I'll live in this house for nothing.

V.: We could keep the baby for eating. O.K.? Well keep the whole family so we can eat them all up. O.K.?

T.: So we can eat them all up?

V.: Yes. We'll eat the daddy. Here. Here. We're hungry, aren't we? We love to eat things, don't we?

T.: We love to eat things?

V.: There. We've got the puppet and we're going to keep him. We can eat them. After I kill them all, I'll save some for me and for you too. There's our telephone and there's our gun to shoot everyone. We'll get the bathtub too. Do you want to do that? So they won't know what they're doing, and after they get alive again, they won't know what we're doing. We'll keep them forever and we'll eat all the family up before they get real again. O.K.?

T.: That's what you want to do?

V.: Yes. We'll cut their panties, and we'll cut off their shirts, and cut off their heads, and eat all of them up. You can eat this one and you can eat this one, and I'll eat the rest of them.

V.: This can be your gun and you can shoot like this. Bang! Now I'll get another gun. All of them will be shot. Then we can have a whole bench. And this can be a ball. And that can be mine, a gun, and we'll bounce these balls on their heads. We can have everything.

T.: You want to bounce the balls on their heads and have everything?

V.: Yes. So if they get real we can have them, can't we? We'll eat them up. We don't have anything else so we have to eat people, don't we? The way bad men do, don't they?

T.: Bad men do that, they eat people, hm?

V.: Yes. We're going to be bad men. And you can be a bad man with us. We can live in this house. And we won't share any of our toys. We won't share anything. We won't share nothing. We'll just have to give them the dirty things to do.

V.: Bang! I won't shoot you. Bang, bang, bang, bang, bang!

T.: Shot them all.

V.: Yes. Now we have everything for ourselves, don't we?

V.: I'll cut off their heads with my knife.

T.: You really are angry with them.

V.: Sure. Cut, cut, cut, cut! All coming off. Cut, cut, cut, cut, cut, cut! There. You're cut, you're cut. You're cut and you're cut and you're cut. Bad family.

T.: You hate the bad family.

V.: Yes. And I'll cut their feet too, so they can't walk. O.K.? Now we're all set. We've got everything to ourselves.

4. In the fourth level of the therapeutic process ambivalences come to the fore again. This time, however, the ambivalence is a mixture of positive and negative attitudes. In her seventh through twelfth play therapy sessions Mary expressed these attitudes.

M.: *(Getting bottle from shelf.)* And another top. *(Feeds baby clean water from small bottle.)* Just a little bottle, she's a little baby.

T.: Just a little baby, that's all she is.

M.: You hold her. Don't let her head come off.

M.: *(Points to baby.)* I'm gonna put this water down her throat. *(Pours teapot full of water on doll's face.)* Her mouth and her eyes. There. Is that funny?

T.: They just don't work for you.

M.: *(Brings jar of finger paint, trying to get some out.)* I can't put my fingers in there 'cause my mamma will say, "Did you do that?"

T.: You're afraid Mamma will be angry?

M.: I know. I'll put a crayon in it.

M.: Well, you hold her. And I'm gonna get stuff for her.

T.: You're gonna fix it all for her.

M.: And she's gonna eat it. It's food.

T.: It's food that she's getting.

M.: But not dirty food. Clean. Clean food.

T.: Just plain dirty food.

M.: Yes. She can't eat with her mommy and daddy.

T.: She can't eat with them.

M.: No. Because she's a bad girl.

T.: She's just bad, so she can't.

M.: No, she's not bad, because . . . because. . . .

M.: *(Shouts.)* Give me the raker! *(A pause.)* This is all dirt. . . . Nice food.

T.: You can't decide whether it's dirt or nice food.

M.: Nice food, not dirty food. We're gonna eat dirty food, my mommy and daddy.

M.: Making a pretty sand pile for you, and my mother and daddy.

T.: Something nice for me and your mother and daddy.

M.: But not for the baby.

T.: Not for her. She gets nothing nice.

M.: Only such stuff, food, that's all. Then she's going right in her bedroom.

T.: She goes right to bed and that's all.

M.: She doesn't really go to sleep, she just stays in there.

T.: She fools them.

M.: Till her daddy comes . . . and maybe he'll let her out.

T.: Her daddy might.

M.: *(Tearfully.)* Her daddy might bring her some flowers. She might be a nice little girl. But she might be a bad little girl

M.: And I got another one of those. Here it is. It's a pie for us. For me and the daddy and you. But not for the baby.

T.: The baby doesn't get anything good.
M.: No. She just gets pie-apple sigologoo. Chicklakalala
T.: She gets something real silly, huh?
M.: Yeah. And she gets a nosy head.
T.: A nosy head too.
M.: Yeah, that's what she gets.
T.: She gets all the bad things.
M.: Nothing good. Only supper.
T.: And that's not good.
M.: No, it's not.

M.: A slap for him. *(Hits the Bobo.)* I'll hit him to you, and then he'll really get a licking.
T.: You'd like him to get hit hard.
M.: Yes. *(Hits the Bobo hard.)*
T.: You'd like to smash him.
M.: He's going to the doctor.
T.: He's hurt bad.
M.: Yes.

M.: Well, I don't like this playroom anyway, with all those dirty old puppets and that old thing. *(Walks to shelves, picks up a puppet and throws it down, slaps the Bobo in passing.)*
T.: You really don't like these things?
M.: *(Anxiously.)* But I can come here again, can't I?
T.: Are you afraid that maybe you can't?
M.: I can still come here, can't I?
T.: Yes, if you want to come again.

5. In the final level of development, negative and positive attitudes become separated and clear, as illustrated in Mary's last few sessions.

M.: No home. No home at all.
T.: Not a real home, hm?
M.: No house like you have. Like kids have.
T.: You don't have a house like other kids, hm?
M.: No. In mine it's just the same old things. All I do is walk around and do nothing. That's all I can do.

M.: *(Plays in the sandbox.)* They're gonna have a new house. I think this house is a music house. Ha-ha, a music house.
T.: That's what. A music house.
M.: It's going to be so big that they're gonna have to put some music in this house. They'll have to have a television too.

M.: And in here we'll have a door. It's gonna be a little hideout. And the kids can see their mother at night. And the kids can fool their mother. But the big people—they can just see from the top.

M.: Now the kids are gonna build themselves another house. And their mother.

M.: I don't like cowboys and shooting. And even animals, if they're big. Every time I hear a noise when I'm up in bed, then I'm scared.

T.: When you hear noises while sleeping, you're really afraid, hm?

M.: Also when I'm bad sometimes and have to sit in a chair.

T.: Oh, when you're bad and hear noises, then you get frightened.

M.: Yes. When I hear noises, then I'm always scared. My mommy comes and says she doesn't hear it, but I do.

T.: You hear it even though your mommy doesn't, and it frightens you.

M.: Yes. And it's really only something like the washing machine or somebody pounding.

T.: It turns out to be something silly but it still frightens you.

M.: Yes.

M.: This is my girl friend. She likes me and I like her too. I'm gonna eat my pie with her.

T.: You like her and so you're sharing your pie with her.

M.: Yes. We'll eat it. She gets half and I get half. She thinks it's too much for me but I've been starving to death so I'll eat it. *(A pause.)* You know, kids just love people but sometimes people don't love kids.

M.: *(Plays in the sand and describes the destruction of a village by a huge storm. The people work together to rebuild it.)* If I helped them, then they'd like me. I'll make a great big cake for them. How deep is my cake gonna be? Oh, my cake, cake, cake. Baking a good, delicious cake. No, I'm gonna eat it all up.

T.: Just for you, that cake.

M.: Not all of it. I'll divide it up with them because they're my friends. Friends, friends. I'm a friend and I'm not gonna eat it all. I'm gonna give them some.

M.: *(Plays in the sandbox.)* A lotta times she dreams about castles. She dreams about all this, only it's too late now.

T.: Is it too late for her now?

M.: Well, maybe not. I'll make one for her. I'm gonna make the castle. I'm gonna make Carol the first castle she's ever had.

T.: You're going to do that for her, hm?

M.: Yep.

M.: See this cake? You can cut it in many pieces. In small pieces for many people.

M.: I'm gonna make a pie so big it's gonna cover the whole place up. The biggest pie you ever saw. There's my pie. And now I'm gonna cut it up in little pieces and share it with all the people. We'll all eat it now.

CONCLUDING COMMENT

The therapeutic process does not occur automatically in a play situation. It becomes possible only in a relationship where the adult responds in constant sensitivity to the child's feelings, accepts his attitudes, and maintains a sincere belief in him.

Through a significant relationship in psychotherapy, the disturbed child experiences a process of emotional growth. He moves from the expression of diffused, generalized, negative attitudes which block him from fully developing his potentials as a human being to the expression of clarified positive and negative attitudes which enable him to feel worthy and to develop in terms of his real talents and abilities. With his self-capacity available and his self-regard restored, he ventures into new experiences and attains new meaning and value in his relations with others.

REFERENCES

1. Anderson, John E. The Relation of Emotional Behavior to Learning. *Yearbk. Nat. Soc. Stud. Educ.*, 41 (2), 1942.
2. Axline, Virginia M. *Play Therapy.* Boston: Houghton Mifflin, 1947.
3. Bernard, Jessie. *American Family Behavior.* New York: Harper, 1942.
4. Horney, Karen. Finding the Real Self. *Amer. J. Psychoanal.*, 9, 3-7, 1949.
5. Horney, Karen. *The Neurotic Personality of Our Time.* New York: Norton, 1937.
6. Kanner, Leo. Behavior Disorders in Childhood. In J. McV. Hunt (Ed.), *Personality and the Behavior Disorders.* Vol. I. New York: Ronald Press, 1944.
7. Korner, Anneliese F. *Some Aspects of Hostility in Young Children.* New York: Grune & Stratton, 1949.
8. Moustakas, Clark E. *Children in Play Therapy.* New York: McGraw-Hill, 1953.
9. ————. The Frequency and Intensity of Negative Attitudes Expressed in Play Therapy: A Comparison of Well-Adjusted and Disturbed Young Children. *J. Gen. Psychol.*, 86, 79-99, 1955.
10. Rogers, Carl R. *Client-centered Therapy.* Boston: Houghton Mifflin, 1951.
11. Snygg, Donald, and Arthur W. Combs. *Individual Behavior.* New York: Harper, 1949.

3

Play Therapy with the "Normal" Child

PLAY therapy is a unique experience for the child developing according to normal social standards and expectations. It offers this child an opportunity to enter into a significant personal relationship with an adult, in a situation where the boundaries are greatly expanded. In the playroom, the child learns to be free to express himself without reservation or condition knowing the therapist accepts him, understands him, and respects his feelings and thoughts. The child soon realizes he will not be reprimanded, punished, belittled, or made to feel guilty or sinful. He can express his anger and fear, be critical and resentful, or act silly, carefree, and joyous. In his play he can carry out his imaginations and dreams, spontaneously and dramatically, realizing there is someone standing by, following his expressions, listening, perceiving, and understanding.

Every child knows personal restrictions at home and in school. To be in a place where one can be fully himself is a rare experience. In the playroom it is possible to be the baby or oldest child or to be one's own self without fear of being examined, judged, or criticized. At school, status is often designated and imposed. The child is frequently assigned his place in the hierarchy. His work is evaluated according to specific norms and standards. In the playroom, the child has a unique status. He makes his own choices and decisions. He establishes his own standards. He can spill and mess, make socially useless objects, draw outside the lines, and do many things that are ordinarily forbidden or condemned. He can flourish in the comfort and safety of a completely accepting adult.

The normal child has an opportunity to explore his feelings and discover how he feels about himself and others. He has the freedom to do what he wants to do and be what he wants to be. He need not submit to the everyday pressures of teachers and parents. The therapeutic relationship sets up no standards, social values, or expectations but honors every wish, need, and expression of the child. Thus it becomes a place where the normal child is able to release tensions and frustrations that accumulate in the course of daily living, to have materials and an adult

31

entirely to himself, without any concern with sharing, being cooperative, being considerate, polite, or mannerly. He can feel his feelings and express his thoughts all the way knowing that he is accepted and revered unconditionally.

The Behavior of the Normal Child in Therapy

Not all children use the therapy experience in the same way. Each child is unique and, in the exact sense, his play differs from that of every other child. Each child has his own way of expressing himself and his own style. He perceives the situation and relates to the therapist in terms of his own particular interests, wishes, and needs. Although each child's play and attitudes in the relationship are distinct, certain general characteristics are often present in the play and behavior of normal children in a therapeutic setting.

These children are conversational and discuss their experiences spontaneously, openly, and directly. They talk about their friends, teachers, family, and important conditions in their lives. They explain their interests and behavior and convey their wishes and attitudes. In contrast, the disturbed child is more devious and indirect in his expressions. He tends to be more forbidding, more prone to attack and threaten to attack, and more likely to use physical barriers to block or restrain the therapist from coming close to him (4).

The normal child enters the playroom and begins immediately to examine the play setting, to test the freedom and limits in the situation, and to relate with the therapist. He often engages in concentrated play, develops projects, and uses a wide variety of materials. Sometimes in the beginning he follows stereotyped forms but as he realizes the freedom, he discards predetermined patterns and forms and creates his own unique and original constructions.

The normal child expresses his negative feelings and attitudes clearly and directly. The themes of his play become direct expressions of his feelings and he continues expressing them until relief and satisfaction are achieved. In one study (3) it was found that children regarded as personally and socially well-adjusted by their teachers and the school psychologist expressed a variety of negative attitudes. These included regression in play indicating immaturity in feeding, toileting, speech, and other developmental tasks; diffuse anxiety indicated by general expressions of unrealistic fears; orderliness anxiety reflected in a compelling need to keep things near, arranged in lines and rows and in a confined space; aggression toward people in general and toward parents and teachers particularly; hostility toward siblings and toward the therapist; and cleanliness anxiety reflected in a compelling need to be clean, to keep play materials spotless, and a fear of getting dirty, spilling and messing or touching and handling such items as finger paints and soft clay. In the study referred to, cleanliness and orderliness anxiety occurred rarely in the play of well-adjusted children; whereas, hostility toward brothers and sisters was the most frequent negative expression. The negative attitudes of normal children tended to be mild or moderate in nature rather than severe. In the setting of play therapy, when these children expressed their negative feelings toward family members and other significant persons in their lives, they felt better and often showed the positive side of these relations.

The normal child is not usually indirect, subtle, or fearful, nor is he cunning and sadistic. He tends to be happy in his play, often singing and humming. He can play alone with equanimity and contentment, working through his ideas and feelings without seeking the support or help of the therapist. He can talk and play with the therapist comfortably without being driven by dependency needs and competitive strivings. He is more apt to participate in activities with the therapist on a mutual basis, though he may disagree with the therapist or question his statements or behavior when it is not consistent with his own views. The normal child is not always deeply serious and intense in his feelings; although, he may, at times, be completely silent and absorbed in a project. He is aware of his feelings, seems to understand his preferences, and usually knows what he wants and what he wants to do.

Perhaps the most important aspect of the play therapy experience for the normal child is the concentrated relationship with the therapist. In the busy life of children, the opportunity rarely exists to be alone for one hour with an adult once or twice a week. Furthermore, it is rare for a child to have a relationship in which he is the center of the experience, where he can express his feelings and be understood as a person, where the adult is fully attending the child, watching, listening, making statements of recognition, and being present in a deeply human sense.

Play therapy is a form of preventive mental hygiene for normal children. It is a way for them to grow in their own self-acceptance and respect, a way to explore feelings and attitudes and temporary tensions and conflicts that cannot be expressed easily and safely in school or at home. Often, threatening feelings and disturbing experiences can be worked through in three or four play sessions.

Many children enrolled in the Merrill-Palmer Preschool Services are seen as part of the current teaching and counseling programs of the school. Before the child is invited to come alone to the playroom, he is introduced to the therapist by his teacher. He visits the playroom with a group of four or five of his peers and his teacher. This gives him an opportunity to become acquainted with the setting and to begin to feel comfortable and safe in it. In the security of his group and teacher, the therapist begins a relationship with him and conveys the possibilities of the playroom. The visit gives the child a view of the situation and enables him to decide on future sessions. The preschool children usually come for four interviews, but the frequency varies with the individual child and his particular interests and needs. Whether or not he comes at all is the child's decision. Usually, after the initial visit, these children are eager to return. They approach their teacher or the therapist on their own. Their requests for the play therapy experience are much greater than the time available by students and counselors in the Counseling Service. These children often express attitudes in play therapy that their teachers had not observed or recognized in the preschool. It happens occasionally that a child perceived as well-adjusted by his teacher reveals disturbing conflicts and problems in the playroom. The therapy experience of these children is discussed by the teacher and therapist and recommendations are made for further therapeutic contacts.

Sometimes the well-adjusted child prefers to use the possibilities of play therapy in a group setting. When it is possible, the therapist makes such an arrangement.

In the following sections, a number of examples are presented to illustrate the nature of the play therapy experience for the child reacting to frustration of a brief nature, the child faced with temporary threat and conflict of longer duration, and the child regarded as adjusted exhibiting severe feelings of rejection, loneliness, and isolation.

THE ADJUSTED CHILD IN BRIEF CONFLICT: JACKIE

When Jackie arrived at nursery school, the therapist approached him and asked if he wanted to come to the playroom. Jackie rushed out the nursery school gate, saying, "I'll bring my book." He talked all the way to the playroom, hurried into the room, and went straight to the dollhouse.

FIRST SESSION, JACKIE

J.:   I want to stay here all morning. Look at the balloons. They're cats.

T.:   Would you be more comfortable if you removed your snow suit?

J.:   No. Eeeee. Look at this boat. Oh! Here's a gun. *(J. walks to the dollhouse).* Smoke comes out of the house. There's a doorway and windows. I see something, a little red chair. Here's a dresser. And what's this? It's a desk. *(J. picks up a nursing bottle, examines it, and replaces it on a shelf. He walks to the work bench.)* Here's a chisel and a screw driver. You know what I'm going to do. I'm going to paint this table because it's rough. Now you watch. *(J. paints the table.)* Oh! You know what? I went to a circus last night. *(J. picks up a gun and shoots various objects in the room. He points the gun at T.)*

T.:   You want to shoot me? *(J. hesitates. He stares at T.)*

J.:   No. I want to shoot the clown. *(J. shoots. Then he jumps on Bobo, the clown comeback toy.)* He's dead. I jugged him in the stomach. *(J. continues punching.)* He's dead. Look I shot him.

T.:   Yes, I see that you did. *(J. gets a tub. He fills it with water and places a boat in it.)*

J.:   See the boat swimming. This boat likes swimming around the water. Now I'll put another boat. *(J. plays quietly for about ten minutes.)*

T.:   Only a few minutes left today. *(J. plays with boats and water for the remaining time.)* We must go back to nursery school now. *(J. hurries out the door.)*

J.:   I'm getting on a bus on Wednesday and go to Pennsylvania but first we're going to East Canada.

COMMENTS

Jackie played happily during the hour. When he began to concentrate on the boat and water play, he remained quiet but otherwise he talked constantly. Most of his expressions were positive. His only aggression was the mild attack on the puncho clown. He seemed to feel immediately comfortable, stating his ideas, making decisions, and knowing what he wanted to do.

When the therapist approached Jackie for the second session, he seemed greatly upset. He began to cry and said he wanted to see his father. As he talked, it became clear that he had been forced to come to school that morning against his wishes, that his father had dropped him off and rushed away. Jackie decided to go with the therapist to the playroom.

SECOND SESSION, JACKIE

J.:   *(Picks up a gun, points at Bobo.)* I shot the wolf. Now I'll shoot the light. *(J. shoots around the room. He aims at Bobo again.)* Gonna shoot this wolf. *(J. hits Bobo on the head. He takes a rubber knife.)* Could this cut?

T.:   Do you think it's sharp?

J.:   A little bit. Now I'll shoot you.

T.:   You feel like shooting everything today.

J.:   Now you're dead. *(J. runs to the door and shoots out. He shoots T. again.)* You're dead. *(J. continues shooting.)* I'm going to shoot the wall. I'll shoot the house. I'll shoot you again. You're dead and can't get up cause I shot you. Here's another knife in case I want to cut you.

T.:   You really feel like shooting up this place and me.

J.:   Yes. I do! *(J. continues the aggressive play for fifteen minutes.)* I'm not going to shoot you any more only the wolf. I don't want that wolf to get near us.

T.:   Maybe it's your daddy you really want to hurt.

J.:   I could shoot him with this.

T.:   Yes. And you feel like doing it.

J.:   I'll shoot the sand. *(J. drops the gun. He takes finger paint and paper and works with these materials for the remaining time).*

COMMENTS

On the way back to nursery school, Jackie talked about his trip to Pennsylvania. His return to the group was peaceful and calm. Apparently through the aggressive episodes in the playroom he had resolved his conflict with his father and his angry, hurt feelings. In the next two sessions he returned to the water and boats and played constructively for long periods of time. The hostility of the previous session had vanished. He described the activities he and his father engaged in together, and it was clear how much this relationship meant to him.

KERRY AND JOHN

Kerry was seen alone once (on a day when John was absent from school) and with John on three occasions. Neither child would come to the playroom alone, following the initial session, but would eagerly approach the therapist when she appeared in the nursery school and beseech her to allow them to come together.

FIRST SESSION, KERRY

Kerry gets into the sandbox and plays silently for three or four minutes.

K.: Here's a pie I made for you. *(T. accepts the pie. K. picks up the bow and arrows. She fails to shoot properly.)* Help me.

T.: This is one way. *(K. shoots one arrow, drops this equipment, and sits at a table with crayons and paper. She works quietly for five minutes.)*

K.: Now you try it. *(K. hands the materials to T.)*

T.: What would you like me to make?

K.: A rainbow. *(T. hesitates.)* Okay, I'll do it. *(K. completes the drawing. She gets swords and shields.)* This is for you and this for me. Now fight! *(K. shouts with delight as the battle proceeds on a gentle basis. K. stops the sword play. She throws darts about four minutes and then takes the family dolls.)*

K.: This is Daddy. This is Mommy. This is Grandpa. This is Grandma. Mommy and Daddy kiss. *(K. embraces figures.)* Hello! Hello! *(K. greets sibling figures.)* Here's where they sleep. Here's a bedroom for Mommy and Daddy and this is one for the children. *(K. plays quietly a few minutes.)* I don't want to play with these any more. *(K. picks up the animal figures.)* A red pig. *(Looks surprised and laughs.)*

T.: Yes, a red one. That seems very funny to you.

K.: Look! A red lamb. *(K. speaks in a loud voice.)* A gray cow! *(K. leaves the animals, goes to the finger paints and works for the remaining time.)* I made three pictures, one for you, one for Daddy, and one for Mommy.

COMMENTS

In this session, Kerry expressed herself freely and spontaneously. Her play was constructive and creative. From the beginning she expressed positive feelings for the therapist, e.g., the gifts of the pie and painting and the sharing of activities with her. Kerry seemed to enjoy and value this session but chose not to come alone again even though the therapist approached her on numerous occasions.

FIRST SESSION, KERRY AND JOHN

J. gets bow and arrows when the children enter.

J.: Kerry, you have to be an Indian.

K.:   I don't *have* to be.
J.:   Will you be?
K.:   Yes. *(J. shoots one arrow and walks to a shelf of toys. K begins punching Bobo.)* Come on boy. Jump up. You're a big boy. *(J. joins her. They jump and ride on Bobo, shouting gleefully.)*
K:.: I'm going to the bathroom. *(J. joins her. K. sits on the stool.)*
J.:   *(J. turns off the light. The room is dark.)* Yeeeeeyeeee.
K.:   Ghosts.
J.:   Wooo! Ghosts! Ghosts!
K.:   Come on, John, the light. Turn it on. *(J. pushes the switch. He shows T. a bandaged finger.)*
J.:   The window was broken and hurt me.
T.:   Is there much pain?
J.:   No.
K.:   I'm cold in here. *(J. turns off the light. He and Kerry pretend to frighten each other. J. notices that when he switches the light on a fan comes on at the same time.)*
J.:   Where is the fan? *(T. points it out.)* Look, Kerry, when I turn the light on, the fan goes on. Did you know that?
K.:   That's no fan. It's a ghost.
J.:   It's a fan.
K.:   Okay. Let's go back to the playroom. *(The children resume the play with Bobo a short time and then play in the sandbox. J. secures family dolls. He hands some to K.)*
J.:   I'd like being father.
K.:   Give me mother. I'd like the boy too. *(J. hands these dolls to K. and the children dramatize several family scenes for T. Then they furnish the house. J. takes tiger and lion and comes behind K.)*
J.:   Wooo! Wooo! Let them fight.
K.:   Mm-hm. *(J. throws the animals in the sandbox.)*
J.:   They are killed. *(K. continues furnishing the house. She places the mother, father, and baby dolls in a bedroom. J. brings a giraffe toy to the doll-house and greets the family.)* Hello.
K.:   Weee! Weee! Daddy, Daddy, giraffe is coming! Mommy, Mommy. *(K. has the baby cling to the father figure.)*
J.:   He won't hurt you. You can ride on his neck.
K.:   Mm-hm. And sit on his head. *(K. puts the baby doll on the giraffe's neck. This play continues until the end of the session.)*

In the second session, the children resume their dramatizations of family scenes, pretend to frighten each other and tease each other. They seem to enjoy the elements of surprise and shock, and in a friendly way they explore the limits of the playroom. The same themes continue in the third session. Some excerpts from this last session are presented.

THIRD SESSION, KERRY AND JOHN

The children enter and take turns shooting the bow and arrow.
K.:   Come on boy. Get up and fight.

J.:   *(J. climbs on a table and touches the ceiling.)* Look, I'm tall.
T.:   Yes. You can touch the ceiling. *(J. takes a container of checkers.)*
J.:   Could I throw them at the target.
T.:   It's up to you. *(J. decides not to throw them. He puts the checkers on a shelf. He takes a dart gun and shoots at the target.)*
J.:   Look, Kerry, I shot it. *(K. collects several guns and knives. She takes two swords and approaches J.)*
K.:   Let's fight.
J.:   No. *(He takes an abacus and counts the beads.)* I like to count. *(K. rides the Bobo. J. joins her. They jump and move around the room with it for ten minutes. Then J. lies on the floor. He stretches out his arms and shuts his eyes.)*
T.:   Are you feeling all right, John? *(J. does not answer.)*
K.:   What's the matter, John? *(K. gently strokes his forehead. J. opens his eyes slightly and closes them again.)* John, are you pretending? *(J. looks at K. again and shuts his eyes.)* I know you are pretending. *(K. gets a sword and slashes at J.'s leg.)*
T.:   John, is something wrong?
K.:   Don't ask him. He's pretending.
J.:   I want water. *(T. gets J. a cup of water. J. rises and goes to the easel. He works a while, then lies on the floor, and closes his eyes again.)*
K.:   John, let's play with Bobo. *(J. doesn't respond.)* John, let's go back to nursery school before we're told there's only a few more minutes. *(J. doesn't respond.)* Let's go and take some toys with us. *(J. rises immediately. They gather up items and after testing the therapist's limits for several minutes, they leave.)*

COMMENTS

The teasing and trickery continue in this session. When the children returned to the nursery school, John and Kerry immediately joined other children and played boisterously and actively for the rest of the morning. John's dramatic flair was apparently intended to worry the therapist. He did not respond to Kerry until her suggestion involved carrying through a forbidden act in taking toys from the playroom to the nursery school. This seemed to be a period in their development when there was joy in testing the limits, in seeing how far they could go, and in getting dramatic effects. Yet all the while, both were aware of the realities and were in full control. They played the game only to a point. They enjoyed behaving in an unconventional manner, and their misdemeanors were calculated to get unusual reactions from the therapist. Having this opportunity in the playroom there was less need to tease and trap adults in the nursery school.

THE ADJUSTED CHILD TEMPORARILY DISTURBED

Children who experience such catastrophes as wars, fires, and floods, serious accidents, and illnesses, or who are subjected to such family crises as divorce and death or frequent changes in neighborhoods and schools often become temporarily disturbed and express considerable aggression and fear. The arrival of a new baby in the family is a common source of such a disturbance in the child's behavior. This event, although usually a joyful and happy experience, often brings a period of stress, even when family relations are rooted in positive attitudes. The arrival of a new family member means that each person in the family will change in some way. Family disorganization may result, at least temporarily, and the older child or children may be faced with the painful experience of feeling replaced.

For neither of the two children, Susan and Stewart, whose play therapy sessions are reported, was the arrival of a new baby a surprise. Both had been informed of the coming event two or three months in advance, and both had expressed pleasure in the prospect.

SUSAN

The nursery school staff described Susan, three years old, as a charming youngster whose winning smile and understanding ways had made her popular with both children and adults. Her mother considered Susan's relations in the family excellent until a new baby arrived. Then Susan became babyish, immature, and constantly whined and complained. The same kind of behavior appeared in the nursery school. Susan's mother, having tried a number of approaches unsuccessfully, telephoned the nursery school and asked what could be done to stop Susan's constant whining which had become a major issue in the family. The mother could not understand how a wonderfully happy and confident child could become so whimpering and clinging in such a short time.

The nursery school staff referred Susan to the play therapist who scheduled three play sessions with her. During the first two sessions Susan appeared to project her negative and hostile feelings onto the humanlike balloon figure, throwing it on the floor, stepping on it, squeezing its head and face, and crushing it inside the vise. Once her feelings were recognized, accepted, and at least partly clarified, she proceeded in the last session to pick up the balloon figure, kiss it, toss it in the air, and dance around the room while she held it in her arms.

A transcript of recordings of the three sessions follows.

FIRST SESSION, SUSAN

(Mother and child walk into the room together.)
THERAPIST: You can use these in any way you like.
(Mother starts to leave room, and child looks at her.)
CHILD: No, you stay here for awhile.
MOTHER: Watch the watch. When this hand gets over here, I'll be back.
C.:   O.K. I'll bounce two balls. Two at a time you did.
M.:   I'll lay down the watch where you can watch it.
C.:   O.K. It's not ticking.
M.:   Want me to put it on you? *(Places watch on C.'s wrist.)* Bye. You can just keep your eye on that watch.

C.:   *(Waves good-by to mother.)* Where's the baby?

T.:   Where do you suppose the baby could be?

C.:   Here? That's the baby. Lookit the big baby. This is a balloon head. Mr. Balloon Head. *(Picks up a balloon in the form of a human figure. Squeezes balloon and cries, "Mommy, mommy, mommy.")*

T.:   That's what it cries. Mommy, mommy, mommy.

C.:   *(Continues to squeeze balloon and cry, "Mommy, mommy, mommy." Looks at T. and places balloon on table. Turns handle of vise.)* What is it?

T.:   You want to know what it could be. It can be anything you want it to be.

C.:   A can opener.

T.:   Is that what it is? A can opener?

C.:   Lookit these soldiers. Are these cowboys or soldiers? What do they look like?

T.:   Cowboys. See the cowboys. Those are all cowboys

T.:   Mm-hm.

C.:   I'm gonna be a monkey.

T.:   That's what you're going to be.

C.:   *(Puts on monkey mask.)* Lookit me. I'm the monkey.

T.:   Susan is the monkey.

C.:   Now I'm gonna be a piggy. I'll say oink, oink. *(Puts on pig mask.)* Oink, oink, oink, oink.

T.:   The piggy goes oink, oink, oink, oink.

C.:   Oink, oink, oink, oink. *(Takes mask off.)* Now I'm gonna be a clown. This goes oink, oink, oink, too. Oink, oink.

T.:   The clown goes oink, oink.

C.:   Oink, oink, oink. *(Laughs.)* Now I'm gonna be a baby and drink from the bottle of water. Shall I?

T.:   That's up to you.

C.:   Should I sprinkle here? Here. Open your hand.

T.:   You want to sprinkle in my hand.

C.:   *(Sprinkles water in T.'s hand.)* Rub them together. *(Drinks from bottle and then replaces it on bench. Turns handle of vise again.)* Now I have to can-opener this. *(Puts figure balloon into vise; it squeaks.)* She doesn't want to be can-openered.

T.:   She doesn't?

C.:   No. I heard my mummy walking. Hey! It's almost up to here. This number right there. *(Indicates number on wrist watch.)* I hear her coming.

T.:   You hear her coming.

C.:   *(Turns handle of vise. Shakes it back and forth. Looks at nursing bottles. Again turns vise handle and looks out window. Picks up figure balloon and squeezes it; drops it and steps on it.)* I'm gonna throw the ball. You kick it like that.

T.:   Mm-hm. That's what you do to it.

C.:   See what you do? Rocky-rocky the baby to sleep. Where's the baby? Where is she? Here's a mirror.

T.:   Mm-hm.

C.:   *(Peers in mirror of dresser.)* Tick-tick.
T.:   That's the way it goes.
C.:   Tick-tock. Tick-tock. There's the baby in there. *(Points to doll-house.)* Baby walking upstairs. One, two, three, four, five. Into your beds. They're in their beds. Into your bed you go, bad girl. *(Baby doll.)* And this one is a big girl.
T.:   A big girl.
C.:   With a round head. Walk, walk, walk. Here's the daddy going to bed now. Walky, walky, walky. Right next to the girl. *(Middle doll.)*
T.:   Mm-hm.
C.:   And here's the mommy. Walky, walky, walky. Right next to the baby. *(Undresses male doll.)* I'm taking his panties off.
T.:   Mm-hm. You're taking his pants off.
C.:   Walk, walk, walk. Walking up to bed, walking up to bed. Three little children.
T.:   Three little children and two big people.
C.:   And another little baby. Here's me. I'm taking her clothes off. I'm going to bed. Now he's up. *(Male doll.)* Up and up and up. *(Dressing male doll.)* Little up, little up. Put your pants back on. Walky, walky, walky downstairs. *(Female doll.)* Walky, walky, walky downstairs. *(Male doll.)* Walky, walky, walky. *(Another male doll. Walks baby doll downstairs.)* I'm climbing up this ladder. Let's climb up the ladders. Just climbing up the ladders.
T.:   Mm-hm.
C.:   And the little one on top of the bed. *(Middle doll.)* The little one sleeps under the bed. *(Baby doll.)*
T.:   One on top, one underneath.
C.:   Two underneath. Here's the bedroom. *(Bends figure balloon and squeezes it.)* I like that noise. Squeak, squeak, squeak. This is a big bed. Here's your bed.
T.:   That's my bed, huh?
C.:   Who sleeps in that bed?
T.:   Anyone you want.
C.:   Me. This is my little chair. *(Crouches and sits on bed.)* How come this doesn't go? *(Points to watch on arm.)*
T.:   You wonder why it doesn't go?
C.:   Oh. Supper is open. Here's your supper.
T.:   Quite a supper.
C.:   That's my mother's watch. Just pretend its your supper. *(Turns handle of vise.)* Zoom, zoom, zoom, zoom. Here's your supper. Eat it up. Don't eat my mother's watch up. Just eat your supper up. Zoom, zoom, zoom. Here's your watch. Zoom, zoom, zoom. Here's your watch.

COMMENTS

Immediately in this session Susan asks for the baby. The therapeutic process begins as Susan expresses strong hostile feelings against her baby sister. Susan's feelings are clearly focused. She squeezes the balloon and mimics the baby, resentfully. The hostility continues with an attempt to crush the baby's head in the vise. Then Susan expresses a desire to "can-opener" the balloon figure representing her sister. Later she drinks from the baby bottle, indicating a strong interest in being the baby herself and being immature. Susan succeeds in her wish to "can-opener" the baby, while at the same time recognizing how the baby would feel under such treatment. At this point Susan shows anxiety. She crushes the baby balloon figure in the vise, steps back, appears frightened, and imagines her mother approaching. Calm again, Susan repeatedly attacks the baby balloon figure, squeezing it, dropping it, and throwing and kicking it. The hostility continues as Susan throws the baby doll under the bed and indicates it is the baby's sleeping place. She places herself between the mother and father, showing she wants to have the favored place.

Second Session, Susan

C.: *(Talks to mother.)* Are you gonna stay here? Here's a balloon. *(Waves a balloon figure at T.)* Good-by *(to mother.)* Mommy, leave your watch here. I want to see what time it is. *(Looks at T.'s watch.)* It will still be there tomorrow. *(Puts balloon figure in upper part of dollhouse. Empties bag of dolls.)* There. In the garbage can. *(Walks to nursing bottles.)* I'm gonna drink from this. *(Drinks from large bottle and replaces it on bench.)* He's gonna shoot you. *(Cowboy figure.)* Bang. Hoppy is gonna shoot you. Shoot you and tie you up. All cowboys are shooting. *(Handles soldiers and shoots T. a few times.)* Everyone is shot. *(Squeezes figure balloon and it squeaks. Walks figure balloon up the stairs of dollhouse.)* Walk, walk, walk. *(Throws figure balloon aside. Sits on floor, fingers stairway. Picks up figure balloon and whispers.)* She's going to sleep. Shall I take her head off?

T.: That's up to you.

C.: *(Places balloon in box with blocks.)* That's a block. *(Picks up figure balloon again, brushes it against T.'s face.)* I wanta take your glasses off.

T.: You'd like to do that, but that's one thing you can't do here.

C.: Let's pretend to play school. O.K.? And you're the teacher. O.K.?

T.: And I'm the teacher.

C.: *(Cuts a piece of paper and folds it in half. Cuts paper along folded line and into quarters. Looks at T., folds paper again and shows it to T.)* I'm gonna give these to my mother. That's for Mother's Day.

T.: Is that a Mother's Day present?

C.: Yeah. *(Cuts another piece of paper in two.)* This is my mother's present, too.

T.: You have quite a few to give your mother. You like to give her things, huh?

C.: *(Holds papers in hand.)* These are my mother's and my daddy's, too. Just for my mother and daddy. *(Lifts comeback toy.)* He's a big clown.

T.:   Mm-hm.

C.:   *(Carries comeback toy to T.)* There. Walk, walk, walk, walk, walk.

T.:   There you go.

C.:   *(Leans against comeback toy, pushing it down.)*

T.:   You want it to go down.

C.:   Yeah. *(Pushes comeback toy into sandbox.)* He's crying.

T.:   You're making him cry.

C.:   Yeah. *(Finally succeeds in pushing comeback toy into sandbox.)*

T.:   There, you have it.

C.:   He's crying. Nobody's taking him out.

T.:   He is just going to stay in there all the time.

C.:   *(Hands T. papers that she has cut.)* Will you fold these for my mother? And my dad.

T.:   For no one else.

C.:   Not even you.

T.:   Not even me.

C.:   No. *(Starts to cut paper again. Continues. Folds one half-sheet in two again and places it on top of the others.)* See? Some's for my family, and not for you, either.

T.:   Not for me.

C.:   No. *(Cuts more paper.)* Only one is for you, and this is all you're getting. Here. None for your mother. No. It's all mine and my mother's.

T.:   Just yours and your mother's.

C.:   I'll be the teacher and gather up your things. O.K., honey. Let's, honey. Yes, honey. Where's that paper? And you, honey. Honey, honey. I'm gonna sprinkle some. *(Drops a handful of sand from sandbox into pail of water. Watches it. Takes more sand and drops it into pail. Looks at T. and laughs.)* It's all getting brown, isn't it? *(Throws more sand into pail.)* The floor is getting wet. *(Continues to drop handfuls of sand into pail.)* It's getting brown water.

T.:   Yes, it is. It's getting to be brown water.

C.:   *(Throws more sand into pail.)* I splashed my shoe. See? *(Sprinkles some sand over comeback toy. Drops more sand into pail and waves her hands in the air.)* I wanta go wash them.

T.:   You want to go wash them? O.K.

C.:   *(Leaves room with T.)*

COMMENTS

Susan begins this session expressing hostility against the entire family. She throws the family doll figures in the "garbage can." Feeling free, Susan regresses and drinks from the large nursing bottle. She eliminates the therapist by having cowboys shoot him and tie him up. Susan returns to the object of her strongest negative feelings, her baby sister. She squeezes and squeaks the baby balloon figure and fluctuates between pulling off her head and getting rid of her by putting her to sleep.

Another level of the therapeutic process begins. Susan expresses positive feelings for her mother and father, making them presents. She shows mixed emotions toward the therapist, telling him there will be no presents for him or his mother and then calling him "honey" a number of times. Though unclearly expressed, there appear to be some positive feelings for the baby as Susan decides to give presents to "my family."

At the end of the session Susan regresses in her play. She drops handfuls of sand in the water and delights in hearing the sound and seeing the brown color. Susan seems relaxed and satisfied as the session ends.

THIRD SESSION, SUSAN

C.: *(Waves good-by to mother and runs into the room. Drops a handful of sand into pail of water.)*

T.: It went right in, didn't it?

C.: Look how much. *(Drops another, larger, handful into pail and laughs.)* A big splash. Splash. The water's getting brown. *(Drops two more handfuls of sand into the pail.)*

T.: It's getting browner and browner.

C.: Mmm. Now I'm making a pie. *(Plays in sandbox.)*

T.: So you're making a pie, that's what.

C.: Here's your pie.

T.: Is that for me?

C.: Mmm. Take a shovel and eat it. Take a spoon and eat it.

T.: You want me to eat it.

C.: *(Throws more sand into pail and smiles at T.)* O.K. Here. *(Gestures toward T. with shovel.)*

T.: You want me to eat with that, huh?

C.: Not really.

T.: You just want me to pretend?

C.: Yes.

T.: Mm-hm.

C.: I'm throwing it all over the floor. *(Throws sand on the floor.)*

T.: You are?

C.: Swoosh, swoosh, swoosh.

T.: You really like that.

C.: *(Continues to play with sand.)* Now this is a little cookie, and I'll put it in a plate.

T.: Mm-hm.

C.: Here. And I'll give you some more. *(Throws more sand into pail.)* It's getting dark blue.

T.: That's what it's getting to be. Dark blue.

C.: *(Fills mold with sand, pats it, and gives it to T.)* Eat it.

T.: You want me to eat it now.

C.: And then I'll give you some more. Eat it up. O.K. Now eat it.

T.: Now you want me to eat it. Suppose that I don't want any more?

C.: Then you won't get any dessert. Now eat it all up. O.K., now take it. Now pick it up now. Hello, hello, hello, hello. *(Dials telephone.)* Pretend I hear the phone bell ringing, and I say "Hello," and you talk.

T.: Oh, all right. We'll pretend that.

C.: Hello?

T.: Hello.

C.: Who is this?

T.: Who is that?

C.: This is Susan, and she's playing here. Good-by.

T.: Good-by. *(Sneezes.)*

C.: God bless you.

T.: Thank you.

C.: *(Picks up large bottle and drinks. Replaces it on bench.)* I like to play here.

T.: You like coming here and playing.

C.: *(Walks over to balloon figure and kisses it. Tosses it into air and catches it several times while dancing around the room.)*

T.: Well, our time is up for today, Susan.

C.: One more bouncy and I'll go up.

T.: O.K., one more bouncy and we'll go.

C.: *(Throws balloon figure into air one more time. Lets it fall on floor.)* O.K. Good-by. Good-by, Mister.

T.: Good-by.

COMMENTS

In this session, a new level of the therapeutic process begins. Susan's feelings are not only more moderate but more positive. Her feelings toward her baby sister indicate a definite change. She takes the baby balloon figure, kisses it, tosses it into the air, and dances around the room.

CONCLUDING COMMENT

For Susan the basic aspects of the process may be summarized as follows: (1) She expresses direct hostility toward the baby; (2) her feelings toward the baby become ambivalent and are unclearly expressed; and (3) she expresses positive feelings and interest in her baby sister and other members of the family.

Susan's mother came in after this last session to tell the therapist that she was happy about Susan, who had again become a pleasant child; that she was no longer afraid to leave Susan with the baby; and that Susan showed affection for the baby and had assumed some responsibility in the baby's care.

STEWART

Stewart was the most popular child in the nursery school. He was considered an outstanding leader by his teachers. He enjoyed every aspect of the school program and played and worked with delight, concentration, and enthusiasm. He initiated the play sessions on his own, asking the therapist if he could come to the playroom.

First Session, Stewart

S.: Look at all these toys.

T.: In here you can use them any way you wish.

S.: We can play games if we want to. Here's a balloon. Let's play catch. (*S. and T. play with the balloon for a few minutes.*) What's this? You push it and it comes back. This is an airplane. My dad helps me make them. Look, a jump rope. Lookit the house. We can play games in here. (*S. enters the sandbox.*) I love to play in the sandbox. I'm gonna play in here. (*S. plays with sand materials for eight minutes.*) Is there water in here? (*S. fills a pail of water and floats canoes. Then he pours water into the sandbox.*) They float in the pail and they float in here too. Watch. People can't float in there.

T.: No. They couldn't.

S.: Children like to float boats. There it goes around. If I fill it with sand it will sink. (*S. fills the boat and watches it go under the water. He takes three more boats.*) Watch them go down stream. All boats go to shore sometime. (*S. puts various objects in the canoes.*) Now these things are having a ride. You can use a paddle and paddle down to shore.

T.: Mm-hm.

S.: This is a school where children go. I'm covering the boats cause they're all going to sleep. And tomorrow I'll play with them. (*Pause.*) Look at the balloons. (*S. plays with balloons for the remaining time.*)

Comments

Stewart began with a feeling of excitement and entered into his play with confidence. His expressions were consistently positive and reflected a certain sophistication. He has a way of observing and making generalizations that seem entirely appropriate. Due to illness, Stewart did not return again for three months. In the interim, two major events occurred in his life: a baby sister had joined the family and U.S. troops were sent to Korea. Two of his uncles were in the army. On his return to school, he approached the therapist again and asked to go to the playroom. Since he was about to enter kindergarten, he was told there was time for only two more sessions. He accepted this arrangement and approached the play materials with an entirely different attitude.

Second Session, Stewart

(*S. enters the room and goes immediately to a shelf with soldiers.*)

S.: These soldiers are marching to Korea. (*S. lines up the figures in the sandbox.*) They are all going to Korea. This is a machine gun they need.

T.: Mmhm, all soldiers head for Korea.

S.: Yeah. That's right, isn't it? If that's the way you do it. Look at this soldier move on his feet. This motorcycle is going too. This is a white guy and another white guy. This one is waving a flag. They are all heading for Korea. This is a drum player with a flag. This man has a rocket. This one throws an arrow. *(Pause.)* Ladies aren't supposed to go to Korea, are they?

T.: You don't believe they will.

S.: The men are all going to Korea. This fireman with an axe is going to chop things in Korea. He is putting a flag in the ground. These men going to Korea are going to shoot the bad guys.

T.: There will be a terrible battle.

S.: They shouldn't be in Korea, should they?

T.: You think they belong in their homes?

S.: They could get shot, couldn't they?

T.: Are you afraid they will get shot?

S.: Are you not going to Korea. *(S. leaves the soldier and plays with Bobo several minutes.)* I'm going to throw a dart at him. *(Pause.)* No, I won't. I can even lift him like this and lay him down like this.

T.: You can do lots of things with him.

S.: Yeah. I can ride him and even put him in the sandbox. *(Pause.)* Who brings these toys here? Do you? Do you make them at work?

T.: No. They are bought at different stores.

S.: A factory makes them—a toy factory. I'm going to let the air out of him and make him a baby.

T.: Do you want him to be a baby?

S.: Yeah. *(S. glances around the room.)* I'm going to feed that baby. *(S. gets a doll and nursing bottle. He feeds the baby a few minutes.)* Can I drink out of it?

T.: If you wish. It's up to you. *(S. drinks from the bottle. He alternates between feeding the doll and drinking himself.)*

T.: Sometimes it's fun to be like a baby.

S.: Yeah. It is fun to drink from the bottle.

T.: You have just about five minutes left today.

S.: I'm going to feed the baby. Where is the bathtub for the baby? Oh! I see it over there. *(S. continues alternating the bottle.)*

T.: A little for the baby and a little for you.

S.: Yeah. *(Pause.)* I'm going to give the rest to her. I am going back to the war. *(S. returns to the soldiers.)* I've got to line up the soldiers. Soldiers aren't supposed to be in wars, are they?

T.: You don't believe they should be.

S.: No. Cause they will get shot. *(Pause.)* If I put them right behind each other they could shoot each other and fall. *(S. suddenly runs to Bobo and hits him repeatedly.)* We had better go back to nursery school right now.

THIRD SESSION, STEWART

(Stewart gathers the soldiers and lines them up in the sandbox. He plays silently for ten minutes.)

S.: Junk.

T.: Junk?

S.: Yes. The war is junk. Where is that garbage truck. *(S. locates the truck and places soldiers in it.)* I'll put them in the junkyard. They all will burn up.

T.: You think that will stop the war to burn them all up?

S.: Yes. He's going in and he's going too. They all fight—even ladies and little girls fight.

T.: So you're taking them all to the junkyard to be burned.

S.: I'm going to put them in the sandbox. They are all getting burned. *(S. puts the truck in the sandbox and pours sand on the figures.)* They all get buried. See. *(S. takes the soldiers out of the truck and buries them in the sand.)* Everyone will be buried and die.

T.: Is that how you feel about soldiers and war?

S.: Yeah. They are all getting buried. I'm putting more sand on and they are all going to get buried under this hill. *(Pause.)* Can I get buried too?

T.: That's up to you.

S.: I'm almost all buried but not quite. *(S. gets out of the sandbox.)* Here is a little girl but I won't bury her.

T.: You'll bury all the soldiers but not the little girl.

S.: Yeah. If they're buried, they can't use their guns.

T.: You bury them so there will be no killing with guns.

S.: I'm making a hill out of them.

T.: Just a few more minutes left.

S.: This one I'm going to free. He'll work on a farm. This one too. None of them are buried. They aren't in a trap. They are all freed.

T.: You want them to go back to their own work on the farms and cities.

S.: Yeah. They all have to stand up and go back to their families. *(S. takes the nursing bottle and places it next to the baby girl.)* That's where the baby bottle belongs. To this baby.

T.: Our time is up now.

S.: We'll go back right now.

COMMENTS

The change in Stewart's play is striking. In his last sessions two central attitudes are expressed. He seems to be struggling with the reality of war—what it means, what it does to individuals and families. He also explores his feelings toward his baby sister. His play conveys an awareness of the tragedy of war and his fear that men will kill each other and that eventually women and children may be destroyed too. In several episodes, he solves the problem of war by destroying all soldiers, but in the end he realizes that killing them is no answer so he returns them to their families on farms and in cities.

His feelings toward his baby sister are ambivalent. He feeds and cares for her while at the same time wishing to replace her, acting the baby himself and drinking from the nursing bottle. After repeating this sequence a number of times, being the baby holds no further satisfaction for Stewart. He places the nursing bottle next to the baby doll and indicates that is where it belongs.

In his play, Stewart explored his fears and worries, his need to regress and his hostile feelings. The nursery school staff had noticed the change in his behavior after the illness. The passivity and aggression lasted only a short time. His teachers felt the combination of the play sessions and the special recognition and attention he was given in nursery school enabled him to work through his temporary conflicts and return to his former creative, happy self and his leadership in the group.

Value of Play Therapy for Susan and Stewart

What these children needed was an opportunity to express their negative feelings in an accepting relationship where they were trusted as individuals and where their feelings and perceptions were respected.

Play therapy provided Susan and Stewart with an opportunity to work out temporarily disturbing feelings and so removed the possibility that these feelings would be repressed, lose their identification with reality, become distorted, and perhaps eventually cause serious damage to the child's sense of self and self-esteem.

Freed from the temporarily disturbing feelings, these children once again were able to use their capacities and talents in work and play and in relations with other children and adults.

The Adjusted Child Severely Disturbed

In the two examples below both children were regarded as well adjusted by the nursery school staff, but in the playroom they expressed intense feelings of rejection and hostility.

Jim

Jim initiated the play therapy experience himself. Daily he pleaded with his teachers to allow him to visit the playroom. Finally, he accepted and agreed to an arrangement whereby he would come once a week for play sessions until the end of the school year. He was seen a total of ten times.

First Session, Jim

J.: I have a Norwegian ski cap. My dad bought it for me. *(Pause.)*
T.: Jim, these things are for you to play with any way you want.
J.: Yeah, I know. *(J. immediately begins punching Bobo, harder and harder.)*
T.: You like to hit him hard. *(J. finally knocks Bobo under a table.)* Ouch! You really socked him that time. *(J. picks up Bobo.)*
J.: Come on, get up! Get up!
T.: You like to hit him.
J.: Yeah. Especially him. *(Pause.)* Where are the darts?
T.: I don't see any here now.

J.: I guess you're right. There aren't any darts. *(J. picks up a truck.)* Say, this is nice. *(J. examines the truck opening the doors, removing the tail gate.) (J. puts a father doll figure in the truck).*

T.: You want to lose him in there.

J.: I'll shut the top down on him. Where's a shovel. *(J. takes a shovel and pours sand on the figure.)* Crash! Boom! *(J. slams the truck doors.)* Keep still you shmoo. Now we'll dump it. *(J. has difficulty dumping the truck.)* How do you dump this?

T.: It's not easy to turn over but I think you can manage.

J.: There. I got it. *(J. approaches the cash register. He plays with it a few minutes. He picks up three knives and throws them across the room. He picks up a toy needing repairs.)* If we had a supply of nails, we'd fix this.

T.: You like to fix things.

J.: And I like to make things too. *(J. begins playing with a ring toss set.)* Oh, I got it in.

T.: Looks like a good game for you.

J.: *(J. tosses two more rings successfully. Then he misses.)* That doesn't count. *(Misses another.)* That doesn't count either. *(J. continues missing.)* Aw heck, I'll try once more. *(Misses again.)* It makes me mad.

T.: Really makes you mad.

J.: *(J. places the rings on the peg.)* Damn darts! I wish they were here.

T.: Damn darts!

J.: *(J. approaches easel and opens jars to paint.)* This is a nice shade of blue. I'm going to mix blue with green and yellow and make a new color. I should have turpentine to thin it.

T.: The paints are mixed with water—not oil. *(Pause.)* Only a few minutes left today. *(J. paints during the remaining time.)*

J.: Can I come back tomorrow?

T.: You can come again next week on Tuesday.

J.: Okay.

COMMENTS

Jim's discharge of feelings onto the Bobo was somewhat violent, indicating a degree of underlying hostility. His negative feelings continued in more direct form in the burying of the father figure and the dumping of it into the sandbox. Acceptance of these feelings by the therapist helped Jim to feel some release and to go on to organized play. Jim seemed confident and self-assured. He knew what he wanted to do and was able to carry through his activities to completion.

SECOND SESSION, JIM

J.: I fight this fellow. *(J. knocks Bobo down.)* Come on. Get up. You're not dead. Down he goes. Up he goes. Come on. You're not dead. One, two, three strikes, he's out. *(J. begins playing with the cash register. He has difficulty opening the door.)* Aw, what's wrong with this thing. I wish you'd get a new cash register.

T.: It annoys you that you can't get that old one to work right.

J.: *(J. picks up a bucket of water. He yells "timber" as he tosses it into the sandbox. He then turns to the easel and paints quietly for about ten minutes.)* You know, on TV they mannapped him.

T.: Mannapped?

J.: Yeah. Mannapped. Not kidnapped, you know. Mannapped. *(J. takes two male figures and drops them into a pail of water.)* Put these old men down in water. Full of water. Be still, you. *(J. pushes the figures down and up.)* Get down there. Get down there. *(J. repeats this sequence several times. He holds the figures under water with a brush. He takes the brush and throws it violently across the room. With a sprinkling can he pours water over the men as they float.)*

T.: You want to cover them and keep them deep down under the water.

J.: *(J. throws the sprinkler forcibly onto the floor. Then for the next ten minutes he repairs broken toys.)* I'll just leave them there for use some other time. *(J. returns to the "men" in the pail of water.)* Stay down there! *(He takes cups of water from the pail and throws them into the sandbox. One cup nearly hits the therapist.)*

T.: Do you want to drown me, too?

J.: Naw. I wouldn't. Cause you're the nice man who brings me over to the playroom. I wouldn't want to hit you with water. I'm getting it all over the sand to goosh it up. *(J. continues throwing water into the sand. He takes the male figures from the bucket and throws them violently across the room.)*

T.: That gets rid of them.

J.: Yeah. Sure does. *(J. climbs into the sandbox and immediately gets out.)* I'd better not get my shoes all muddy. *(J. shovels sand and throws it hard against a wall.)*

T.: We have about five more minutes, Jim.

J.: *(J. picks up two knives. He throws them across the room.)* Bang! Boom! If I had real knives I'd throw them in the dart board and make them stick. *(J. picks up a girl doll and throws it against a wall.)* See her leg, I broke it off.

T.: Yes, it's gone now.

J.: I'll get these girls too. *(J. throws them across the room.)* That takes care of them. *(J. continues throwing items to the end of the hour.)*

T.: It's time for us to leave now.

J.: Bye. Bye. *(On the way out, J. shoves Bobo into water on the floor.)* Ol' fighter, down you go, right in the water.

COMMENTS

This session again was characterized by considerable expression of hostility. For the most part it was of diffuse, general nature, such as throwing the bucket, slamming the brush across the room, scooping up sand and throwing it against the walls. At times the hostility was more focused, e.g., Jim's "drowning" of the men in a bucket of water, dragging the "ol' fellow" in water, breaking off the leg of the girl doll, and "getting rid" of all the girl figures. These acts perhaps convey Jim's negative feelings toward his father and sister.

In contrast, there were many episodes of constructive, organized activity such as the painting and the repairing of broken toys. It is possible that others' (teachers and parents) perception of Jim as a quiet, placid boy have kept him in such a role and prevented him from expressing assertive strivings and aggressive wishes.

THIRD SESSION, JIM AND HENRY

J.: Oh, good, the darts are here today. Whoever gets the bull's eye wins. *(Jim and Henry throw the darts. J. sticks one in the dart board.)*

H.: You win.

J.: No. Whoever gets the bull's eye wins. *(J. throws one in the bull's eye.)*

H.: There, you did it. *(H. picks up the darts.)*

J.: Hey, I want the darts. You don't know how to play.

H.: You don't know how either. *(H. leaves the darts and plays with the cash register. He is still holding three darts. J. pulls these darts away from him and hits him with his fist. H. pushes J. into a chair.)*

J.: Oh! Too bad, Hen. You don't know how. *(J. scores another bull's eye.)*

T.: You got it that time.

H.: Look I'm see saw. Just like See Saw Marjorie Daw. *(H. gets a balloon and tosses it into the air.)*

J.: If you're not careful, you'll bust it, Hen. You don't want to get killed, do you?

H.: I'm going to blow it up and bust it in your face.

J.: Hey, look at that. Three out of one, or one out of three, I should say. *(J. approaches H. with a dart and punctures the balloon.)*

H.: Why did you do that, Jim?

J.: I wanted to bust it. *(H. gets a gun, points it at J., and shoots.)*

H.: That was too bad for the balloon. *(J. returns to dart throwing. He stops and kicks the waste basket, spilling its contents onto the floor.)*

T.: Are you trying to show how tough you can be. *(J. approaches H. who is playing with tinker toys. He grabs at the box. They struggle for several minutes. J. succeeds in getting the box.)*

T.: You seem to be keeping Henry from doing what he wants.

J.: I'm strong. *(J. dumps tinker toys onto the floor and resumes the dart game.)* Hey, Henry, better watch out. You might get hit with a dart.

H.: I'm not afraid of you. *(J. secures the girl figures and throws them violently across the room.)*

J.: I just feel like throwing things today. *(J. throws the father figure against the door.)*

T.: I see that you do. You want to throw the father and sister dolls. *(H. secures more male figures, hands them to J. and tells him to throw them. J. throws these items and begins pounding on the house with a wooden hammer. H. joins him.)*

J.: One, two, three, six. *(J. kicks tinker toys across the room. H. puts on a mask and approaches the therapist.)*

H.:   Boo. *(J. approaches H. and raises a dart to stick him.)*
T.:   No, Jim. I can't let you do that. I'll have to take it from you.
J.:   I was only teasing.
T.:   I know you like to tease but from now on you'll have to leave the darts in the board when you aren't playing the game.
J.:   Okay. I'll play nice with them. *(Pause.)* Sometimes I'm so unhappy. I feel like kicking.
T.:   When you get angry with people why don't you tell them. *(J. punches Bobo to the end of the hour. H. is painting.)*
T.:   Well, it's about time to go now.
J.:   Can I come back again?
T.:   Yes, next Tuesday again. You know, in here it's all right to get mad and throw things, but you understand why I had to limit your use of the darts?
J.:   Yes.

COMMENTS

In this session Jim's hostile expression continued. It is significant that, in the playroom, he is assertive and aggressive and tries to dominate Henry, whereas in the nursery school he is submissive in this relationship. He seems to be trying desperately to convince Henry and the therapist that he is a strong, skillful boy. In consistently attempting to show Henry his superiority, he reflects his own uncertainty and his feelings of inferiority. In spite of Jim's assertiveness and willful, demanding ways, Henry maintained his independence and would interact with Jim only on equal terms.

Perhaps the most significant episode was the setting of the limit with the darts. This involved a situation in which the therapist's concern was for Henry's safety. Initially, Jim may have interpreted the limit to mean that the therapist cared more for Henry. Jim directly verbalized his unhappiness. This gave the therapist an opportunity to encourage Jim's expression of anger and to reach an understanding with him.

FOURTH SESSION, JIM

J.:   *(J. goes immediately to the darts and begins throwing. He sighs heavily when he misses.)* Those don't count. Monkey face. *(J. takes a tray of silverware.)* Mm. This one smells. It smells funny. It would be good for feeding Jeffie. He's my baby.
T.:   You think he should be fed with a smelly spoon?
J.:   You always tell me to play any way I want to.
T.:   Well, that's so. *(J. takes the girl figures and throws them on the floor.)*
J.:   Wait a minute. I didn't break this one. *(He throws it harder.)* Now I broke it.
T.:   You got rid of all the girls.
J.:   Ha! Ha! See, saw. *(J. begins punching Bobo vigorously.)* Knock him on the nose. *(J. kicks Bobo around the room. He stops by the easel*

and paints two pictures.) You know, once I struck a match. I'd like to do it here. Do you have one?

T.: No. I do not. *(J. goes back to painting. He jabs the brushes violently into the jars. He paints his hands.)* Real good and yellow. Now a little bit o' green. *(He returns to his painting and works peacefully for five minutes.)* It's a pretty picture, isn't it?

T.: You like it very much.

J.: Maybe I'll be an artist. I'll make another one. You'll have to watch and see what time it is.

T.: Okay. We now have about five more minutes.

J.: About five more minutes. *(J. continues painting. He mixes colors together.)* This is a real pretty shade. *(As he uses the mixed colors, he empties them in a bucket of water. When he finishes, he washes all the jars and replaces them on the easel.)*

T.: Our time is up now, Jim.

J.: Okay. Goodbye.

COMMENTS

In the first part of the hour, the general hostility and attack on the girl figures continued, but in the latter part Jim began to express some positive feeling. He became warm and friendly in his comments to the therapist. When he painted at the end of the hour, he was composed and peaceful, used delicate strokes, and made "pretty" pictures. He seemed to realize that other children might not want to use his mixed paints, so he dumped them out, washed the jars, and replaced them. There seemed to be a definite shift in this session to positive feelings and a movement toward a healthy and constructive relating to people and situations.

FIFTH SESSION, JIM

(J. begins the session playing with a cash register.)

J.: This is a cute thing. Look, 90 cents. Let's play money. Pretend you come to Waukegan and you want something and I am Jim, the owner.

T.: Okay.

J.: What do you want to buy?

T.: Maybe a gun?

J.: All right, ten dollars.

T.: Sounds like a lot of money.

J.: Yes. Excuse me, it's the telephone ringing. Oh, Dee. Okay, come over later. I can't talk now.

T.: You really like to play store. *(Pause.)*

J.: I'm going to punch that. *(J. hits Bobo hard many times, knocks it down.)*

T.: You hurt him?

J.: Mh-hm. Hey, two knives. I'm going to cut something up. I'm gonna cut that house. Cut! Cut! Cut! Cut the house up. I cut the house up. *(J. drops the knives and picks up two tractors.)* I like these. *(J. plays with the tractors a few minutes and then takes the darts. He throws them and goes to the sandbox.)* I'm gonna play here. *(He gets into the sandbox for the first time. He builds a castle and hums and sings.)*

J.:   There. Doesn't it look like a castle. It's a big one. Now here's a little teeny weeny one. *(J. leaves the sandbox, secures a gun, and shoots the therapist.)*

T.:   Do you want to shoot me?

J.:   No. This can't hurt anybody. *(J. goes to the sandbox shoots the castles and stamps on them. Then he approaches Bobo.)* He's going to get a punch into his nose. *(J. picks up Bobo, punches it hard and jumps up and down on its head. He repeats this sequence. He takes a sprinkling can and pours water over Bobo.)* That's all. I'm not going to water him any more. *(Pause.)*

J.:   Say do you have a television.

T.:   No. I do not.

J.:   You should buy one. Laurel and Hardy is real funny.

T.:   You really like television.

J.:   Yes. My sister does too. She got sick last night. My dad called her a dope. My mommy did too.

T.:   How did you feel about it.

J.:   I didn't like it very well. She is my own sister.

T.:   You don't like your own sister treated that way.

J.:   No! She's not anyone else's sister. *(J. gets knives, cuts the sand, and buries the knives.)* I'm gonna crash everything before I go. *(J. gets the sprinkler and pours water on the sand.)*

T.:   We'll have to leave in a short while. *(J. goes to the easel and paints during the remaining time.)*

J.:   Will you take the paper off so I can take it home?

T.:   Yes.

J.:   I'm having lots of fun over here.

T.:   I see you are, but it's time to stop for now.

COMMENTS

In this session there was much more organized, constructive activity. The intensity of the hostile expression diminished considerably. Jim related an episode in which he supported his sister, indicating his capacity to empathize with her when she is under fire. His interaction with the therapist is now friendly rather than rooted in anger. Even when he "shot" the therapist he assured him the gun was harmless and would hurt nobody. He ended the session painting freely and enjoying the experience.

SIXTH SESSION, JIM

(J. begins immediately punching Bobo.)

J.:   He's a fighter.

T.:   You like to sock him.

J.: Punch. Punch.

T.: You hit him hard that time.

J.: I'm gonna make this a punching bag.

T.: You like punching him hard?

J.: Wee! Bang. Now I'm gonna dig in the sandbox. *(J. procures sand tools.)* Here are all the tools I need. *(J. works quietly in the sand about ten minutes.)* I like this sand better than the nursery school. You know what we saw on television last night? We saw Dean Martin and Jerry Lewis. Jerry Lewis flew in the air on a kite. *(Pause.)* The more I learn about highways the better I like them. When I finish the highways, I'll put cars on them. Look, I'm down to the bottom of the sandbox and I made a little hole. *(Pause.)* Do you have any children?

T.: There are children in your house, I know.

J.: Mm-hm. I have a sister and a baby. I'm the one that goes to nursery school. She goes where the big girls go.

T.: Is that okay with you?

J.: No. I don't like it.

T.: You think you should go to the big school.

J.: Pretty soon I'm gonna go there. *(J. returns to the Bobo and punches it vigorously for a few minutes. He takes a rubber knife.)* This is what I'm gonna do with this knife. Gonna cut the house. Cut the chimney.

T.: You want to cut it all up.

J.: I'll leave all the knives in here. *(J. goes to the easel and paints quietly for about eight minutes.)*

J.: I'm gonna play with the tinker toys now.

T.: You like tinker toys.

J.: Yup. I like playing with them. I'm gonna make a tall, huge tower. *(J. works to the end of the hour.)* Now, isn't that just peachy dandy?

T.: It is peachy dandy.

J.: Hey! I'm gonna take my painting home this time.

COMMENTS

In this session, Jim continued to play in a concentrated, positive fashion. The few episodes of aggressive behavior were of short duration. He expressed confidence in knowing what he wanted to do and seemed satisfied with the results. His interaction with the therapist continued on a friendly basis. His decision to take the painting home indicates an acceptance of his work and a wish to share it with his family.

SEVENTH, EIGHTH, AND NINTH SESSIONS, JIM

In these sessions, the only aggressive acts were punching of the Bobo. He worked for long periods of time with the paints, tinker toys, and sand equipment. In two lengthy episodes he talked about his baby brother. He indicated he enjoyed feeding the baby. He played with a baby figure, feeding and bathing it gently and lovingly. He described a family trip, spoke positively of a cousin who had visited him, and talked at length about several television programs. He approached the playroom in a tranquil mood and seemed to be in harmony with himself and his environment.

TENTH SESSION, JIM

J.: This is the last time I come.

T.: Yes. How do you feel about that?

J.: *(J. does not respond. He walks slowly around the room, handling certain items gently and replacing them. He stops at the darts about ten minutes and plays with the cash register about five minutes.)*

T.: You want to try all the things you've done before. *(J. gets the sand tools and begins digging.)*

J.: Will you get me that truck over there? *(T. procures the truck and hands it to J.)* This is a truck load for my backyard. Good, black dirt. *(As he plays, he sings "Happy Birthday" several times.)*

T.: You like having birthdays, huh?

J.: Yeah. Look, I'm a rocket. *(J. runs back and forth across the room for several minutes, screaming gleefully. He then goes to the easel and makes two paintings.)*

J.: I want to leave now.

T.: You have about ten more minutes but we can leave now if you wish.

J.: I want to go back now.

T.: All right.

COMMENTS

In this last session, Jim was happy and spontaneous. His play indicated an acceptance of the terminal meeting. When he had taken his last look at some of the items and participated in his favorite activities, he was ready to leave.

In the nursery school, with the exception of minor arguments and conflicts, Jim related with other children on a positive basis. His teachers reported that he continued to be a well-adjusted child throughout the therapy sessions. They saw no evidence of emotional disturbance. Even so, the content and feeling in his play, particularly in the initial meetings, indicate underlying tensions and conflicts especially toward his sister and father—feelings that possibly were alleviated through his frequent and intense hostile expressions in the accepting atmosphere of relationship therapy. These angry feelings may never have been deterrents to his growth, but the fact remains that he came to terms with them in the playroom and went on to more positive expression and activity.

SALLY

Sally was seen in four sessions. Following the play therapy meetings, a referral for long term therapy was made to the counseling service. The play interviews with Sally reveal the depth of her loneliness, feeling of rejection and wish to retaliate.

First Session, Sally

S.: What is your name?

T.: My name is Mr. Moustakas.

S.: That's a funny name. *(Pause.)* I wanta make a house in there. *(S. begins furnishing the house.)* Some of these are broken.

T.: Yes. I see.

S.: Somebody must have broke them. *(S. begins sucking her thumb.)* Who else was here?

T.: You think some child came and broke them?

S.: I—Yes! Let's make this house together. You tell me where things go. Where should we put this table?

T.: Now, let's see.

S.: Right here. Well have a far-away living room. And we're going to have to make a bathroom too.

T.: Yes. That's important.

S.: So everybody can have a bathroom. You could fix it, couldn't you?

T.: What would you like me to do?

S.: You make this chair stand up.

T.: Where shall I put it.

S.: Put it in here. Now where shall I put this? In this kitchen. Aren't we making a nice house? Where could I put these dishes and cups?

T.: Where?

S.: In the drawer in the kitchen. *(During the next twenty minutes this pattern continues as Sally puts the furniture in the house. Then there is a shift in her play. This part of the session follows.)*

S.: Isn't it a hard time to make a house?

T.: It takes a lot of work.

S.: It takes a lot of work to build a house. No people in this house. *(S. takes all the family figures and places them in a corner of the playroom.)*

T.: They all get out.

S.: I smack those right away.

T.: Feels good to do that.

S.: Yeah. *(S. climbs onto T.'s lap. She leans against him and hugs him.)* Now, I'm gonna paint. *(She copies a picture from a book.)* I'll cut it around in a circle and take it home. To the teacher I'll show it.

T.: You want to show it to your mother and teacher.

S.: Yeah. I can feel the black. My hands get black.

T.: Does it feel bad?

S.: I don't wanna get them black. *(S. washes her hands a number of times.)* You help me finish the house now.

T.: The time is almost up for today.

S.: Let's get the house finished. Let's hurry. You gotta hurry. We gotta finish before our time is up. We needs lots of bathrooms to scrub and make things clean.

T.: Lots of places to scrub.

S.: Now, doesn't it look like a nice house?

T.: A real nice house.

S.: The people aren't in it. You know, my house is gonna be all cleaned up. Am I gonna be here another time?

T.: Yes, if you wish.

S.: Am I gonna be here every time.

T.: Several more times. (As T. and S. start to leave, S. picks up a toy rifle and shoots T.)

T.: You shot me.

S.: Don't say that any more.

T.: I won't say it again.

S.: I don't want to get up close to you.

T.: You want to stay far away.

S.: Yeah.

T.: All right.

COMMENTS

Perhaps the two most significant episodes in this session are Sally's rejection of the family figures and her comment to the therapist that she prefers to be separated from him. She seemed extremely anxious while she furnished the house. She talked constantly. She asked repeated questions. She kept seeking the therapist's help without wanting or needing it. She sucked her thumb during most of the hour. Also, she seemed to be compelled to put things in the right place, to keep them neat and orderly, and to keep herself and her clothing clean. She apparently wanted to be close to the therapist, to include him, and share with him, but underneath there seemed to be growing doubt, suspicion, and distrust.

In the second session, she did not speak at all. She began by placing the family figures in a corner of the room and repeated in a similar manner the furnishing of the house. She seemed lonely and deeply depressed. The therapist accepted her decision to remain silent. He stood by, watching and attempting to understand her behavior.

THIRD SESSION, SALLY

(In contrast to the silence of the previous hour, Sally immediately began talking.)

S.: We're gonna have to build the house again.

T.: That's what we'll do this time.

S.: Yeah. (S. removes her coat.) I left my boots in the car.

T.: But you didn't get your shoes wet.

S.: No. (S. starts furnishing the house.) You can't have any of my toys. You can't touch any of these.

T.: Not anything?

S.: You can't touch anything.

T.: You want everything for yourself.

S.: You don't touch a single thing. Keep your hands off. Cause you—I don't like you. You keep your hands off.

T.: You don't like me at all?

S.:   Cause—cause you cause I don't know what you'll do every time I come.

T.:   You never are sure what I might do?

S.:   No. Why is the stairway broken? *(Pause.)* Well, people. *People!* They're gonna have to jump down.

T.:   They'll tumble all the way down.

S.:   Yeah. All the way down. Now, where did we have the bathroom?

T.:   Hard to remember.

S.:   Where did we have everything? I think I remember. Help me make it. You take these toilets.

T.:   Where shall I put them?

S.:   Right here. Close in line.

T.:   Line them all up.

S.:   Yes. You take some things and I'll take some things.

T.:   What shall I take?

S.:   You can take just what you want.

T.:   What would you like me to take?

S.:   You can take anything you want, I said. I said you can take anything.

T.:   Supposing I take a table. Where shall I put it?

S.:   Put it right here. Now take some again. Take something. Take something again. *(Sings.)* Take something again.

T.:   Shall I take this mirror?

S.:   They don't have a roof.

T.:   No roof.

S.:   Just half a roof. There's a big hole to look through.

T.:   They can look out and see the sky.

S.:   No, they can't.

T.:   It's shut off from them.

S.:   Shut the sky off. This mirror is just for me so I can see myself. *(Pause.)* Do you want *me?*

T.:   I care about you.

S.:   Then you can take anything you want.

T.:   All right.

S.:   And you want me to take something I want.

T.:   Yes. I want you to take something you want.

S.:   Yes. *(S. rearranges the beds. Looks at T. for about a minute.)* Now what *should* you—what do you *want* to take?

T.:   Maybe I'll take this.

S.:   Okay. *(Pause.)* I'm going to live right here all the time.

T.:   All the time? Yes! I'm gonna stay forever and ever.

T.:   Will you never leave?

S.:   No. I'm not gonna come out of here forever and ever.
      Not forever and ever.
      Not forever and ever.
      Ever and ever and always.
      Not ever.
      Not ever.
      Not forever and ever and ever and ever.

T.: For a long, long time.

S.: Yes. And you'll never calm down.

T.: You want me to stay wild.

S.: Yes. I want you to stay wild.

T.: Forever and ever and ever.

S.: Forever and ever and ever. *(Pause. An angry expression suddenly appears on Sally's face.)* Get out of here!

T.: You want me to leave?

S.: Yes. Stay out in the hallway.

T.: But I want to be here with you. I'll sit far, far away if you like.

S.: Sit way—sit way far. Not in the little chair. Stand up! Stand up and get tired.

T.: Over here in the corner?

S.: Yes. Don't sit on a chair. Don't sit there.

T.: Not on anything, and far away from you?

S.: Yeah. You can't be close to anything.

T.: You want me away from everything?

S.: Yeah. Now you don't have anything

T.: Away from everything. Out in the cold.

S.: Move further away. Now you can't—now you don't have anything. You're out in the cold.

T.: Away from all good things.

S.: All pretty things are away from you.

T.: Nothing left for me.

S.: No. Can't have anything. *(Pause.)* You can have some of the dirties.

T.: Only dirty things for me.

S.: You can have this dirty thing. That's the only thing you can have. *(S. picks up a gun and shoots T.)* There. Want me to do that again?

T.: It's up to you.

S.: I will do it. *(S. shoots again.)* Again.

T.: Bang.

S.: You won't—don't talk to any people. You must watch me.

T.: You don't want me to say anything.

S.: No. Can't talk to anybody. I'm gonna shoot you again. There. You're dead. You're dead. You can't talk to anyone. Cause I got a little girl and you can't have her. Get out in the hallway and sit.

T.: But I want to be here with you.

S.: Why?

T.: Because I care about your feelings. I'm interested in you.

S.: You can't touch anything. You can't touch anything. Not a single thing. *(S. takes clay.)* I'm gonna play with the clay. And I'm gonna give you this. Cold clay. And you won't have any nice warm clay. There, I'm gonna put this in your face.

T.: Just cold clay.

S.: I'm gonna put this in your face. *(S. approaches T.)*

T.: I understand your wanting to, but I can't let you.

S.: I'll make a little ball and shoot you. You're gonna be dead on my birthday.

T.: I'm gonna die then?

S.: Yes. *(S. laughs nervously, shoots T.)* There. I'm finished. And you can't talk even. You can't say a word. You're gonna have a hard— you're gonna have a hard time. *(Pause.)* You're gonna be alive.

T.: You've decided I'm to live?

S.: Yes, you're gonna be alive. And Santa Claus won't bring your little daughter anything. I'm gonna tear your daughter's bed. I'm telling Santa Claus she's bad.

T.: My daughter is bad?

S.: Yes. She gets nothing.

T.: Poor little daughter.

S.: Poor little daughter. *(Pause.)* I'm gonna tell Santa Claus my brother is good.

T.: Your brother is the good one.

S.: And your boy daughter and girl daughter isn't good.

T.: No good at all.

S.: No. *(S. takes clay again.)* I'm gonna cut this clay up. *(S. smears clay onto the floor.)*

T.: You're smearing it on the floor.

S.: Yeah. Nobody won't know who did it.

T.: You don't want them to know. Maybe they'll think you're a bad little girl.

S.: Don't you tell them.

T.: You don't want anyone to know?

S.: No. They'll have to sweep it up. It's gonna be all splattered on the floor. How long do I have?

T.: About ten minutes.

S.: I better hurry up then. *(Continues smearing clay for a few minutes, then stops.)* I want to make something before I go. Write my name on this paper.

T.: All right.

S.: Cause I wanta take it to school. *(S. draws.)* I'm making cookies. *(Pause.)* I'll tell *your* daddy that you're bad.

T.: My daddy?

S.: Yeah. I'm gonna use up all the red paint so no one else will have it. *(S. uses red paint. She dips a brush into yellow paint.)* I'm gonna put this on your hands and you're gonna eat it. I'm gonna make you eat it. *(S. approaches T.)*

T.: You can use it in other ways, but I don't want it on my hands.

S.: You're gonna have to take it home to your brother.

T.: To eat.

S.: My brother—I'm gonna take this home to my brother.

T.: To *your* brother?

S.: Yes. I wanta wash my hands. Come with me. No. You stay here.

T.: All right. *(S. returns.)* It's about time to leave. *(S. picks up a balloon and breaks it in her hands.)*

S.: I broke it. Goody. I broke it.

T.: You're glad.

S.: I'm glad I broke it. Nobody can fix it.

T.: Nobody can ever put it together.

S.: No. I'll break another one. I'll break all of them.
T.: Just one more. Then we'll have to leave.
S.: I broke it.
T.: You broke another.
S.: I broke two balloons. I broke two good ones. Goody.
T.: You're happy now.
S.: And *they* won't have any yellow balloons and no blue balloons.
T.: That's the end of them.
S.: I didn't want anyone else to have them. They can't see them. They can't ever see them.

COMMENTS

In this session, Sally explores more fully the nature of her separateness, loneliness, and feelings of rejection. She wants the therapist's friendship and in many episodes approaches him in a positive manner. She is afraid of his rejection, however, and decides to push him out of her life, makes him feel removed and cold as she has felt in her relations, and gives him the ugly, dirty, and broken items. She expresses her feelings of being bad and unwanted in the family. She is undoubtedly the girl daughter who causes trouble, who will get nothing, and whom no one loves, in contrast to the brother who is good, who gets beautiful things, and whom everyone loves.

Sally wants to attack and hurt others as they have hurt her. She feels safe in the playroom. She feels a sense of belonging and a sense of harmony. She wants it to be her place and to possess the items in it. She wants to remain "forever and ever and ever." In the final episodes she expresses hostility against her brother and against people in general. She leaves clay smeared all over the floor so that others will have to clean it up and breaks balloons so others cannot see or use them. She expresses negative social attitudes but is unable to accept responsibility for her acts and does not want anyone to know what she has done.

FOURTH SESSION, SALLY

S.: You have a new orange balloon.
T.: Yes.
S.: I might break it.
T.: I know. You could if you wished. *(S. gets a cup of water.)*
S.: I might spill this on that rug.
T.: The colors on the rug fade when water is spilled on it. I'll just put it out in the hall.
S.: I'm not wearing a dress today because I got my pink one dirty.
T.: I see.
S.: I can wear dresses only when I keep them clean. *(S. takes clay and smears it on the floor. She empties water on Bobo.)* It's going all over him. Write my name on this clown. Right here. Write Sally Johnson, three and a half.
T.: Anything else?

S.:   There's nothing else I want you to write. *(S. tears clay into small pieces, throws them on the floor, and sprinkles water over them.)* I like to puddle on the floor.

T.:   That's what you like to do?

S.:   Come with me. I wanta go wash my hands. *(On the way back, S. approaches the rug.)* I'm gonna spill water right here.

T.:   You'd like to spill it all over but I can't let you.

S.:   I can do it anyway. *(S. gets a cup of water.)*

T.:   I know you know how to do it, but the colors would fade.

S.:   And make it ruined.

T.:   Yes.

S.:   I'm gonna spill it on you.

T.:   If I don't let you spill it on the rug, you want to spill it on me?

S.:   I'm gonna. *(S. throws water at T. and runs for more.)*

T.:   If you do it again, Sally, I'll have to ask you not to use water at all today.

S.:   I want to spill it on the rug. I want to ruin it. I want to ruin it.

T.:   You want to destroy it?

S.:   It's going to be ruined.

T.:   You're determined to ruin it, but I can't let you. *(S. gets several cups of water and lines them up.)*

S.:   I'll spill them all over the floor. *(S. throws two cups on the floor and the third on the rug. She screams gleefully.)* That's all ruined. It's gonna be ruined. Ruined!

T.:   You've ruined it now.

S.:   Yeah. Goody.

T.:   You're happy now?

S.:   Yeah. But you aren't.

T.:   You want me to be angry with you?

S.:   You are kinda angry.

T.:   You think I am?

S.:   Yeah. I'll cut this crayon.

T.:   You want to keep on ruining things?

S.:   I think you're angry. I wanta go back to school.

T.:   You have reason to leave now since you think I'm angry?

S.:   Yeah. *(Period of three minutes' silence.)* I don't want you to be mad at me.

T.:   You wish I wouldn't be.

S.:   But you really are.

T.:   You think I'm angry because you did something I told you not to do?

S.:   Yeah.

T.:   You wanted to make me angry.

S.:   You are angry.

T.:   You want me to be angry with you.

S.:   I want to ruin it more.

T.:   You want to ruin the rug more?

S.:   It is ruined. It's gonna be ruined. It's gonna be ruined.

T.:   'Til there's nothing more to ruin. *(S. walks out.)*

COMMENTS

In this session, Sally continues to try to prove to herself that the therapist rejects her. She hopes to convince herself that this is like all the other relations in her life. But when the therapist holds firmly to his feelings of acceptance and respect for her, Sally becomes upset. She throws water on him and "ruins" the rug, feeling certain that these acts will cause him to expel her from the playroom. The conflict which has emerged between therapist and child is the main theme of the session. The working through of this conflict to a positive solution would have been of crucial significance to Sally's experiences with other persons; but Sally walked out, ending the session. The nursery school staff suggested to Sally's parents that she continue the play interviews through the guidance clinic of the school. The parents refused, however, and Sally's experience in therapy ended. The therapist spent one morning in the nursery school following the last interview in an attempt to convey to Sally his continued feelings of regard for her even though they would not meet again in the playroom.

REFERENCES

1. Hartley, Ruth E., Lawrence K. Frank and Robert M. Goldenson. *Understanding Children's Play.* New York: Columbia University Press, 1952.
2. Moustakas, Clark E. *Children in Play Therapy.* New York: McGraw-Hill, 1949.
3. Moustakas, Clark E. The Frequency and Intensity of Negative Attitudes Expressed in Play Therapy: A Comparison of Well-Adjusted and Disturbed Young Children. *J. Gen. Psychol.,* 86: 79-99, 1955.
4. Moustakas, Clark E. Situational Play Therapy with Normal Children. *J. Consult. Psychol.,* 15: 225-230, 1951.
5. Moustakas, Clark E., and Henry D. Schalock. An Analysis of Therapist-Child Interaction in Play Therapy. *Child Devel.,* 26:143-157, 1955.

4

Psychotherapy with the Disturbed Child

THE CASE OF HANS

THE case history of little Hans published by Freud in 1909 (1) was the first formal presentation of psychotherapy with a disturbed child. It is a highly speculative account of an analytic relationship between a father and his young son. Though it is often referred to as a classical case in child analysis, Freud saw Hans just once, for only a brief visit. The analysis was conducted by Hans' father, who was not a psychoanalyst. According to Freud, he was qualified to do the analysis because of his authority as a father and as a physician. Advice as to the general line of treatment was received from Freud primarily through the mail. Freud's suggestions were based on the father's observations and interpretations. On the occasion Freud saw Hans, the boy had to contradict his father on a matter of discipline, an incident which the father had repressed.

How qualified was the father to conduct the analysis? From the father's notes one can see inconsistencies and contradictions between the mother and father in their relationship with Hans. Since the mother had been analyzed by Freud himself one might assume that her approach to Hans was a healthy one. Although the parents eventually divorced, Freud attributes little significance to this. Yet it implies an unhappy, disturbed marital relationship. Freud himself remarked, at one point, "Hans' father was asking too many questions and was pressing the inquiry along his own lines instead of allowing the little boy to express his thoughts. For this reason the analysis began to be obscure and uncertain."

Freud claims that the case supports his theory of the universal, unconscious nature of the castration complex. Yet there is evidence in the father's notes that Hans' castration anxiety was an induced fear, a learned pattern rather than an instinctive one. Also, it was not Hans' father but his mother who threatened castration. She warned Hans when she found him playing with his penis that if he continued to do so she would have it removed. On the basis of the data presented, it would seem that Hans was frightened into developing a castration complex.

66

Freud speaks of the sexual enlightenment of Hans as a significant step in the resolution of his phobia. Yet Hans rejected many of his father's interpretations partly because they differed from his mother's explanations. For example, Freud says, "I proposed to his father that he should inform Hans that his mother and all other female beings, as he could see from Hanna (Hans' baby sister), had no widdler at all." Yet Hans' mother told him that baby girls and mothers had different and smaller widdlers than boys and fathers. She pointed to Hanna's naked figure as evidence of this.

In another reference to sexual enlightenment, Freud says, "We are aware that by a process of careful induction, he had arrived at the general proposition that every animate object, in contrast to inanimate ones, possesses a widdler." Yet Hans continued referring to widdlers on trains and other inanimate objects long after Freud made this observation.

Freud told the father to tell Hans that the reason he was so afraid of horses was that he had taken so much interest in their widdlers. Hans considered this a silly interpretation. Freud also told Hans that he knew even before Hans was born that there would come a time when his father would have a little boy who would be afraid of him precisely because he was so fond of his mother. Hans' response to this was: "Does the Professor talk to God as he can tell all that beforehand?"

With all the emphasis on sexual enlightenment, Hans was not permitted to observe his father or mother in the nude. Freud's suggestions were continually circuitous and indirect. Though the intellectual content was given in a matter-of-fact way, the parents apparently were inhibited when it came to their actual behavior with Hans.

If this case is classical, its significance lies in teaching us about the impact of the personal relationship rather than in verifying the instinctive and universal nature of oedipal and castration complexes. We learn of the potential damage of frightening children with threats of castration, of the emotional disaster which results when mothers *encourage* boys to sleep with them and caress and fondle them excessively, of the effects of inconsistent and contradictory child rearing practices, of the unhealthy consequences of fathers analyzing their own children, and of the importance in child psychotherapy of not asking too many questions and not pressing the inquiry along the lines of the therapist but of allowing the child to express his own thoughts in his own time.

THE DISTURBED CHILD

Since the publication of the case of little Hans, numerous reports have examined the behavioral dynamics, motivations, attitudes, and self-perceptions of the disturbed child. Intensive experiences in psychotherapy, consistently point to the fact that this child lives in a restricted circle. He sees himself as an inferior person, unloved, inadequate, and afraid of the consequences of his behavior. He is threatened by criticisms and punishments which are reminders and mirrors of his inadequacies, reinforcing his own feelings of insecurity and sometimes terrifying him. Reward and approval are also threatening because they are perceived as attempts to change or modify him. However inadequate he may feel, he will struggle to maintain his own picture of himself in spite of all allurements.

The disturbed child is often so afraid to try new ways that he continues to operate within the safe and static patterns of his life. As paradoxical as it is, one way to reach him and enable him to actualize more fully his capacity for self-growth is through a significant relationship in which he is accepted as *he is* and held in esteem.

The therapist does not offer reward and approval, nor does he extol punishment and criticism. He is not involved in thoughts about modifying the child or in ways of pressuring him to change. He approaches the child with a sincere belief in him. He recognizes him as a person who has capacities for working out his difficulties. He respects the child entirely—not merely his momentary expressions of good will, his gentleness and politeness, but also his fears, hatreds, resentments, and destructive behavior. He consistently encourages the child to state his perceptions of himself and others. It is the child's view that matters.

The disturbed child often views the relationship with the therapist as quite different from any other he has known. He uses it in diverse ways. He expresses and explores underlying attitudes which in the past have seemed too threatening to reveal. He expresses himself fully without feeling ashamed and guilty. He projects his feelings and attitudes through media such as paints, clay, sand, and water using these materials symbolically, giving them personal meanings. In the process, he learns to make decisions and to act spontaneously and confidently. His experience in therapy involves gradual attempts to grow within himself to self-awareness and a realistic understanding of his life.

Some children may remain completely silent in their first few play sessions. They speak only with great difficulty to the therapist. Their initial reactions are made cautiously and deliberately. They use a small area in the room and a few toys. They often want to be told what to do and what not to do. Other children may keep up a rapid-fire flow of questions and conversation during their early sessions. Some children are immediately aggressive. They want to destroy the play materials and sometimes they want to destroy the therapist.

Whether seemingly passive or stormy, it is through individual ways of reacting to the situation and to the therapist that each child works through his attitudes and reorganizes them, so that he has a better understanding of himself as a person and of the world of reality in which he lives.

THE REACTIVE RELATIONSHIP INVOLVING DISTURBED CHILDREN

Most relationships with disturbed children involve stimulus—response interactions. The therapist responds to the child's words and feelings by listening, accepting, understanding, clarifying, or interpreting. The child then reacts with further expressions of fear, anger, depression, anxiety, or guilt. Thus an interaction sequence is initiated which has its significance only within the therapeutic relationship and which leads to the resolution of emotional difficulties, reduction of tensions, clarification of ambivalences and distortions, and change in feelings and attitudes toward a positive orientation to self, others, and life. Essentially the therapist responds as a specialist, as an experienced worker who selects and responds to some particular aspect of the child's behavior which he believes to be therapeutically significant. He responds through interpretations, questions, reflections, empathic listening or in some other way which will lead to further release of tension or clarification of the emotional difficulty. The child then reacts to the therapist's comment with an elaboration of his central concerns. A chain of associations results which constitutes a continuous theme. The specific sequence of interactive episodes ends when one or both individuals are satisfied that the communication has been successfully completed, that the tension has been reduced, the anxiety alleviated, and the goal achieved. Then a new sequence begins.

In such a situation, the therapist is aware of himself as a therapist and conscious that he is acting in terms of a particular theory of personality development. He assumes certain functions and applies particular concepts and principles in order to bring about significant changes in the child's behavior and attitude. He may function as an empathic therapist, as one who tries to understand, as an accepting counselor, or as one who reflects or interprets in order to make underlying themes or defenses open and clarified. He may respond in such a way as to facilitate the release of the child's accumulated hostile or anxious feelings. When he responds in these ways, he is motivated by the desire to achieve certain goals. He focuses on the problems, the feelings, the disturbances and the concrete perceptions, thoughts, and needs of the individual. He looks upon the client's strivings and goals. He clarifies or interprets in order to bring about important personality changes and to remedy and correct the psychological problems of an emotionally disturbed child.

Reactive relationships in child therapy fall into two general categories. In situation A, the child's problems and distortions are clear. The therapist sees the central emotional difficulties reflected in the child's expression and play. He responds to these cues from the child. This leads to specific interactive episodes between the therapist and the child through which rigid defenses are replaced and the child's sense of self is strengthened. In situation B, the therapist responds to the child's stimulations but the child does not focus on his difficulties. His behavior is activity-centered rather than problem-centered. In both relationships, symptoms disappear, problems are resolved, and attitudes change, but in the latter there is no direct connection between the changes which occur and the content or method of therapy.

PROBLEM-CENTERED RELATIONSHIPS

This section illustrates the type of relationship which focuses directly on the child's behavioral difficulties and problems. Most therapeutic relationships involve frequent episodes of problem-centered interaction. The emphasis is on specific problems in the child's life, e.g., school phobias and failures, night terrors, and disturbed relationships. The aim is to remove the symptoms, alleviate the tensions, and strengthen the self through the child's expression and examination of significant personal experiences.

BILLY

Billy was brought to the counseling service by his mother following a particularly disturbing incident which occurred in nursery school. His teacher complained bitterly that he was the most belligerent, aggressive, and temperamental child she had ever seen in the nursery school. She suggested to his mother that she keep him home until he learned something about sharing, cooperation, and respect for the rights of others. Billy's mother did not feel that he was selfish and unmanageable, although she recognized that he was immature in some ways. She believed his immaturity was due to the fact that everyone at home catered to his whims. She described her husband's attitude as follows: "My husband follows him around and jumps to everything he dictates. He'll say, 'Please, Billy, may I go?' 'Please, Billy, don't ask me to read another story tonight. I'm so tired.' 'Please, Billy, let me watch my program.' It's sad but it's true. He's just that way. The sun rises and sets with Billy as far as he's concerned."

EXCERPTS FROM THE PLAY SESSIONS

In the first two sessions, Billy expresses many feelings of anxiety and some hostility. He enters the playroom, moves from item to item, and is critical of the toys.

BILLY: What else—that's silly. What else? What else?— that silly clown. What else? Silly, Silly, silly.
THERAPIST: Lots of silly things.
B.:   Why do you have them down here?
T.:   Well, to play with if you want.
B.:   What's this gun for? *(Pause.)* What's this truck for? What's this? What's this?

The repetitive questioning continues for ten minutes. Then Billy takes a sprinkling can and pours water on the items he called silly. He justifies this behavior by saying they were broken anyway. He continues asking about items in the playroom while gradually approaching the sand. After many questions, he begins pouring sand into a truck, "because it needs dirt inside." He picks up a male doll figure, throws it down hard, saying, "Boy—not a good boy."

(The second session begins again with Billy's questions.)
BILLY: Where are the knives and forks? What did you do with them? Why is the doll house here?
T.:   For you to play with, any way you want.
B.:   What's this? A door and another door. Well, what are these stairs?

Who broke them? Some egg beaters. They don't work. What's this? What's this? Where did this doll house come from? *(Pause.)* What are these? Balloons? Blow them up. Why did they go back down? *(Pause.)* Can I get that bottle?

T.: Whatever you wish, you decide what to do.

B.: What's this?

T.: What would you say?

B.: A gun. Where's the alligator? *(Billy continues his questions for about six minutes.)*

T.: I think you just can't make up your mind what you want to do.

B.: What? *(T. repeats)* Yeah. I don't know. Paint a picture? What?

T.: Very hard to decide what to do.

B.: Why do you have a mother giraffe?

T.: For you to play with, if you wish.

B.: I think I'll paint. O.K.?

T.: If you want to. It's up to you.

B.: Where's something so I won't get my clothes all dirty? *(T. gets an apron.)* I don't need it on because I'm not going to spill—I'm a big boy. I'd get this color, O.K.? Dear, dear, dear. How can I wipe this off? Dear, dear, you see, I'm not spilling—I'm a big boy. Look all these planes are burning up.

T.: All burning up.

B.: Now they're all burned up. Another picture to paint.

T.: O.K.

B.: This is going to be another big thing, burning up some more airplanes. Here's one—you see that one.

T.: Mmhm. It's being all burned up.

B.: Yeah. Now you see this one, see that one. Why is it dripping? Now I can't paint that one. Get another one. *(While T. gets paper, B. quickly picks up a nursing bottle, drinks from it and replaces it.)*

B.: *(Continues painting.)* You see, there's another airplane getting burned up-see—ouch—eeeeee. Here's another. Oh, boy, just look it there. The engine getting burned up. *(B. gets paint on hands. Grimaces in disgust.)*

T.: You don't like getting your hands painty? *(Billy paints some toy animals. He picks up a knife.)*

B.: I'm a soldier—I'll cut this house down.

T.: You're chopping up the house.

B.: I'm hitting the house up. *(B. punches the comeback clown.)*

B.: Guess what I did—I hit that man down. *(Hits him again.)*

T.: You really knocked him down.

B.: Because he was a bad. He was a bad man.

T.: A real bad man.

B.: Yeah, he was bad. You see, I hit this man here. Now watch what I'm going to do. See what I did— I hit that soldier in the river.

T.: Knocked him off.

B.: Now they're all dead. Watch, I'm going to hit that train. Now I'll hit that off. And that off.

T.: You're knocking all the furniture off.

B.:   And that's my brother and he's a soldier too so he gets hit down.
Bang.

Billy continues this aggressive play for the remainder of the session.
In two instances at the end of this session he refers to mother, saying
"See what I did. That mother is dead cuz I hit her down. I killed the
mother cuz she was going to put her baby to bed so I killed her." Later,
he yells, "I'm going to pick up his mother and I'm going to—" *(He drags
the figure across the room.)*

COMMENTS

These two sessions illustrate a process which occurs frequently. Billy
begins the experience with a deep feeling of anxiety. He moves nervously
from one item to another. The feelings of diffused anxiety are reflected in
his constant questioning, his inability to decide, his wish to be dependent
on the therapist, and his desire to be told what to do and how to use the
play materials. His insistence that he is a big boy and a good boy seems
to cover up his feeling of being small and bad. He does not wish the therapist to know how he really feels. He drinks from the nursing bottle
when the therapist turns his back. The expressions of diffused anxiety
continue until about the middle of the second session when Billy displays
a great deal of hostility directed toward almost everything in the room
and particularly toward the mother figures. He is delighted when he
burns the airplanes and chops up the house, and the animal and the
human figures. He enjoys beating the "bad man" and dragging, scraping,
and killing the mother figures. The therapist participates in this process
by responding to Billy. By encouraging him to continue to express his
anxiety and hostility, the therapist helps him release his tense, pent-up
feelings and reduce his tensions and insecurity. The therapist accepts
him as he is, enabling him to bring to awareness some of his hostile feelings toward adults, and particularly toward his mother. Thus a new level
of the therapeutic process begins. The child moves from the hidden and
indirect feelings of anxiety and hostility to direct open expression. He begins to face his feelings toward real people in his life and to come to grips
with his extreme aggressiveness at home and in school.

After this second session, Billy's mother stated, "When my husband
came home last night he wasn't able to read to Billy and everything. He
had sore eyes. Well, it's the first time this has happened. Usually he
says, 'Let's read or let's play,' and afterwards he puts him to bed. If I try
to do anything at all he'll say, 'Go way, leave me alone. Daddy is going to
read to me and put me to bed.' Well last night I said 'O.K. Billy, let's go
up and get ready for bed.' And he kissed his daddy. I read to him and he
went to bed without any fuss. It's the most surprising thing ever. He understood why his father couldn't read. I just can't get over it."

In the next several sessions, Billy's aggression continues. He attacks
human figures and "drowns" them in a tray of water saying, "I'm going
to stick those bad men in it. Now watch. They're not my friends." The
therapist remarks, "You want to put them all down under the water."

This episode continues for a large part of the session as Billy lifts the figures in and out of the water. He then secures the animal figures and continues his aggressive play.

T.: You knocked him down.
B.: Well, he's dead.
T.: You killed him.
B.: *(Knocks another animal figure off the shelf.)*
T.: You knocked him down too.
B.: He's not my friend.
T.: You want to hurt anyone who's not your friend?
B.: The baby is my friend. *(Billy returns to the human figures and continues the drownings. He then takes a wooden hammer and pounds the figures.)*
T.: You want them really dead.
B.: They are dead.
T.: You felt like killing them.
B.: I killed them.
  (He takes other human figures from a shelf.)
B.: These are my friends. I'll give them some food. They're friendly. Now they'll go to sleep. They're fast asleep. *(Pause.)* A lot of fun in here.

During the next several sessions, Billy vacillates between burying, drowning, and chopping the human figures and protecting, feeding, and comforting them. In one episode, he shouts, "I want them all dead." He pours several pails of water over the drowned figures and chops them with a shovel.

  (In the fifth session, Billy overcomes his cleanliness anxiety. He gets into the sandbox [for the first time] and piles the sand in a corner of the box.)
B.: Getting more and more. More dirt.
T.: Lots and lots of dirt.
B.: All the dirt. Is that enough?
T.: It's up to you.
B.: Yeah. That's enough. Get some water. *(Mixes sand and water)* Grind it all up. I'll make meatballs. Hey, look. That's mud now.
T.: You've made it into mud.
B.: *(B. takes "mud," dumps it into the doll house and says with glee:)* Getting it all muddy. Here and here.
T.: Messing and dirtying it all up.
  (B. puts mud into every room of the house.)
B.: I'm going to burn, burn it. Now watch. I'm going to burn that house.
T.: Feel like burning it all up.
B.: All up. Get the fire going. *(B. spreads mud on the floor. He squeezes it, rinses his hands in it. He returns to the sandbox and mixes more sand and water. He sings gaily.)*

Get the place full of dirt. Dump it on the bad men. Cover them all up. Cover some more. Cover all the rest.

T.:   You're burying every one.

B.:   Yeah, I gotta cuz they're bad.

T.:   Billy, it's time for us to leave.

B.:   O.K. Make sure and don't touch that dirt because that dirt is for to keep the bad men covered. Don't touch that dirt, will you? Leave it that way.

COMMENTS

The therapist-child interactions continue as Billy further explores his hostile feelings. His behavior becomes more violent as the therapist recognizes his feelings and accepts his need to hurt and destroy. Along with the intense negative feelings, protective, warm feelings emerge. At first, these expressions occur with the baby and later with other figures. There is a definite ambivalence in Billy's play at this point as he vacillates between burying and drowning the family figures, the "bad men," and feeding and caring for them as "friends." As therapy progresses, differentiation occurs from the diffused, indirect, generalized expression to a focused, direct expression of negative and positive feelings. Billy seems to be differentiating and separating the positive elements and the destructive forces in his life. He comes to terms too with his cleanliness anxiety, messing, and spilling in the sand, freeing himself from the inner restriction and severe conscience which equates being free with being bad. Freed from the distortion, Billy burns the house down and removes the shackles of his imprisoned wishes. From this point, the severe intensity of his feelings lessens and he expresses himself with a degree of control, relaxation, and quietude.

Throughout this period, Billy's therapist remains close to his expressed feeling. She responds empathically, conveys understanding, and offers support. Frequently she reflects the content of Billy's statements and encourages him to recognize the nature of his feelings, to own them without fear, and to express them to their ultimate or deepest level. The therapist relates, not to Billy as a whole person, but to those aspects of his behavior which are specifically tied to his problems—his rebellious nature and his basic fears of being bad, small, unlovable, and without value. In time, Billy makes decisions for himself and acts without needing constant approval from the therapist. He learns to trust himself and to use materials in his own way.

The next episodes revolve around Billy's newly developed freedom. He plays with sand, water, and paints—mixing, and making many different constructions and designs. During many sequences, he mixes the paints together, works freely with finger paints, and uses clay. He participates in activities which he has avoided in the nursery school. In the midst of the constructive play, hostile behavior toward human figures is expressed. In one session, he fills a garbage truck with mud and places two human figures into it. The following sequence occurs:

B.:   Stir them all up.
T.:   In the dirt.
B.:   Yeah, the garbage truck is going to grind all those bad men up. *(Pause.)* How can I get all this in? There. *(He drops them in.)* Put them down. Eeeeeee. *(Billy shoots the figures through a gun, drowns them, buries them, chews up the figures with an alligator puppet—all with vehemence and angry expression.)*

Following this sequence, Billy focuses his hostility on "boys and girls." He doesn't want to share anything he owns with them. The playroom, he feels, should be his alone. If others keep coming, he plans to "shoot them," and when they fall, "'I take one of these knives and chop them." He expresses hostile feelings toward the therapist. He gives orders, tells her what to do, shoots her and attacks and chops her with a toy knife.

B.:   I'll shoot you. There, I shot you. Now hold the gun. *(Billy takes a dart from the board and moves toward the therapist.)*
T.:   You feel like sticking someone, maybe me.
B.:   Yes, stick your hand out and I'll stick you. *(B. pushes dart toward T.)*
T.:   I can't allow you to do that, to hurt me.
B.:   Why can't I hurt you?
T.:   I can't let you.
B.:   I think I'll chop down the house and make holes in it.

(B. mixes paint and sand.)
B.:   I'll pour this on your dress—shall I?
T.:   No, I'd rather you didn't.
B.:   Why?
T.:   I don't want it on my dress.
B.:   Drink it. *(Pause.)* Just pretend.

(B. takes a bottle of water. He pours some on T. T. moves away.)
T.:   You want to pour water all over me, but I can't let you do that either.
B.:   I'm not going to do it anymore. *(B. pours water on doll house.)* *(B. stops to look into the furnace room. He tells T. to get in all the way on top of the fire.)*
T.:   You want to burn me up.
B.:   Yeah, and all the little kids you see. They can get in too and burn up.

(B. enters the playroom crying.)
T.:   You don't want to stay here with me. *(B. continues crying.)*
T.:   It's upsetting being here with me.
B.:   I don't like you.
T.:   You seem to be very angry. *(B. continues crying. Takes dragon puppet.)*
B.:   Sometimes dragons bite people.
T.:   Maybe you'd like the dragon to bite me.

B.: *(B. takes knives.)* Knives make holes in people—I'm going to chop you up.
T.: You're feeling so angry with me. You'd like to cut me up. *(B. hits T.)*
B.: You really want to hurt me.
     (B. nods his head. He takes a pail of water and splashes it around T.)
B.: Someday Jimmy is going to come and play with me and we're going to make cement and put your head in it. Then we'll put you in the cement mixer and cut you all up.
T.: Get rid of me once and for all.
B.: And when Mommy and Daddy come down to breakfast they'll eat it and get sick.

After this episode Billy's hostility centers on his mother, at first only in the playroom and later in direct meetings with her.

Billy attempts to throw a jar of black paint at T. T. limits this behavior. Billy hesitates. He makes threatening gestures, then angrily opens the jar, and begins smearing with aggressive strokes. He shouts, "I'm making this for my mother. A nasty high black mountain."

On arriving at the counseling building Billy repeatedly irritates his mother. He teases her, and refuses to go to the playroom. He pretends he is too frightened to go alone. They argue in an apparently playful way and kiss each other several times before parting, but the affectionate gestures do not conceal the intense hostility. One day Billy is unable to control his fury. He grabs two magazines which his mother has been reading and throws them to the floor. She tells him sharply to pick them up. He refuses. She shakes him. He begins screaming, squeezes her arm, and pinches her. She announces angrily that they will have to leave. Billy continues hitting his mother and screaming. As they go out the door, his mother remarks to the therapist, "This time I'd really like to spank him, but I guess that's my problem."

In the following session Billy leaves the playroom, stating he has to go to the lavatory. Instead, with a gun in his hand, he goes upstairs. The therapist follows. Billy points the gun at his mother, shoots her, and then returns to the playroom. The conflicts between Billy and his mother continue over many weeks. Interspersed with the hostile episodes there are positive interactions, e.g., Billy's mother reads to him and plays with him while waiting for the sessions to begin.

In one of Billy's last sessions, he mixes black paint in the baby bottle and hands it to the therapist saying, "Drink it. I want you to get sick because *(laughing)* I don't like you. . . ." Then with a serious smile he says, "You know I really do." There are other positive interactions between Billy and the therapist though the hostile ones continue. Often in his play, he gives a party and invites the therapist. He serves her favorite meals and expresses a desire to help her.

During the last four months of therapy (the sessions continued for approximately one year) Billy's attitude takes a definitely positive turn. He begins playing in a concentrated fashion, compared to the scattered and fragmentary play in the previous sessions. His play becomes imaginative and dramatic. It conveys a social relatedness and interest. Billy plays for long periods with the puppets. He develops programs and performs for the therapist. In one session, referring to the therapist, he remarks that he has a friend whom he likes very much. Another time he is mixing "cement" to hold together the block buildings he has constructed. He says, "This is for the little children who can't build one of their own." At the end of one session, he cleans off spots of paint he has made on a table. As he works he remarks, "When the other children come, they will say, 'Billy made a big mess.' So I'm cleaning up. Then the other children will come and say, 'This table is so pretty' and they'll play." One day he is singing as he works, "Some mud—making a castle. How do you make castles? You pile the sand up. Nice rich dirt. Five gallons of dirt to take it where we're building. My mommy doesn't care if I put my knees on this dirt—she doesn't care. Castle of sand—goes together with mud. Pat-a-cake, pat-a-cake, bake me a castle as fast as you can."

In his final session, Billy plays quietly with trucks, sand, and blocks, making roads, sidewalks, curbs, and buildings. It is serious, concentrated play. He speaks to the therapist only a few times during the hour. He seems especially happy and satisfied. He hurries upstairs to say to his mother, "You should see how well I played and what a good time I had."

Billy's sessions ended when he entered public school. His mother decided it would not be possible to bring him anymore. She was satisfied with the progress he had made. He was now playing cooperatively with other children and was not as demanding at home.

Two years later Billy's mother called. She said everything had gone well in school and at home, but his current teacher did not understand him. A visit was made to the school in an attempt to convey certain insights to the teacher. Six months later Billy's mother reported that he had had a delightful school experience after the visit but his new teacher was having a similar difficulty. Again, a visit was made to the school. A year later Billy's mother called, this time to say, "For a change I'm calling to say that Billy is happy and doing well both in school and at home." At this writing, Billy is in the fifth grade. From his school records, it is clear that none of the difficulties he encountered at nursery school have recurred, except briefly in the first and second grades.

COMMENTS

The relationship between Billy and his therapist contained certain consistent conditions. Billy entered with deep feelings of self-rejection, dependency, uncertainty and anxiety which were expressed in the diffuse hostile attacks on the playroom and play materials, and in the constant repetitive questions. The therapist accepted him as he was, with all his doubts and aggressions. She responded to his questions, his demands, and his "acting out," by showing that she understood him and by encouraging him to express even his most severe feelings. She helped him to reach new levels of understanding. She showed Billy that she valued him and cared when he suffered. Through the relationship, Billy came to perceive himself as a positive, loving person with potentialities and talents. In time, his anxiety was alleviated. He began to face directly the nature of his real relationships, particularly with women. His hostility toward his mother, teacher, and therapist (all women) reached a peak in his constant attacks on the therapist and his search for ways of painfully eliminating her. Later, when he found the courage to face his feelings, he approached his mother directly and let her feel his anger and resentment. Finally, positive feelings emerged and his play became constructive and imaginative. He was able to concentrate and complete activities. He wanted to do things for other children. He related to his mother in a positive fashion. He expressed his feelings of affection for the therapist. Although negative feelings toward his mother and other women still remained, his attitude was now frequently one of acceptance and love. His feelings had undergone a change from diffused hostility and anxiety to positive and negative feelings, differentiated and clarified. Thus, within an important relationship, the therapist's attitudes and responses had stimulated the child in such a way that he had largely resolved his emotional difficulties, reduced the tension and suffering in his life, and developed a positive attitude toward women and people in general.

The Case of Carol

Carol, an only child, four years old, was referred to the play therapist by a community agency. Mrs. L., Carol's mother, was considerably worried about Carol's recent complaints of stomach pains during mealtimes. Also, Carol's habit of twisting and pulling her hair had become so serious that she was partially bald.

Family background data included the following: the mother's repeated statement that Carol looked and acted like a stepsister whom the mother hated, the mother's strong emphasis on cleanliness, the degradation she felt in her own family experiences where her stepparents were alcoholics and her home was usually littered with scraps of food and dirt, the parents' belief that Carol was incapable of loving them or anyone, and the crowded conditions in the family's seven-room house where they lived with three other families.

Mrs. L. was seen regularly by a caseworker. The play therapist had two interviews with Carol's mother. The first of these was held before Carol's first play session. After the final play session a second interview was conducted. Attitudes expressed in the last interview will be described later. A summary of Mrs. L.'s attitudes toward Carol, as expressed in the first recorded interview follows:

"I can't accomplish anything with her. She just won't listen. You have to use force. You just can't treat her nice and expect to get results. . . . I punish her frequently, and then she becomes a very, very good girl, but it makes me feel like a worm afterwards. But then, at her age, she just can't understand anything but that kind of treatment. . . . She's just very selfish, and that's all there is to it. What makes me so mad is that she's so quick to notice when someone else is selfish, but she herself continues to be a selfish person. . . . She just seems to be getting worse and worse. . . . She's pulling her hair out all the time, and she always complains about her stomach at meals."

Carol's mother saw her as a selfish, inconsiderate, disagreeable, unruly child with stomach pains and hair-twisting symptoms. The therapist found her to be a frightened, lonely, love-hungry, confused, and hostile child. Carol had twenty-one play therapy contacts. During this time she expressed her attitudes of resentment, hatred, loneliness, and fear. She explored these feelings and attitudes, expressed them again and again, and re-explored them.

Tremendous feelings against the mother were prominent in these sessions. Carol struggled to free herself of these torturing emotions and eventually gained a degree of emotional and intellectual insight within herself. This meant that Carol could see herself more clearly as a person and understand how her relations with others might improve through a sincere desire to share and cooperate. During the first few contacts Carol often spoke in a language of her own that was not understandable. Later she expressed herself clearly and intelligently. After the fourth play session the mother reported that Carol's stomach pains had disappeared. Carol expressed more respect for herself and a greater affection toward others. As a way of illustrating Carol's growth, excerpts from the recorded play sessions follow.

FIRST SESSION, CAROL

(Mother enters the room with Carol.)
M.: Isn't this lovely?
C.: Mm-hm.
M.: Do you like this?
C.: Mm-hm.
M.: Now you play down here. O.K.?
C.: Mm-hm.
M.: Then I'll go see Mrs. D. O.K.?
C.: Mm-hm.
M.: All right.
C.: Mm-hm.
M.: And I'll come back and get you. O.K.?
C.: Mm-hm.
M.: He's going to watch you, darling. O.K.?
C.: Mm-hm.
M.: O.K.?
C.: Mm-hm.
M.: O.K.?
C.: Mm-hm.
M.: Do you want to kiss Mommy? *(Kisses Carol's cheek.)* O.K.?
C.: Mm-hm.
M.: I'll be back. O.K.?
C.: Mm-hm.
M.: All right. Bye-bye.
C.: Bye.
M.: *(Walks out of the room after looking back at Carol.)*

Throughout the session Carol constantly refers to worn toys and at the end says, "I guess the kids don't break 'em. I guess the people who bring 'em in just break 'em first and then let the kids play with 'em."

SECOND SESSION, CAROL

C.: I'm gonna use this stick to paint with.
T.: You are?
C.: Mm-hm. I'm not messing up my hands. I'm gonna use all of these.
T.: All the colors, hm?
C.: That's what I'm gonna do. Use all of them. That's what I always do. *(Pause.)* We have much troubles. Much troubles.
T.: You really have troubles, don't you?
C.: Mm-hm. I'm gonna wash my hands.
T.: You don't like to have your hands dirty.
C.: I don't much. No, I won't wash my hands now. I'll wait before I go upstairs.
T.: You're going to wash them before you go upstairs, hm?
C.: I don't want my mommy to see them dirty.
T.: You don't want her to know about it.

C.: *(Picks up nursing bottle and chews on the nipple. Drinks for a while and then starts chewing again.)* Looks like I'll have to stay here nineteen years.
T.: A long, long time, isn't it?
C.: Just for this old bottle.
T.: That will keep you here if nothing else does.
C.: Yes. *(Laughs and continues to drink. Chews nipple for quite a while.)*
T.: Just keep working and working and working on it, hm?
C.: My mommy is going to have to wait until I get to be four years old.
T.: She'll have to wait until you grow up to be four, hm?
C.: Yes. *(Sighs heavily and continues to chew nipple.)*
C.: I'm gonna shoot up this whole place.
T.: Just shoot everything, hm?
C.: Yeah. *(Laughs shrilly.)*
T.: Shooting all over.
C.: *(Laughs.)* I'm shooting everybody in the place.
T.: Everybody is being shot down, hm?
C.: Everybody except my girl friend.
T.: She's the only one you won't shoot.
C.: Yeah, I'm gonna shoot you now. *(Laughs.)* Why don't you fall down?
T.: You'd like me to just fall.
C.: Uh-huh. After I shoot you, you can stay up just one minute. Then you be dead. *(Shoots at therapist and laughs.)* You don't get up.
T.: Not ever to get up.
C.: You never get up. Nobody's gonna see. I'm gonna shoot the lights off.

COMMENTS

The mother seems considerably anxious in leaving Carol, asking repeatedly for permission to leave. Left with the therapist, Carol chatters incessantly, points to the toys but does not play with them, and in other ways shows diffuse anxiety. At the end of the first session she expresses hostile feelings toward adults, rather tentatively but directly, saying that people who bring children to the playroom (in Carol's case, her mother) break the toys first and "then let the kids play with 'em."

Carol conveys the attitude that her home is filled with troubles and shows fear of her mother. She becomes immature in her play, drinks from the nursing bottle and chews the nipple. She shows hostility toward her mother and implies that her mother is responsible for her immaturity, saying, "My mommy is going to have to wait until I get to be four years old."

Carol's negative expressions become more generalized. In her play she shoots all the humanlike figures in the room, except one doll which she identifies as her girl friend. She is especially vehement against the therapist, shooting him and telling him to die and never get up. At the end of the second session she shoots off all the lights, so that no one will see the "crimes" she has committed in her fantasy.

FOURTH SESSION, CAROL

C.: *(Designates an area while playing in the sand.)* That stuff you see is halfway up to the north.

T.: Halfway up to the north, hm?

C.: Yes. And this north has a monster. The other north has nothing in except trees.

T.: Nothing but trees.

C.: The other north is wild.

T.: Two norths. A wild one and a peaceful one.

C.: You can get lost in it. You could get lost all over till you go straight. Then you could get to the cars. You get to the cars, and then walk a little further, and then you get to my farm. You got a driveway going up there. 'Way up on the hill.

T.: Mm-hm.

C.: Yes. Mine's 'way up there on the hill.

T.: Your farm's up high?

C.: No. I changed it to a house.

T.: Just changed your mind.

C.: Ain't it looking perfect now? This is where the seeds grow. And they're gonna grow up, and stuff is gonna be all around here. Don't you see? Don't you see the house here?

T.: Mm-hm.

C.: And there's going to be stairs going up here.

T.: I see.

C.: And this is going to be a room right through part of the house. This was the rough place, but you can pat it right down like this. It's a house. It's a house. Don't you know?

T.:   It's a house.

C: It's a house. Not a real toy.

T.:   It's a real house.

C.:   Yeah. The whole thing is big. It's all one house.

T.:   Mm-hm. And this house is gonna storm now.

T.:   Really going to storm.

C.:   Many years ago it stormed down.

T.:   It was all broken down then.

C.:   Yes. You see, this part's gonna come off.

T.:   Tear right down.

C.:   Just this part. Just the roof.

T.:   Mm-hm.

C.:   And there's a safety zone down here to save the people. The people come down to here after the storm. Then they come back here and build it up again. Then the storm comes again and blows it away. Then the people come and put it up again.

T.:   Mm-hm.

C.:   This part here is gonna be a secret panel so the people will never know what a big house.

T.:   They'll never know the truth about it.

C.:   That's right. At night is when the storm comes up, and then comes the morning, and then they can build it up safely so that it won't come down again.

T.:   Mm-hm.

C.:   It all looks different now.

T.:   Not the same any more.

C.:   Don't you know what happened in the storm? It all fell. This is gonna be a special one. She didn't like the other one, and she never will.

T.:   She never liked it.

C.:   It'll be all zoomed up here. You wouldn't like your house to fall. Well, the storm—. She must have got the bad lady. Her didn't like anybody except the house cooker.

T.:   She liked only the house cooker.

C.:   Mm-hm. Who cleaned her house. She didn't like the strange people. They got her then. They got her right down, and that was the end of her. No. That wasn't. That was the end of the people.

T.:   All of them died?

C.:   Except the good ones. It all happened years and years ago.

T.:   Many, many years ago.

C.:   That's when I was a baby. And the storms came and tore everything apart. Now the whole thing's crashed down. *(Stands back and surveys sand pile.)* I'm all done with that. That finishes that job. *(Picks up clay and flattens two small pieces of clay.)* Everything's always the same.

T.:   Nothing ever changes here.

C.:   I have to shine my glasses. Some glasses she gave me. I'm gonna tell her this is no good. It's not even glass.

T.:   She gave you some pretty poor glasses, hm?

C.: I'll take 'em back. They're not even glasses. There. Now listen, I want some good glasses back. *(Pretends to open package.)* Same old glasses!

T.: She's given you the rotten ones again.

C.: I'll take them back and see what she'll give me this time. Oh, lookit. Oh, oh, how pretty shined they look. But they're still the same old thing.

T.: You've been cheated so many times, haven't you?

C.: I'll take them back. Now let me try these. They look shiny. But they're no good.

T.: Every time they look so good, and they turn out to be bad.

C.: Well, this time she gets some good ones. Now what is she going to have for lunch? *(Continues to play with the clay.)* Half a motorcycle and a little butter. I guess I'll wrap it up. She told me that I'd like it. If you don't eat it, you're gonna get a licking. Let's see if this would be butter. Oh, it should be. It's good work stuff. Aah, gee, that's supposed to be butter? That's butter I'm getting? Oh, I hate it, I hate it. Turn it over. Mix it up. Are you gonna eat it? I wouldn't. What's supposed to be? Now he'll find out what he's getting. But he won't like it. She sure don't fix his lunch. She fixes it the rotten way. He's gonna fix his own, and he won't fix another rotten one. This man sure is a good kind. Good as gooder. *(Pause.)* Oh, this tastes so good. Now I'm gonna kill some of this clay if she don't know any better. She sure gave me some rotten stuff. I'll see what she says about this piece. If you couldn't eat it, then you can't. Let's see what she says about this stuff that she wanted. If she do that again, she'll get some bad. Oh, what she does! One slice she gives. One slice and one slice and one slice. Oh, I hope you got the good food you wanted. Did you want good food? You're getting it. Here, I'm giving it away. She won't like it but she gives mine away, and I don't like that. It's a good thing you're sitting over there, because I don't want to get any cutting on you. *(Looks at therapist.)* You might get cut open.

T.: I might just get cut open if I weren't over here.

C.: Mm-hm. Might get cut and ruined. Do you mind if I wrap it up and throw it away? I don't want it any more.

T.: That's up to you.

C.: She'll find out it was me.

T.: And are you afraid?

C.: She gave me dumb. Well, she's gonna have dumb right back.

T.: You'll give it to her right back, hm?

C.: If she gives it to me again, she's gonna get it right back.

T.: You mean you'll give it to her if she does it again?

C.: She will. You should hear her when she starts. She started it years and years back.

T.: It all started a long time ago.

C.: Yes, now you see what she says about this stuff. She's not gonna like it.

T.: You won't let her get away with it, hm?

C.: She won't never get away with it with me. I'll tie her up and say that I'm moving.

T.: If you have to, that's what you'll do.

C.: I'll move even if I don't have to. I'll move anyway. *(Picks up small nursing bottle and sprinkles clay.)* Squirts, squirt. I'm gonna squirt her. See how she gets it now.

T.: She's getting it now, hm?

C.: She will get it. She won't like it the way I'm gonna fix it. She'll get it the same old way.

T.: You'll give it to her just like she gave it to you, hm?

C.: Because I don't like her. I won't eat her food. I'll eat the other people's food. Their food is better.

T.: Her food makes you feel bad.

C.: I'm gonna cut her open and see her. Here's your old sicky food.

T.: You'll cut her right open and give it back to her.

C.: She'll say, "Ah, what kind of food is this?" And she'll say, "That's good; it must be good." But it won't be.

T.: If she says it's good, it probably won't be.

C.: Probably I'll put poison in it. I'll put it in it.

T.: Poison in the food.

C.: Yeah. And if she says it's good, she'll find out.

T.: She'll find out if she eats it.

C.: How you like this food? It won't make you die. This will be much gooder. Some of this is so good. And some of it's got poison in it.

T.: Some is good and some is bad, hm?

C.: She'll say it's all good when it isn't. And she'll eat it. Aah! I'm dying. Thought it was good food. Some good food you called it. Rascal food. Now I'll put some good food in it. Some real good stuff. I'm gonna cut her open and get all that bad food out. And put some good food in. It's good food, but she thinks it's poison. She thinks she's dying. She's just making herself dead.

T.: She thinks she's dying and making herself dead.

C.: Mm-hm. She won't be. She'll be alive as anything. This is good food. I'm getting hungry as could be, so I better eat this good food that I got her. Wow! I'm afraid! I hope I don't die.

T.: You're afraid to eat the food, is that it?

C.: No, thank you. Now I've got a good bite to eat. So I guess I'll go on to the good part. *(Runs back to play in the sand.)*

COMMENTS

Carol expresses a number of mixed emotions in this session. She creates two norths, a peaceful one and a wild one, which in her own mind may represent her ambivalent feelings toward her own home situation. She makes a house in the sand, destroys it, builds it again, destroys it, re-enacting this play sequence a number of times.

Carol's despair and loneliness seem very great as she looks at the therapist and says, "You wouldn't like your house to fall." She conveys the emptiness of her emotional life and attributes it to the fact that "she must have got the bad lady," who didn't like anybody and was interested only in cooking and cleaning. Carol indicates it all happened when she was a baby, "and the storms came and tore everything apart."

Carol's anger becomes direct and she shows, possibly, how her mother has always deceived her and cheated her. Her feelings are severe and intense as her sarcasm mounts. She reveals hatred for her mother, who has always tricked her and withheld her love. In the play situation Carol retaliates, expresses hostility toward her mother, and poisons her. Later in the session Carol shows the positive side of her feelings toward her mother in her desire to be loved. She takes "all that bad food out" and gives the mother good food.

FIFTH SESSION, CAROL

C.: *(Kneels in sandbox and builds with the sand.)* Four years ago a rock—a rock felled on this house. So we call it a part of the house.

C.: *(Plays in the sandbox.)* She turns it up herself, and she plays all around and has a lot of fun. That's the way it should be. She used to laugh, but not Mama.

T.: She laughed, but her mama didn't, hm?

C.: Her mama used to holler all she could. She'd holler and holler and holler. All she wanted was a house. Not a big house. Just a little girl's size.

C.: *(Plays in the sandbox.)* Now she says now it looks like a house. She screams out, and ever since she's crying. It's different, this house. First the daddy left the mother, and now the mother left the daddy.

T.: Mm-hm. Daddy left Mommy and Mommy left Daddy.

C.: So you know what she did. She built herself a house her size. She crashed down the house to make her own house.

T.: She made a house all of her own.

C.: Nobody lived in it except her, and everybody's happy now. Except her. So she's cut hers off again.

T.: She didn't want her house attached to theirs.

C.: So she moved it down to California, and they didn't like it. But she loved it. And they didn't like it.

T.: So she moved away.

C.: And she brought water for her house. A little water. Water in a tub for her house. All around the house, water, water, water. And her house is bigger. And her house is bigger and bigger and bigger. Finally she wanted it hooked on again. So you know what she did? She moved again and hooked hers on. So they were glad. And their family wasn't happy, and she was happy. Before, they were happy and she wasn't happy. So what's the difference?

T.: She's happy now, and they aren't.

C.: So she crashed her house down again and made another one. If they wanted to hook on, she didn't mind.

T.:   She would let them hook on, hm?
C.:   Only how could they hook on, the way they had built it?

SIXTH SESSION, CAROL

C.:   *(Builds large mounds in the sand.)* I want to be warm.
T.:   You want to be warm.
C.:   It's rock cold.
T.:   Cold as rock.
C.:   Colder than rock.
T.:   Mm-hm. Quite cold.
C.:   You'll never know.

SEVENTH SESSION, CAROL

C.:   *(Sits in front of the dollhouse and plays with doll figures.)* My hands are ice cold. What kind of water is this? It's so cold. Turn on some hot water. No. We don't have any hot water. But there was hot water. It was hot water. It's just so cold. If you do what I say, you can get out of there and have hot water. Now do you understand? So they had to do what she said.
T.:   They have to do what she says in order to get warm water.
C.:   They can't do what she says. We're stuck in with glue. Too bad we can't. Be quiet, they shout. So they did be quiet. They can't hear my noise, but they can hear their noise. See what they did? They told you to get out of the house. Now get out! And I mean get out. *(Pause.)* Finally. But—hey, hey, it's cold out. It's cold out anyway. Be quiet yourselves. This house is not for big people like you. So they took a gun and shot them one by one.

C.:   *(Still playing with doll figures.)* They're *so* cold here. Even the horses had to go outside. It's lucky they had a heater. But she got colder and colder. She just couldn't stand it. She just couldn't stand it.

C.:   *(Handles clay at workbench.)* I guess I'll put on these aprons. Aprons, aprons, aprons. Guess I'll put on two aprons, because I'm gonna get awful dirty. *(Picks up scissors and jabs at clay.)* Zhoop, zhoop, zhoop, zhoop, zhoop, zhoop. Oh, goody! She's stabbed. She used to dream about it. So Mommy could fix it up so she liked it. How did she dream about it? How did she used to do it? She used to say, "Give me the porcher, porcher, porcher." Boy! Was that ever good.

EIGHTH SESSION, CAROL

C.:   *(Plays with doll figures while sitting in front of the dollhouse.)* She calls them good, only they're bad. Because Mom calls them good, but she calls them bad. They don't agree on that. *(Pause.)* Here's another one that she likes. But Mom says this one's bad too. And she likes the bad ones.

T.:   She likes the bad ones, does she?
C.:   Mm-hm.

NINTH SESSION, CAROL

C.:   *(Plays with the clay and the vise.)* I'm gonna smash it in two. Wanta see me smash it?
T.:   You're going to smash it in two, hm?
C.:   *(Pushes the clay into the vise.)*
T.:   Carol, you have only a short while longer to play. Just a few minutes more.
C.:   A few minutes? I don't care about that.
T.:   Just a few minutes.
C.:   It's long enough. Isn't the Fourth of July long enough? It's long enough. I have to grind this up now. *(Puts more clay into vise and handles it for a few minutes.)* I'm through. Can't stay here all day. Next time I come, I'm gonna do it backwards. Start with the clay, then the dollhouse and the sandbox.
T.:   You know exactly what you're going to do.
C.:   And after that I'm gonna start with these balloons.
T.:   You've got it all planned out.
C.:   Yeah. I started it all.
T.:   And now you're going to finish it.
C.:   Mm-hm. It's all in pieces now.

COMMENTS

Carol shows how lonely and cold her life has been; in her play "she used to laugh," but "her mama used to holler." She seems to indicate strained relations between her parents, their rejection of each other and of her. Carol makes a house in the sand "all her own" but is dissatisfied and unhappy with it. She is uncertain. She wants to be near her parents and love them. Yet she is afraid. In her play she fluctuates between moving away from them and staying near them, exclaiming, "If they wanted to hook on *(to her house),* she didn't mind." In earlier play sessions Carol was determined to move away permanently.

Carol repeatedly expresses her feelings of loneliness. "My hands are ice cold," she screams, and later, "But she got colder and colder. She just couldn't stand it. She just couldn't stand it."

She expresses hostility toward adults again in her play, shooting all the adult doll figures one by one.

She regresses in her play and speaks immaturely.

Carol plays out her conflicts with her mother numerous times and shows how strongly they disagree. As the ninth session ends she shows growth in her ability to decide and play, saying, "Next time I come, I'm gonna do it backwards. Start with the clay, then the dollhouse and the sandbox. And after that I'm gonna start with these balloons."

Tenth Session, Carol

C.: *(Plays with the clay and vise.)* You put this in here. This is the last time I'm getting into this. This is the only time. Then I'll forget about the whole thing.

T.: Mm-hm. This is the last of it then.

C.: I don't care about cutting. I just cared about the clay.

C.: *(Still playing with clay.)* Squawking all the time. I don't like that.

T.: You don't want that, hm?

C.: Squawk, squawk. That's all they figure. They just can't help it. Squawk, squawk. That's all they can squawk. Squawk, squawk. That's all they'll get back. If I don't get it, then I won't give it. I get squawk, squawk. Something else. That's what I'd like. Something else.

T.: You wish they'd give you something besides squawking.

C.: Talk, talk. Squawk, squawk. That's what they do. I'll put a snake in there. See if that squawks. I think the snake does. Water snake, water snake. You go in there. I'm home, snake, and my mama won't let me go out any more. Squawk, squawk. Squawking all the time.

Eleventh Session, Carol

C.: All you do is sit, sit, sit. Well, I don't want you to do anything more.

T.: You feel that's enough.

C.: Just that and nothing more.

Twelfth Session, Carol

C.: *(Plays with doll figures at the dollhouse.)* Everybody's going to be naked in the family.

T.: A whole family without clothes.

C.: Then the boys can see the girls, and the girls can see the boys.

T.: Each one can see the other.

C.: And I can see all the little children with their clothes off. And then they're gonna take all the people's clothes off. Not just dollies. All their clothes are gonna come off. The children will see each other.

Thirteenth Session, Carol

C.: *(Plays with the clay and paper towel.)* I think I'll wrap this up for lunch today.

T.: That'll be your lunch, hm?

C.: Yes. I guess I'll have this for us to eat. I got it all wrapped up. He only has to go to work. To work, to work, to work, to work. She bothers me every day. *(Pause.)* It's so quiet around here today. That's what I want. Just so much peace and quiet.

T.: That's what you want most. Just peace and quiet.
C.: Because the old mother hollered at me every day. Hollered every day. And all she wants is peace and quiet.

C.: No home. No home at all.
T.: Not a real home, hm?
C.: No house like you have. Like kids have.
T.: You don't have a house like other kids, hm?
C.: No. In mine it's just the same old things. All I do is walk around and do nothing. That's all I can do.
T.: Just walking around with nothing to do.
C.: I'll stop now. I'm going upstairs.

FOURTEENTH SESSION, CAROL

C.: *(Plays with clay at workbench.)* Look. What a silly. What I'm doing! I'm cutting.
T.: You're cutting and being silly.
C.: No. I'm not silly. Now, I'm having good things to eat. And I'm selfish. I don't want anyone else to eat my things. *(Pause.)* Do you want something to eat?
T.: Do you suppose that I would?
C.: Yes. You might like this to eat at home.

FIFTEENTH SESSION, CAROL

C.: *(Plays with the clay.)* You know, I live alone.
T.: All by yourself, hm?
C.: But I have two sisters who live down the street. We fight once in a while, but we get along most of the time. *(Pauses as she fingers clay.)* I don't like boys. They're nasty.
T.: You don't like boys.
C.: Well, really they don't like me. Maybe I'd better go back to work. I'm gonna have lunch. Would you like to eat with me?

COMMENTS

Carol again expresses feelings of anger and resentment against her parents. In her play she refers to their constant quarreling and indicates their frequent criticisms of her. She retaliates with "Squawk. Squawk. Squawk. That's all they'll get back."

Later Carol removes the clothing from all the doll figures and implies that if all people were "naked" (perhaps she means without fears and defenses), we could see each other as we really are.

Hostility toward the mother reappears. Carol wishes to escape her mother's persistent admonitions. In a whisper she says, "It's so quiet around here today. That's what I want. Just so much peace and quiet." She indicates the tragedy of her home situation, telling the therapist that she has no home at all, not like other kids.

As the sessions continue, Carol becomes more relaxed and spontaneous in her play. There is even a childishness about her. In previous sessions she has acted more like a miniature adult. She acts silly and laughs continually.

Carol recognizes her selfishness but justifies it, indicating that she has never had good "food," but "now I'm having good things to eat." When her feelings of selfishness are accepted, she offers to share her "food" with the therapist.

SIXTEENTH SESSION, CAROL

C.: *(Plays in the sandbox.)* They're gonna have a new home. I think this house is a music house. Ha ha, a music house.

T.: That's what. A music house.

C.: It's going to be so big that they're gonna have to put some music in this house. They'll have to have a television too. They're gonna crowd the house.

T.: They want to crowd the house, hm?

C.: But I'll fix it. That piano goes out farther. I'll put it back a little.

T.: Mm-hm.

C.: All right. A nice little room. How do you like it? Don't it look nicer with the piano spaced out farther?

T.: More space there, hm?

C.: And in here we'll have a door. It's gonna be a little hideout. And the kids can see their mother at night. And the kids can feel their mother. But the big people—they can just see from the top. And if the mothers go through there to the hideout, then— bang. The whole house gets on fire.

T.: That's what would happen, hm?

C.: The whole house would catch fire. Now the kids are gonna build themselves another house. And their mothers.

T.: Just for the kids and the mothers, hm?

C.: No. Just for the kids. And it's gonna be just right.

T.: It'll have plenty of room, hm?

C.: Yes. Right back here to the house. And they like to play. Right to the back of the house.

T.: That certainly will be roomy for them.

C.: The kids are gonna have a good time. They'll have pianos. They'll have hundreds of pianos.

T.: Hundreds of pianos.

C.: Yeah. For a nice big house.

T.: They'll enjoy themselves then, with all those pianos.

C.: All the kids will be climbing around the pianos and jumping up and down on them and having fun.

EIGHTEENTH SESSION, CAROL

C.: *(Plays in the sandbox.)* And then she dreamed another story.

T.: She dreamed another story.

C.: This is gonna be the whole story she dreamed. She read it in a book once and said, "I'm gonna try and dream it." Then she thought maybe I should get a record of it first and see if it's scary. I don't like anything if it's scary.

T.: You don't like scary things, hm?

C.: No. I don't like cowboys and shooting. And even animals, if they're big. Every time I hear a noise when I'm up in bed, then I'm scared.

T.: When you hear noises while sleeping, you're really afraid, hm?

C.: Also when I'm bad sometimes and have to sit in a chair.

T.: Oh, when you're bad and hear noises, then you get frightened.

C.: Yes. When I hear noises then I'm always scared. My mommy comes and says she doesn't hear it, but I do.

T.: You hear it even though your mommy doesn't, and it frightens you.

C.: Yes. And it's really only something like the washing machine or somebody pounding.

T.: It turns out to be something just silly, but it still frightens you.

C.: Yes. It rolls me back.

Nineteenth Session, Carol

C.: (Plays in the sandbox.) This isn't a free country. Nobody gets free here. But I made this. I made all my people, but I didn't make them right.

T.: You made them, but they didn't turn out the right way.

C.: I know things that they don't know. Ha ha ha.

T.: You know some things they don't.

C.: This is my girl friend. She likes me, and I like her too. I'm gonna eat my pie with her.

T.: You like her, and so you're sharing your pie with her.

C.: Yes. We'll eat it. She gets half and I get half. She thinks it's too much for me, but I've been starving to death, so I'll eat it. (Pause.) You know, kids just love people, but sometimes people don't love kids.

Twentieth Session, Carol

C.: (Plays in the sand and describes the destruction of a village by a huge storm. The people work together to rebuild it.) If I helped them, then they'd like me, and it will never be crashed again. I'll make a great big cake for them. How deep is my cake gonna be? Oh, my cake, cake, cake. Baking a good, delicious cake. No, I'm gonna eat it all up.

T.: Just for you, that cake.

C.: Not all of it. I'll divide it up with them, because they're my friends. friends, friends. I'm a friend, and I'm not gonna eat it all. I'm gonna give them some.

C.: (Plays in the sandbox.) A lotta times she dreams about castles. She dreams about all this, only it's too late now.

T.: Is it too late for her now?

C.: Well, maybe not. I'll make one for her. I'm gonna make the castle. I'm gonna make Carol the first castle she's ever had.

T.: You're going to do that for her, hm?

C.: Yup. And tonight it's gonna be filled all around with pretty water.

C.: See this cake? You can cut it in many pieces. In small pieces for many people.

T.: That's the way you want to cut it, hm?

C.: The big chiefs get the biggest pieces. Yes, the biggest chiefs always get the biggest pieces.

FINAL SESSION, CAROL

C.: *(Plays in the sandbox.)* Nobody knows what I know. Nobody knows what I know. *(Chants.)* Nobody goes where I go. Nobody wants to go where I go. Nobody wants to go where I go. *(Pause.)* You take the dirt, and you take the water, and you mix it together. Water and sand. Rub it, squeeze it, mix it. That's what you do in here. You mix things the way you want. I'm gonna make some pie, I am. And then there won't be any more time. I'm gonna make a pie so big it's gonna cover the whole place up. The biggest pie you ever saw. There's my pie. And now I'm gonna cut it up in little pieces and share it with all the people. We'll all eat it now.

T.: It's time to leave now, Carol.

C.: G'by.

T.: Good-by, Carol. It's been very nice knowing you.

COMMENTS

These sessions are characterized mainly by Carol's exploration of the positive feelings within herself toward herself and other people. She builds a music house with blocks, where children are close to their parents, play games with them, and have fun with them. She makes the house a spacious one, and "the kids are gonna have a good time."

Carol describes her fears of animals and loud noises and recognizes that they are foolish. In her play she shares her pie reluctantly, because "I've been starving to death."

In the twentieth session Carol creates a village in the sand. She decides not to destroy the homes this time and realizes that "if I helped them, then they'd like me." She makes a huge cake in the sand and decides at first to eat it all up, as her "selfish" feelings momentarily return, but later she says, "I'll divide it up with them (all the people), because they're my friends." She now sees herself as a friend, someone whom people care about and regard as important. And in the play experiences Carol indicates that it's not too late, her dreams can still come true.

Finally Carol expresses a positive friendly attitude toward people, saying, "I'm gonna make a pie so big it's gonna cover the whole place up . . . and now I'm gonna cut it up in little pieces and share it with all the people."

During the therapy experience, Carol expressed her deep resentments and fears in her relationship with her mother using clay and sand to symbolize these attitudes. She was able to talk about her fears that food would be poisoned and also her resentment toward her mother for giving her bad food and so little love. After she had expressed her feelings that she had been cheated and deceived, the food for her was no longer a source of anxiety. It now held a more realistic place in her total life situation. As Carol clarified and reorganized these attitudes toward herself, she became more accepting of herself and her mother. Acceptance of herself and her mother enabled Carol, then, to move out of her inner world and express feelings of affection and friendliness toward others. Many of these positive feelings and explorations were dramatized in her play in the sand. Following the fifteenth play session these socialized attitudes were most clearly revealed. In her play Carol expressed a desire to help people, to do things for them and with them, and to win their friendship and their love. Carol's perceptions of herself and others were now both more positive and more realistic. Her mother's perceptions of Carol were also different.

In the therapist's first contact with the mother, the mother described Carol as selfish, inconsiderate, disagreeable, and unruly. Quoted statements from the therapist's last contact with the mother revealed new attitudes. "It is not very difficult to see Carol's growth. For a long time now we have had to punish her very little. Her manners are improving. She just seems to do things much better. She seems to just get along better with everyone. . . . My husband says she's been acting a lot smarter and has noticed lately that she's using big words when she speaks. . . . I think sometimes when I look at some other people's children that Carol is almost perfect. . . . For four years of her life Carol showed us very little affection, but in the last six months she has begun to kiss us and to hug us. My husband is much warmer to her now, and he spends much more time with her. . . . Last night she said, 'Dear God, please don't let there be any more trouble between my mommy and daddy,' so it shows that she does have a great deal of consideration for us."

TASK-ORIENTED RELATIONSHIPS

The task-oriented relationship focuses on activities, projects and plans which the child selects and initiates. The child enlists the cooperation and participation of the therapist in the achievement of his own specific purposes and goals.

DENNIS

Dennis was referred to the counseling service by the visiting teacher of his school. At the time of referral, he was ten years old. He was seen by three different therapists. The first two experiences were relatively brief and were broken off. The final contact continued for approximately one year and was regarded as valuable by Dennis's mother, the visiting teacher, classroom teacher, and principal. The following discussion refers primarily to Dennis's experience during his last year of therapy.

Interviews with Dennis's mother disclosed the following picture of Dennis at the time of referral:

He was considered a slow, resistant boy who "has to be pushed into doing everything he is supposed to do and never does the right thing at the right time." His mother stated that, "When you try to reason with him, it is like talking to a wall!" Dennis spent most of his time at home watching television. He rarely participated in any family activities and had no friends in the neighborhood. His mother felt that Dennis had no reason to complain about school because he had "a very good teacher whom he could respect and like." She indicated the problem which precipitated the referral, as follows: "He is soiled *every night* and occasionally during the day. This started about two years ago. The bed-wetting we can overlook but the soiling is disgusting. We've tried everything we know to stop it but nothing has been successful. He's had a thorough physical examination and there's no physical basis for the soiling. Our other children won't have anything to do with him."

The school staff believed Dennis to be an "extremely disturbed boy." The following problems were mentioned, "regression, playing with much younger children, thumbsucking, daydreaming, tardiness, soiling, and bullying." His teacher indicated that he had no friends in his class, that he was lazy, that he had to be constantly reminded about his work, that he was slow in everything he did, and that he was especially unclean. Dennis was failing in every school subject. His grade norms at the beginning of the sixth grade were as follows: reading 4.4, spelling 3.1, study skills 4.2, arithmetic 5.2, and social studies 5.1.

Only one positive characteristic was mentioned by both the mother and the school—that Dennis was a generous boy, spontaneously sharing his possessions with other children.

Dennis's therapeutic experience was comprised of certain projects, plans, and tasks. These generally took the form of groups of questions and problems in geography, history, reading, and arithmetic which he assigned to himself and to the therapist. Sometimes he developed the plan of work before arriving. At other times he dictated the assignments on arrival. Sometimes he requested that the work be done independently. At other times, he and the therapist worked together. Over a number of sessions, he brought his stamp collection and some booklets and books on the history and value of stamps. Dennis and the therapist spent many hours discussing stamp collecting; often child and adult worked on puzzles and constructed color designs and geometric figures in accordance with formulas and plans which Dennis devised. During the last two months of therapy Dennis used almost the entire time to improve his reading comprehension and speed. He selected passages from a number of reading texts, and asked the therapist to time him, and to test his comprehension.

The specific nature of the task-oriented relationship is illustrated in the verbatim excerpts which follow:

(Dennis enters the play room.)
C.: Well, what are we going to do today?
T.: Whatever you'd like. This is your time.

C.: Let's talk.

T.: All right.

C.: Let's go way back in history. We're studying about it in school. I'm going to be studying about Italy next week. *(Period of silence.)* I can't think of anything to talk about. *(Pause.)* I can't think of one thing to say. Can you?

T.: I'd rather discuss something you suggest.

C.: I can't think of a thing.

T.: We can just sit here if you'd like.

C.: Good. *(Long period of silence.)* Do you want to read?

T.: O.K.

C.: You be the teacher and I'll be the student. I'll read to you. Now you be ready to ask me some questions. *(Dennis reads passage from a history book, then answers correctly questions asked by the therapist. Dennis begins to discuss school work.)*

C.: I don't like spelling. I like social studies and I like art more than any other subjects. *(Pause.)* I'd like being the teacher for a change. *(Dennis asks therapist questions from a reading text.)*

T.: You like to ask questions you think I'll miss.

C.: That's right. I'm going to give you a test next week. A whole bunch of arithmetic problems, and social studies, and other questions. Now I'm going to read like my friend does. *(C. reads two paragraphs silently, then aloud.)* Notice how he reads?

T.: Seems to read fast, without pausing.

C.: Yes.

T.: You'd like to be able to read like that.

C.: Not much. *(Pause.)* Let's name the ships in the book. *(C. names each of the types of boat.)* I have so much fun making up names for these. That's what we'll do next week. *(C. begins reading again.)* Stop me when I make a mistake or do something wrong.

T.: I'd rather you stop yourself.

C.: The teacher always stops me.

T.: I'm a listener, not a teacher.

C.: Be a teacher—all right? *(C. begins reading again.)* That reminds me I have three China dogs at home. The set cost me three dollars. Two have been broken. *(Session is about to end. C. examines darts and board .)*

C.: Oh, boy, darts. Maybe we can play with them next week.

T.: You're making lots of plans for next time.

C.: Yeah.

DISCUSSION

This first session sets the pattern of the relationship between Dennis and his therapist. Dennis decides on the activities of the hour and makes future plans. The therapist responds to Dennis by answering his questions and accepting his decisions, but he insists that Dennis lead the way, be responsible for his choices and act in a self-dependent manner. The therapist is willing to participate in Dennis's projects and plans but he does not make decisions or direct in any way. His attitude and re-action to Dennis make it possible for Dennis to do what he really wants to do, namely, to work on school subjects, and to be one who teaches and directs as well as one who learns.

C.: Today I'm going to make things with the tinker toys and you tell me what they are. *(C. makes an object.)* Do you know what this is?

T.: An automobile?

C.: Right. *(Claps hands.)* *(C. makes another object.)* Now what's this?

T.: A tommy gun?

C.: No, a car fan. *(Continues working.)*

T.: Looks to me as if you make these up as you go along.

C.: Yes—sort of. Know what this part is for? A drinking fountain. You turn this and water comes out. You can put coke or ginger ale in it and have it right in your car.

T.: Sounds like your own invention.

C.: Let's work on the blackboard. You be the teacher and tell me to write words on the board.

T.: All right. Write some words on the board.

C.: *(Writes a number of words.)* There, teacher. I'm only in the first grade—pretend. Now you say cross out all the i's.

T.: Cross out every i.

C.: O.K. now every e. *(This continues until every letter is crossed out.)*

T.: It feels good to be in command and tell the teacher what to do.

C.: Yes. Now I'm going to ask you two questions.

T.: Is your teacher one who answers questions?

C.: Very seldom. That's why I'm asking you. I'm going to make a pic-ture on the board. This is a river. We'll call it the Nile River. O.K. Now what's this?

T.: A delta?

C.: That's right. Now this.

T.: A tributary? *(C. continues drawing.)*

C.: Now how's that, teacher. You say, "It's good."

T.: It's good.

C.: Thank you teacher. Now you say, "It's time for arithmetic."

T.: It's time for arithmetic.

C.: Arithmetic—oh, boy! We'll make some clocks. And you ask me to put the right time on them. *(C. completes problems correctly.)* Now it's time for geography. You ask me to draw a delta, a tributary, a lake, a river, and an island. *(C. proceeds to draw these.)* Now we have a few more minutes. Let's play tic-tac-toe.

Dennis enters with a clipboard. He has prepared four pages of arith-metic problems of increasing complexity. He takes the difficult papers himself and gives the therapist the others. When the problems are com-pleted Dennis corrects them.

C.: Now I'm going to give you a little test. Draw eight boxes on this paper. In the first one draw these lines. *(C. illustrates on the black-*

board.) In box #2 write this and in box #3 write this. Can you figure out what you're doing!

T.:   Looks like you're doing to me what your teacher does to you.

C.:   It's just a small test. Take each of these designs now and complete a picture out of them. *(C. continues assigning similar tasks to the end of the session.)* I'll have a new test ready for you next week.

T.:   You're already thinking ahead to testing me.

C.:   You had them all correct today. So next week I'll have to work out some hard ones.

Dennis arrives with another assignment containing arithmetic problems and geography and history questions. Child and therapist work together. When this is completed, Dennis writes numbers on the blackboard.

C.:   I'm going to write some numbers that look like letters. You tell me what the letters are. *(Dennis makes up several other assignments during the hour. One of these requires the therapist to identify geometric figures.)*

T.:   You're getting tricky on these.

C.:   That's what my teacher likes to do.

T.:   Tries to trick you. Likes to see how many she can get you to fail.

C.:   Yes.

T.:   I think you like to be the boss and tell me what to do.

C.:   It's lots of fun. *(Pause.)* Next time I'll bring my stamp books. It will take the whole time. We have fifteen minutes. Let's play tic-tac-toe. *(C. and T. play together to the end of the session.)*

T.:   I think you get angry when you lose.

C.:   Ha ha. You burlap you. I'm mad at you.

T.:   You feel better when you win.

C.:   Darn it. I'm no good. I don't like cheaters.

T.:   You think I'm a cheater.

C.:   Oh. No. I'm the one. *(Puts his head on the therapist's shoulder, gets up to leave.)* Just wait until next time.

In the next two sessions, Dennis brings history, geography and arithmetic questions and asks the therapist to assign them to him one at a time. Both sessions involve teacher-pupil relationships with Dennis shifting roles from time to time. He enjoys being the tricky teacher who gives the orders as well as the bright student who executes them. Dennis gives the therapist an exercise which requires folding sheets of paper into eight equal parts. He then makes peculiar figures that look like different letters and asks the therapist to tell him what letters are represented.

He sometimes becomes anxious when a task is completed and he is thinking of something else to do. He seems to want to be constantly active.

These sessions end with the game of tic-tac-toe. He takes the games in stride, enjoying them but not making the winning or losing an important matter.

During one hour Dennis and the therapist cut and paste geometric patterns made from colored paper. Dennis decides the pattern and gives directions for the work. Toward the end of the session he makes a stage with large blocks and boards and performs a puppet show for the therapist.

For the next several sessions, Dennis brings his stamp collection and stamp books. He and the therapist work together putting stamps in the appropriate places.

C.:   My dad has a set of these stamps—all of them. You know how I started my collection? I used to take stamps off old envelopes I found and put them on sheets of paper. My dad said, "Maybe you'll get a real stamp book for Christmas." And I did. That's where I get a lot of them—from him. He has a very large collection.
T.:   Do you have any which he doesn't have?
C.:   No. *(Pause.)* He gave me this one and this one. I'd been looking for them for a long time.
T.:   He's really been helpful.
      (Dennis describes the circumstances under which a number of the stamps were printed—the dates, occasions, and conditions.)
T.:   You learn a great deal from stamps.
C.:   It helps you to know where the countries are located and the capitals and what they produce. Also you learn words of different languages. Could you help me with that? *(Dennis looks up a number of foreign words and asks the therapist for translations. In a notebook he writes the word, when the therapist can translate it, and its English equivalent. Then he continues putting his new stamps in the albums.)*
C.:   You know you're such a nice guy.
T.:   Because I talk with and do things with you. *(Pause.)* Isn't anyone else willing to do this?
C.:   Maybe, but I don't ever sit down and ask.

Dennis and the therapist continue the discussion of stamps. Dennis points out the fine discriminations between the many stamps which look the same. He explains the special terminology of the philatelist and tells where stamps are produced and how much they cost. Dennis encourages the therapist to begin a collection and offers his "doubles" as an inducement.

By the end of the fifth month of therapy, certain aspects of Dennis's behavior are clear: He has never been late in coming. He always calls time himself at the end of the session. He concentrates on his work until it is completed. He is careful to return the items he uses, to clean up at the end of the hour, and to wash the blackboard when he uses it.

Talks with Dennis's mother and the school staff at this time revealed that the bed-wetting and soiling had stopped but the other problems persisted. Dennis was still failing in all school subjects but arithmetic (in which he had improved considerably) and art.

Following the conversations about stamps and stamp collecting, Dennis decides he wants to play games with the therapist. One of these is illustrated in the following excerpt:

C.: I know a new game that we can play. But you've got to help me play it. It takes two to play. Will you?

T.: Yes, if that's what you want to do this time.

C.: *(Dennis makes rows of dots and explains the game to the therapist.)* We have to make squares out of all these dots. The one who puts the last line across making the square counts it as one point and has another turn. The one who completes the most wins the game. *(Play begins)*

T.: It looks like you have me trapped on this one.

C.: Thank you, 1-2-3-4-5-6-7-8-9. I like that.

T.: You're really forging ahead. *(Game continues.)*

C.: Who is winning now, sir?

T.: You, by a great margin.

C.: Go on—please continue. O.K. Thank you. Twelve more points for me. That one goof did it.

T.: You're making fun of me now. *(Pause.)* You take advantage of every mistake.

C.: Go ahead. Your turn.

C.: Look at all these boxes I have clear around the edge. Who would you say is winning?

T.: I guess you've won.

C.: *(Emphatically.)* Thank you, sir. We have time for one more game.

During the second game Dennis makes up a special rule in order to avoid defeat. However, as he leaves he seems upset. The following week he enters the playroom prepared to play the same game.

C.: This time we won't go outside the outer edges. Because I was actually cheating last week. I wanted to win so I went to the outer edge.

T.: But you were angry with yourself in spite of winning.

C.: Yes. This time I'm going to be a good sport.

T.: You think it's wrong not to be a good sport.

C.: Yes. We'll just play this one game today.

C.: Today I'd like to make some designs like we made at school. We need colored paper, crayons, and scissors *(C. procures these materials.)* I want you to make one too. *(He begins making a pattern.)* You have to fill your whole paper to get a good design. I'll have to bring the picture I did at school for you to see. It was quite good and was put in the showcase. Notice how this point touches this point. Now you color whole page.

T.: Yes. And you end up with an unusual design.

C.: Yes. *(Dennis spends remainder of the time making designs. He insists that the therapist complete one. The next two sessions proceed on a similar basis. Then Dennis devises a boat race game which he and the therapist play.)*

For the next two months, the entire time is devoted to work on arithmetic. Dennis asks that increasingly difficult problems be assigned to him. While he works he sometimes gives the therapist assignments. During this period he covers decimals, percents, simple and compound fractions, mixed numbers, and the areas of triangles, circles, and squares. Sometimes he writes story problems. He makes such comments as, "This will help me to learn a little faster in school." Even when the problems represent a new skill and are difficult for Dennis he prefers to struggle with them himself rather than be helped. The last ten minutes of these sessions Dennis often plays darts with the therapist.

After the "arithmetic" hours, Dennis brings a stamp book and asks to be quizzed on its contents. He is preparing to take his Boy Scout examination for a merit badge. The following week he excitedly reported to the therapist that he has passed the oral test and will be awarded the merit at the next Court of Honor.

During the final two and a half months of therapy, Dennis uses the time to improve his reading vocabulary, word recognition, reading comprehension, and speed. He brings assignments with him, and asks that he be timed and questioned on the passages. He selects and tries to recognize difficult words in the reading texts. At the end of this period he is able to read orally in a fluent manner whereas earlier he read unevenly and often would be completely stopped by a single word.

At the end of the school year Dennis was given an achievement test by his classroom teacher. In the final conference with the school staff, Dennis's achievement scores were reported as follows: Reading 7.4, spelling 5.4, study skills 7.1, arithmetic 8.6, and social studies 6.9. Thus he had improved in every area beyond the expected average increase. There was no question in the teacher's mind regarding his promotion. The teacher stated that Dennis had been elected president of the graduating class—the vote being almost unanimous. Also, he was playing baseball regularly after school with his own age group. He had been involved in only one aggressive incident and had been tardy only once during the past six months. There was no recurrence of his soiling in school and he had improved considerably in cleanliness and in appearance. In short, every problem which had been a concern to the school had been corrected or largely resolved.

Dennis's mother reported similar improvements at home. In the last interview she spoke of Dennis in positive terms, mentioning his help in caring for the garden, painting the garage, and carrying through with other responsibilities. Changing her earlier attitude, she felt that Dennis's teacher did not understand him and was partly responsible for his regression at the beginning of the year. She was pleased that Dennis had become a participating member of the family again and expressed complete satisfaction with the changes in his behavior.

COMMENTS

It is possible to explain the change in Dennis's attitude and behavior on the basis of his special relationship in therapy. Here was a person who respected him, gave him complete undivided attention and participated in his games, tasks, projects, and plans. Here was someone with whom he could talk and share his interests and ideas at a time when no one else would understand and accept him. He needed someone who would interact with him, and respond to his thoughts, feelings, and suggestions. He needed a personal relationship in which he was trusted, valued, and accepted. He needed someone who would let him lead the way, and let him be important in making decisions and plans. The therapist responded to Dennis on this basis, respecting his requirements, his demands, and his ways.

Dennis never directly worked on his problems. He rarely mentioned them. There was never any expression of deep feelings of anxiety or hostility which one might have expected from his background of personal deprivation and rejection. His problems, symptoms, and underlying tensions were not reflected at all in the relationship.

Dennis and the therapist related in terms of Dennis's preconceived plans and projects, the tasks he needed to achieve, and his goal of academic improvement. Dennis enacted many roles in the relationship. He was the stimulator, the initiator, the director, the law-giver and statement-maker, the teacher, and the parent as well as the student and the son. He needed to let someone else feel how it felt to be the follower, the one who is told what to do, the one ordered into activity and made to follow expectations. Dennis needed to gain respect and confidence in his ability to face tasks and problems and to see them through successfully. In short, he used the therapy experience to improve his relationships and his skills. He did this, not by examining and expressing the conditions which prevented him from making a satisfactory adjustment at school and at home, but by being the well-adjusted person in charge of his life, and by expecting the therapist to respond to him in this new role. He became a competent, self-dependent person by practicing behavior, which gave him a sense of self-adequacy and self-fulfillment.

REFERENCES

1. Freud, Sigmund. "Analysis of a Phobia in a Five-Year Old Boy." In *Collected Papers,* Vol. III. Ernest Jones (Ed.). London: Hogarth Press, 1949.
2. Horney, Karen. Finding the Real Self. *Amer. J. Psychoanal.,* 9, 3-7, 1949.
3. Moustakas, Clark E. *Children in Play Therapy.* New York: McGraw-Hill, 1953.

5

The Creative Child in Therapy

INTRODUCTION

EVERY year children are seen in therapy who do not fit the usual categories of disturbance, who do not show the extreme hostility or withdrawal patterns readily recognized as symptoms of psychosocial illness. When these children are judged according to ordinary standards and norms, they are sometimes labeled as "bizarre" or "hopeless" unless they happen to possess talents which are not only peculiar but also have prestige value. To be understood, these individuals must be seen in an entirely different sense, and related to uniquely because their orientation and structuring, their patterns of expression, are so completely unusual. If not related to as real persons, their developing potentialities remain unrecognized and hidden. Only the person who meets them as real persons discovers their unique and self-fulfilling nature.

These individuals are not nonconformists. They do not act in protest against their environment or against authority, but they *are* peculiarly different and *do not* conform to the usual behavioral manifestations and expectations. Because they remain unaffected by the typical therapeutic strategy and management, they are apt to threaten persons who treat them as nonconformists or as disturbed children.

To conclude that children referred for therapy are healthy, self-fulfilling individuals in spite of the peculiarities and in spite of the problems others seem to have in relating to them is a conclusion hard to come by. To relate to them in a fashion that does not follow the prescribed theory and technique is also a challenge difficult to face or even to recognize. It requires a willingness to plunge into an unknown journey and take untraveled pathways in contrast to the comfort and safety of a previously tested process. The usual procedure is to look upon these individuals; in traditional ways and thus not meet them as real persons, as healthy individuals. Or, after failing to relate to them in any significant sense, there is a tendency to classify them as beyond the realm of therapy or to recommend them for special training and institutionalization.

This paper points to another reality, the experience of relating with these children creatively, the reality of meeting the "bizarre," "peculiar," "hopeless," or "nonconforming" child in a person-to-person relationship.

TWO DIFFERENT RELATIONSHIPS IN THERAPY

I have come to believe that two essentially different relationships can occur in child therapy. The first is a creative relationship in which two persons meet, as whole persons, immediately, without anticipations, expectations, or preconceived ideas but as two human beings who have come together to create and share in a vital life process. The second is a reactive relationship, in which the adult responds to the stimulations of a particular child and the child responds to the stimulations of a particular adult, thereby initiating an interaction sequence which has its significance only within a relationship and which leads to the resolution of emotional difficulties, reduction of tensions, clarification of ambivalences and distortions, and reorganization of feelings and attitudes.

THE CREATIVE RELATIONSHIP

When two persons meet in a creative relationship, there is a continuing sense of mutuality and togetherness throughout the experience. Therapist and child are involved in a process of self-fulfillment, a growth experience which has a wholly positive orientation and direction. There is constancy and consistency of self within which new patterns, images, and configurations appear. Together, therapist and child create unique themes of life, whether it be in the realm of deep mutual silence, in their dramas of important personal figures, or in their fresh expressions. Such a relationship cannot be understood by studying the behavior of the adult and the child. Behavior in the creative relationship is only an external fragment of the total experience. It includes, in addition to the unique individuals, certain transcendental qualities which connect these two persons with all of human life and human welfare.

The whole idea of errors or mistakes in the creative relationship is irrelevant. It is not possible to do right or wrong in such a relationship. It is a matter of being, of presence, of thisness, of a life being lived rather than a matter of individuals acting and being acted upon. All references to responses and their correctness or incorrectness are inappropriate. These are judgments valid to a reactive situation where definite goals exist and where the therapist's behavior can be rated in terms of its contribution to the realization of these goals.

In the creative relationship changes do occur. It is inevitable that when individuals really meet as persons and live together they learn in suffering, frustration, and despair as well as in joy and fulfillment. It is my contention, however, that the creative relationship does not address itself to motivation, learning, and change but only to the interests, capacities, and ways of two persons. The reality of the creative relationship in therapy cannot be understood on the basis of the changes which occur. The changes are not the basic process of the relationship, not even a goal or focus of the relationship. Attempting to understand the creative relationship on the basis of motivation, strategy, goals, and outcomes is futile. Such terms are meaningless. They relate to outside-of-life situations and can be used to understand about, or learn about, or study about something discrete, static, and nonexistential. The creative relationship can be considered only through denotation or utterance, or through pointing to it, and can be known only through living it! It is my belief that such a relationship cannot be brought about no matter how fervently the therapist may desire it or how rich his background of experience in such relationships. The creative relationship *happens*. But once it occurs, the therapist can decide to participate in it as a matter of choice.

The creative relationship in child therapy is similar to Buber's I-Thou relationship. Buber (1) presents this relationship as follows:

> When *Thou* is spoken, the speaker has no *thing:* he has indeed nothing. But he takes his stand in relation. . . . If I face a human being as my *Thou,* and the primary word *I-Thou* to him, he is not a thing among things, and does not consist of things.
>
> This human being is not *He* or *She,* bounded from every other *He* and *She,* a specific point in space and time within the net of the world; nor is he a nature able to be experienced and described, a loose bundle of named qualities. But with no neighbour, and whole in himself he is *Thou* and fills the heavens. . . . The *Thou* meets me through grace—it is not found by seeking. But my speaking of the primary word to it is an act of my being, is indeed *the* act of my being.
>
> The *Thou* meets me. But I step into direct relation with it. Hence the relation means being chosen and choosing, suffering and action in one; just as any action of the whole being, which means the suspension of all partial actions. . . . The primary word *I-Thou* can be spoken only with the whole being. Concentration and fusion into the whole being can never take place through my agency, nor can it ever take place without me. I become through my relation to the *Thou;* as I become I. I say *Thou.*
>
> All real living is meeting.

The creative relationship in play therapy is not the external butterfly, the fleeting life of Buber's I-Thou, but is an enduring and sustained mutuality, a oneness of continuing substance. It is an experience between two persons—not experiencing each other, but relating as persons. It is an experience of participation, a meeting of real persons—not a transitive managing or perceiving of something or someone.

In a time when psychologists and psychotherapists are focusing primarily on the motivational aspects of behavior, David Levy (3) has shown the value and necessity of considering the dimension of capacity. He points out that emphasis on motivation and personality dynamics is a professional bias and, like all biases, contains its weaknesses and pitfalls especially when used as the sole basis for understanding psychotherapy. Levy describes the importance of seeing the use of capacity in psychotherapy when this is the basic dimension involved, rather than reacting to the client in terms of his unconscious motivation or defensive behavior. He states that factors related to capacity, when appropriate, should determine the approach to the child undergoing treatment.

There are two essential differences between the creative relationship I refer to and Levy's recognition of capacity. Capacity is only one dimension in the over-all pattern of the relationship. I believe it is unified in experience and cannot be treated as a separate entity. Secondly, capacity in the creative relationship refers to the positive expression and actualization of potentialities. Although Levy defines capacity in terms of the individual's ability, fitness, and endowment, all of his examples involve incapacity and limitations of the individual rather than potentialities. All of his examples (though not his discussion) show the therapist reacting to limited capacity rather than participating in a shared experience. These differences between the use of capacity as a single variable and its integration within a whole constellation of patterns are presented solely to point to two major differences, not to minimize Levy's insight nor to idealize the creative relationship. I believe that both are realities in psychotherapy and that each has its place. But they are different.

THE REACTIVE RELATIONSHIP

In the reactive relationship, the therapist responds, not as a person whose skills and potentials, talents and interests are unified in self-consistent patterns, but as a specialist, as an experienced or trained worker who selects and responds to some particular aspect of the child's behavior which he believes is therapeutically significant. He responds through interpretations, questions, reflections, empathic listening, or in some other way which will lead to further release of tension or clarification of the problem. The child then responds with an elaboration of his central concerns. Thus a chain of association begins which constitutes a continuous, reactive situation. Both child and therapist are responding to discrete behavioral expressions, initiating a reactive, interactive situation which is completed when one or both individuals are satisfied that the communication has been successful, that the tension has been reduced, the anxiety alleviated, and the goal achieved. Then a new sequence begins.

In such a situation, the therapist is aware of himself as a therapist and conscious that he is acting in terms of a particular theory of personality development. He knows that he must assume certain roles and apply particular concepts and principles in order to bring about significant changes in the child's behavior and attitude. He may function as an empathic therapist, as one who tries to understand, as an accepting counselor, or as one who reflects or interprets in order to clarify underlying themes or defenses. He may respond in such a way as to facilitate the release of the child's accumulated hostile or anxious feelings. In every case, he is motivated by a desire to achieve certain goals. He focuses on the problems, the feelings, the disturbances, and the concrete perceptions, thoughts, and needs of the individual. He looks upon the client's strivings and goals. In short, the therapist reacts by clarifying, listening, accepting, or interpreting to bring about personality changes and to correct psychological problems and difficulties.

Summary and Concluding Comments

Reactive and creative relationships are different realities which show up in distinctly different patterns. Both seem to be important relationships in our culture and both occur in therapy with children. The creative relationship involves two persons who meet as persons and express their individual nature. When changes take place, they do not affect the nature of the relationship. The reactive situation focuses on the behavior of the two individuals, their responses to each other, and the changes which result from this interaction. In both relationships, the problems the child faces are resolved. In the creative relationship, this is incidental to what exists positively and unchanging, whereas, in the reactive situation, the problems and the process of their resolution are the central theme. Since the creative relationship is based on the mutual sharing and relatedness of two human beings, there are no criteria of evaluation or assessment, of success or failure. Since there is no goal, there is nothing to judge or evaluate. The essence of the relationship is its quality of wholeness and oneness. The relationship cannot be isolated into discrete, measurable units. It is a matter of *this* rather than unconscious, elaborate motivations. It is not something. It is not a thing. It is *this*. It is a process of life being lived rather than a matter of unconscious, elaborate motivations and the dynamics of interactive behavior.

The therapist cannot bring the creative relationship into being but he can let it happen and he can choose to participate in it. He can turn a creative relationship into a reactive one by treating the person as an external, as a separate entity, as an individual for professional study. On the other hand, if the conditions of therapy constitute a reactive or stimulus-response situation, it is not possible to make it otherwise. Though it may start in this way, it may, through its own evolvement, come to be a true meeting of two persons as persons, a creative relationship.

Illustrations of the Creative Relationship,* David

David was referred to me by his parents. He had been extremely unhappy in school due to a disturbing relationship with his teacher. At home he was constantly on the verge of explosive behavior. His mother felt that the accumulated tensions of the school day caused his outbursts at home, his vomiting, and his difficulty in sleeping. His father believed that his attempt to conform in school made him argumentative, resistant, and rebellious at home. Both parents regarded David's behavior as situational and temporary. For them, he had always been a loving child of a serious temperament, but enthusiastic, satisfied, and joyful in his relationships with children and adults. They felt he had an unusual sense of inquiry, a deep perceptiveness and sensitivity, and a way of seeing integration, unity, and wholeness. They hoped he would be able to develop these talents in school.

---

* Since the reactive relationship is illustrated in previous chapters, examples are omitted here.

David's teacher believed he was a "disturbed" child, "confused in his orientation," and unable to adapt to school standards and requirements. He questioned David's ability, wondering whether he could complete the academic requirements of the grade. School standards based on a typical curriculum, competition, and the use of reward and punishment were in conflict with parental views that the child should be free to create an individual, unique curriculum, and to explore and experiment on the basis of his own interests and potentialities. His parents also believed that learning should be a cooperative, not a competitive, endeavor. While David's parents believed in autonomy, spontaneity, and individuality, his teacher believed in social conformity and adherence to school rules and standards.

THE CONVERSATIONS

David, nine years old, came for a total of eight visits. He usually remained at The Merrill-Palmer School the entire day, bringing with him a folder of books and working by himself. His "reading materials" were references in geography, anthropology, physics, chemistry, and electronics. I informed him that I would have an hour free in the morning and one in the afternoon when we could meet if he wished. I showed him the playroom and my office and indicated we could meet in either place. He considered it strange that I should offer him the playroom with its toys and materials, and announced immediately, "I'll come to your office."

Throughout the first hour, David sat silently. I felt that we were together in this. There was a feeling of identity and communion which made words unnecessary. In the afternoon, we sat together again. At the end of the second hour, he expressed his views on religion. His main complaint against the school was that it required Bible training of him. He felt this to be a violation of his own beliefs. As he talked, he decided to discuss his religious beliefs with his teacher, Mr. Locke.

Since it is difficult to convey the nature of this experience and the evolvement of the relation without quoting from our talks, excerpts from the remaining meetings with David are presented.

THIRD SESSION, DAVID

(David looks through the window to the trees, the parking area, and the people for the first fifteen minutes of the session. Then he begins to speak:)

DAVID: Well—he didn't change the Bible much. He just didn't have me do it in the workbook.

MR. MOUSTAKAS: He doesn't seem to understand what we're trying to do, does he?

D.:   I couldn't tell.

MR. M.:   In any case, he couldn't or wouldn't let you do what—

D.:   Uhuh. He doesn't—the whole thing is against—you know—it's against the way I believe.

MR. M.:   He doesn't see that your beliefs are different from his.

D.:   I can't really tell—I mean—I wished he didn't hide his feelings.

MR. M.:   You'd like to know his real thoughts but he covers them up.

D.:   I can't tell what he's thinking, or anything, you know. *(Pause.)* I suppose he understands what we want—he just doesn't understand how to carry it out maybe. He hides his feelings and you can't tell what's happening.

MR. M.:   He doesn't discuss things with you?

D.:   Not a word—doesn't even change the expression on his face.

MR. M.:   It's difficult to approach him.

D.:   *(Sneezes.)* That's hard on the tape recorder, isn't it? *(Laughs.)* I think they're fun to work with, you know. If you take the erasing device—like making a steady ah-h-h-mm-m-m-m, and then a steady whistle right over it, it might sound something like this. *(Makes sound.)* *(Pause.)* I don't know what would make a difference with him. *(Pause.)* There's nothing very interesting in school. It's all boring stuff. And then he has those rules you have to follow. He whips boys when they break certain rules. He whipped Donald 'til he cried. He was crying when he went into the bathroom. He took him in at recess time and whipped him again.

MR. M.:   It hurts to see another boy being hurt.

D.:   He just ruins those kids doing that. He got Tommy. He's a hot-tempered guy—you know. He'll stand right up to the teacher and say: "I don't feel like it." He gets whipped a lot. He gets into trouble that way. I can see why he does. I just can't stand it, you know.

MR. M.:   That's something you don't believe in, kids being pushed around.

D.:   But Mr. Locke has a lot on his mind too.

MR. M.:   And it's not so easy being a teacher.

D.:   And sometimes those boys are—especially Donald. *(Pause.)* Sometimes he makes the kids hand the walnut stick to him.

MR. M.:   That must be awfully hard to do.

D.:   Help murder yourself. It's like committing suicide on a small-size scale. *(Pause.)* Tommy's so used to being pushed around he's not himself any more. I mean he's kind of dumb-witted sometimes, it seems like. He probably cares, but he tries to laugh it off. I mean he doesn't seem himself. You know what I mean.

MR. M.:   I can see that it upsets you when you see someone treated that way.

D.:   He has all those rules, you know, laws we call them.

MR. M.:   It seems to be pretty hopeless as far as you doing things in school you particularly like, working with materials that really interest you.

D.:   I want to get something over here. I wonder if I could take a home course instead of going to school. I have a book here that tells about it, and your parents don't have to have a teaching certificate. *(David hands booklet to Mr. M.)* My dad doesn't seem to like it. You see, I'd be in the fifth-year course.

MR. M.:   And you think this is the solution to your school problem?

D.: I think it's good, but I don't have any other kids to do it with. *(David takes the booklet and reads outline of content for the fifth-year course.)* I wish there were some other people to do it with. Everything is so boring in school, except two subjects, English and arithmetic. These are real good. I like them. Memorizing the Bible verses are just a waste of time as far as I'm concerned. I guess he's trying. He starts out pretty good, taking me off the workbook, but he still wants me to do the Bible study and the quiz.

MR. M.: Have you ever told him you don't believe entirely in what his Bible says?

D.: No, not directly, but he knows.

MR. M.: He knows from knowing you.

D.: He's talked with my mother and father too. He knows what we think.

MR. M.: That's important.

D.: Yeah, it is. Otherwise, how can he change? *(Pause.)* The only way you can tell whether he's angry or not is by his red face. He covers up like I was telling you.

MR. M.: It would be good if he would openly express his feelings.

D.: Maybe, too, he doesn't change because we don't pay the full fee for my schooling.

MR. M.: Is that your idea or your parents?

D.: Both.

MR. M.: You think he would change if you paid him a fee?

D.: I don't know. He might.

MR. M.: Sometimes money does influence people.

D.: Yeah. I don't know whether it's true about Mr. Locke. *(Pause.)* Kids build up tensions in school. My brother is right now. He's got so much inside. He goes wild at home. He has the same attitude I do—I mean—only his teacher is a little easier to work with because she expresses her feelings. *(Pause.)* I get irritable at home too.

MR. M.: Because you're unhappy in school.

D.: Uh-huh. I feel bored at school. I feel all—well, you know. Nothing to do.

MR. M.: And you just about burst.

D.: Yeah. I wish we could start a school at home, but nobody else is interested.

COMMENTS

In this conversation, there is a mutuality, a shared relatedness between child and adult. There is a relative absence of commenting by the adult. He does not *respond* because there is nothing to respond to. He is already there. He is participating directly in the experience. His thoughts and feelings are interrelated with the child's within the experience. There is an underlying, transpersonal sense and a mutual inner understanding. The adult's verbal expressions are not responses to the child but continuations of a theme or pattern. They are not reactions to what has gone on before, not even related, except as next steps in a central theme. It's as though child and adult were painting a picture together, or writing poetry or composing a symphony, and the different patterns were emerging even while the expressions were being formed. The patterns, fitted together, show up in some sense of closure. They are the many facets of an over-all experience being explored by child and adult in creating a completed picture. For example, the conversations on the Bible include numerous thoughts and feelings which are woven into a holistic view as child and adult together try to perceive this personal experience. They think congruently and in a similar manner. An incident which clearly illustrates this is the moment of the child's sneeze. Both adult and child realize it will be recorded and laugh simultaneously before any words are spoken. Between them there is a relatedness, connection, and continuation.

There is a relative absence of questions, explanations, or justifications. The numerous unfinished phrases and sentences (complete in the shared experience if not in the language) also illustrate the communal nature of the relationship. Many of their comments are connected with "and." There is frequent use of "you know" and "you know what I mean," indicating that child and adult know and understand each other. There are many silences during this session. These were peaceful moments when there was a complete sense of interhuman feeling. Thus the conversations are the work of two persons in a relationship, seeing and exploring patterns of a human experience.

In the sessions which follow, they explore further the nature of the child's school experience, the values and conditions present, and the real identity of the teacher. As the child expresses and portrays his life in school, a pattern is formed which enables him to perceive school life differently and with a new perspective.

FOURTH SESSION, DAVID

(David sits quietly. He and Mr. Moustakas look through the office window for about ten minutes. Then David begins to speak:)

D.: Well, about the Bible, he's awfully hard-headed. I went in to tell him for the first time that I thought his religion was different from mine. I told him I thought they believed in the Bible *word for word* as rules, and we took it as a general guide. And finally we got around to my saying that, at bottom, I said it would be all right—if I just *dropped* the Bible altogether. And he said, "Oh, no, David, uh-uh." He says, "I don't think it would be good for you to drop your Bible study because after all *(long pause)*, wouldn't the other kids think you were getting something special?" And I said, "Well, yes, I guess they would from their point of view because they don't like it either." Not exactly like that but you know. And he said, "Now we took all the trouble to make a school of our own and—and to—just so we could have Bible because none of the public schools have it." And he said, "Now I don't think it would be right to drop the very— to drop the very subject we were made special for."

MR. M.: I see. And you couldn't say anything to that.

D.:   He had to—I guess he had to leave then.

MR. M.:   It was of value to have talked with him.

D.:   To see what he thought. Yeah, there was big value in that.

MR. M.:   Now you seem to understand his thinking.

D.:   Yeah. That's right. I guess because I opened up to him, he opened up to me. He thinks it would be a shame to—*(Pause.)*

MR. M.:   Yes, be in school without having Bible.

D.:   Uh-huh.

MR. M: Yet he was trying to understand your point of view.

D.:   This time I think he was.

MR. M.:   He knows that it's meaningless to you, that you do it only because it's required.

D.:   Yeah, he knows that. *(Laughs.)*

MR. M.:   He's no longer trying to convert you. *(Period of silence.)*

D.:   At least I know his feelings. I think he knows mine. The things he wants to bring up with me, he can, and I can do the same, you know.

MR. M.:   You're no longer so much in the dark with him. It seems to be the most open he's been with you all year.

D.:   And the artificiality is going away now too.

MR. M.:   He's being a real person. *(Period of silence to end of the hour.)*

FIFTH SESSION, DAVID

D.:   We talked again. I said, "Wouldn't it be all right," I said, "if I drop *all* the Bible. I'm still doing the quiz and I'm doing the book and they, they don't mean anything to me. It's against my beliefs and it's a waste of time, as far as I'm concerned." And I said, "Maybe I could—could—well," I said, "I'm not too good in penmanship. Maybe I could work on my penmanship during that time." And uh, he said, "Well, you just can't drop it, David. I did take you off the workbook, but that's as far as I can go."

MR. M.:   I guess he feels pretty strong about Bible.

D.:   Yes, they are pretty strong beliefs. *(Period of silence.)*

MR. M.:   It sounds to me that you've given him a lot to think about, and even though he didn't go along with your suggestion, he is interested in you.

D.:   I notice he's been trying to treat me real nice, you know. *(Pause.) I* do the same things but he treats me differently. But he kind of gives me the feeling that he's not doing it because he wants to. He's doing it because—

MR. M.:   He thinks he should.

D.:   Yeah. It seems like it, anyway. I mean, just from my being with him. He really cares to be friendly with me but he does these things because he thinks he should. *(Pause.)* It sort of embarrasses me, halfway between embarrassed and self-consciousness.

MR. M.:   Makes you stand apart from the others.

D.:   You know what I mean. You've had people be real nice to you because—I can't find the words.

MR. M.:   Yes, I know.

D.:   Well, if they saw you coming in real—coming in why they glance at you, stand up real quick. That sort of exaggerated—stand up real quick and say, "Hello! Hello! Hello!" All that, you know. It's a kind of artificial life, the way they do it. *(Pause.)* He believes in the things he does, like the Bible and spanking, very strongly.

MR. M.:   Not just an application of rules, but he personally believes in their value.

D.:   He does believe in them so strongly. *(Period of silence.)*

D.:   *(Pointing out the window.)* Right out there. That scene out there would be good to paint especially if we didn't have these cars out there blocking off our view. See how the wind moves the trees and the clouds. *(Pause.)* It's funny how he looked—different —when we talked. Some sort of sign.

MR. M.:   Maybe it is different for him to talk that way, for him to be open. You've given him a chance to really know you.

D.:   Uh-huh.

MR. M.:   Perhaps it isn't artificial, but his way of beginning to relate with you.

D.:   He doesn't quite know how to go about what he's doing.

MR. M.:   Yes. And he's really trying to be genuine.

D.:   Perhaps I'm rushing it too fast. He's never been hateful but just—

MR. M.:   Lukewarm.

D.:   Like someone acts toward a semi-friend. *(Long period of silence.)* *(Child and adult sit silently looking through the window for the remainder of the hour.)*

COMMENTS

Up to this point, much of the content of the talks refers to David's struggle to relate with his teacher. In a sense this is his "problem." But it is not a problem in the ordinary sense nor is he seeking a resolution as such or looking for responses from the therapist. Rather, David's explorations are ways of perceiving the various aspects of his experience to form a view consistent with the realities of the situation. He is relating the school experience to his own values and convictions and trying to see if he can be a self-consistent person in school. It is a matter of seeing relatedness and difference in his experience with his teacher, a matter of relating to his teacher, essentially, substantially, genuinely rather than tangentially, manipulatively, and superficially. The discrepancies he notes are not aspects of a distorted view or ambivalences to be resolved but, rather, they are realities with which he must live. He is trying to live with them in a healthy fashion while, at the same time, not violating his own beliefs.

SIXTH SESSION, DAVID

(David enters and begins talking with excitement in his voice).

D.:   Well, at last satisfaction. We had a talk for almost two hours after school. We each discussed our point of view on religion. Now we really understand each other. He is a fundamentalist and he takes the Bible word for word. But we take it as a picture-word of history, like literature. I asked him if someone acted out the Bible, word for word, would he be perfect. He said, "Well, I should guess so." I asked, "You mean that he would stop growing?" Then he said that, "Only Jesus was perfect." I told him there were places in the Bible which said that Jesus was not perfect. And I said, "You know the place where Jesus said, 'Don't call me good. There is only one who is good and that is God.'" He said, "Well, how do I know." *(Pause.)* He's not being artificial now. He's really being friendly. We found it very hard to discuss our religion. When I made a point, I had to explain the base of it, and then that base and that base, the whole thing in order to get one point across. It was hard to talk with him. I know how I feel with my religion, but I don't know how to put it into words. *(Pause.)* I have lots of special feelings that there are no words for. Like when I'm here with you. This room gives me a special feeling—not good or bad, just a full feeling—all over—and it is very comfortable. When I'm in a dark, eerie, dingy basement—that's another special feeling. It's a nice dinginess, a great dinginess, not good or bad. *(Pause.)* I had a dream last night in which I was completely free in space, not affected by gravity. It was a special feeling. I can't describe it. In my dreams, trees have animal heads and dog tails, sort of cartoonlike. I wish I could give people a mental picture of my dreams but I can't. If others could see inside me, they could know my feeling. There are no words to give a picture of how you feel inside. *(Pause.)* Right now, as I look out the window, I don't see a road that looks like a T. That's what I've been taught is there. When I was little I didn't have to think about it. Sometimes I still don't. *(Pause.)* I can be in a trance and not know what's going on around me. Someone can even ask me questions which I answer without even knowing it, when I'm open to nature. But people expect you nowadays to see things in a certain way. Sometimes you have to think and concentrate to see things as they really are to you. Out there, right now, I see a fuzziness in that place where the road is—its brickiness and grayness is blending with the buildings and the trees and everything outside merges, comes together and becomes alive, all living things. *(Pause.)* Psychologists, you know, try to figure out what other people are thinking and feeling, mind readers, you know. Even if someone wants to keep a secret in their minds, psychologists try to know it.

MR. M.: There is no privacy any more.

D.: But maybe they'll never be able to read your mind unless you let them. *(Period of silence.)*

D.: *(Pointing out the window.)* Look, everything so fresh and green. That's a special feeling. It sort of brings me close to everything, you know, feels sort of spiritual, everything I see. Everything seems like it's available and the way things are. It seems natural, like I've seen it all my life.

MR. M.: Something very close and yet familiar, unlike what most people see.

D.:   See that road out there? You might think it was something different if people didn't call it a road and say what it was for. You might
see it as a pattern or a contrast to something else out there. You
could put it in your own thinking and imagining. You could make a
design that fits with everything else.

MR. M.:   Yes, everything comes together.

D.:   And you just see designs. If you really look, you can see a design in
everything—like that curving branch and the ones below it form a
pattern. If you don't separate them, they fade together in a dimension. You see designs in the formation of everything out there.

MR. M.:   It's different from—

D.:   What others say are real things. It kind of takes it away when
you're told it's not that way. When I was littler, I didn't have a
learned sense of perspective and I saw things differently.

MR. M.:   Now you have to concentrate to see the shape and form of
things as they really are.

D.:   Yeah. There's a particular feeling that comes along with those designs. Everything comes together. It seems like everything is available. I just look at all of it like it was together and I'm kind of glad
I'm in the world, you know.

MR. M.:   It's a beautiful feeling when we don't have to see life separate
and apart, to just be free to experience life in all its availability.

D.:   Mmmhuh. *(Pause.)* Daddy says he's heard of people who dream of
chicken-skinned tunnels. First came the skin, then the muscles,
then the blood and the water, and on down to the dirt, you know.
(Period of silence.) I didn't think about these feelings when I was
little. I started wondering why I had these feelings when I was bigger. But I've never talked about it to anyone. I couldn't explain it,
except to my parents. It's a rather homey feeling. Like you were all
cozy-cozy, drowsy. Not only that, I don't know—I can't.

MR. M.:   Qualities of experience that cannot be put into words.

COMMENTS

There is a definite shift in this talk. David seems to have completed
his portrayal of school life so that it forms a self-consistent and self-conscious picture. From the external side of it, the Bible study and boring
subject matter must continue, but David seems satisfied now that he is
related to his teacher. Though there are differences between them, he
feels there are understanding and respect. David did not miss a day of
school since this talk, whereas earlier he had missed several days each
week. The vomiting, night terrors, and explosiveness had disappeared
after our third talk. None of the external signs of disturbance reap-
peared over the duration of our visits which continued for approximately
two more months.

The shift in this conversation (and this is the central theme of the remaining talks) is to an expression and exploration of the creative experience, i.e., to a discussion of special feelings which accompany raw perceptions, feelings for which there are no words, matters of personal presence

and being, not in terms of good or bad, or separate parts of living things, but of patterns, unity, design, availability, and togetherness of human life, perceptions unencumbered by training, teaching, or conditioning.

This was a mutual experience, events being realized and shared between child and adult, an organic tie which can barely be sensed in the literal transcript of the recorded talk.

SEVENTH SESSION, DAVID

D.: I've been wondering maybe I shouldn't come for any more of these interviews with you. School's almost out and we're going to be having lots of tests.

MR. M.: I guess you'll want to concentrate on these. Do they upset you like they did?

D.: Uh-uh. I'm used to them now.

MR. M.: Just take them as they come along without worrying about them.

D.: I guess so. *(Period of silence.)* Sometimes I can't think of a word.

MR. M.: And you wish you could.

D.: Yeah. But my words, you know, are word-forms. *(Pause.)* The dreams, I wish I could relate these better, and things of feeling like my religion. I can't describe my feelings.

MR. M.: Do you think you would have a better life if you could?

D.: I wish I had words like the Wintu Indians do. They have words for feelings. It's like saying, "Going downstairs." They would say, "Going downstairs him," you know. Sort of brings past and future together in the present, like "going downstairsness," or "going downstairsness him," instead of saying, "He is going downstairs." It brings all of time together.

MR. M.: Sort of unity of time in one experience.

D.: And with the spiritual. It's not motion like our words say, like going and coming and moving.

MR. M.: But a feeling, an experience, a togetherness.

D.: Of past, present, and future.

MR. M.: Without words there's no way of bringing all of time together. *(Pause.)* This is the way you see the life outside the window.

D.: Yeah. I was thinking just then about it. I am seeing something out there, not anything special but looking and having that feeling. Sort of like music and a drowsy, you know, like rocking to sleep. You know, those branches swaying *(snaps fingers)*, only there's more to it than that. Something else, I can't explain it. Sort of a very dingy feeling. No, not that either. That's the way I say it but that wouldn't explain it to other people. I can't even say it at this point.

MR. M.: But there's something there you feel and know even though you can't explain it.

D.: Yeah. Patterns and contrasts of color, everything all together. It is so very good—I'd sort of be lost without it really.

MR. M.: It brings you in touch with life.

D.: Mm-huh. I have this feeling when I sit in church on a sunny day. Sort of in touch with all spirit, God, and all the people. *(Period of silence.)* Especially I have this feeling in the spring when new shoots are out.

MR. M.: When everything is coming alive, growing, open.

D.: Yeah. *(Sighs.)* That's the best I— *(Period of silence.)* I wonder if everyone doesn't have this experience sometime. I've watched my sister. It's as though you were watching yourself. It's very—very—it brings you close to spiritual things. You're not in touch with any matter except the matter you see.

MR. M.: Really fundamental.

D.: Yeah, spiritual matter yet the body is there. *(Pause.)* When I was little, I believed that everything had a spirit. I still do.

MR. M.: And it gives great joy to have this all come together in spirit.

D.: Sort of brings me in touch with everything. The whole pattern seems to represent God. Everything has a spirit.

MR. M.: That certain inner quality that makes it special or unique.

D.: Yeah. I believe everything has a spirit, except manmade things like bombs.

MR. M.: Anything that destroys has no spirit.

D.: Except maybe a degenerative spirit.

MR. M.: Like viciousness and cruelty.

D.: Yeah, right in the middle of my picture——it breaks up because something bad is happening

EIGHTH SESSION, DAVID

D.: I just had a talk with Mr. Smillie. It wasn't a scheduled one but I just started in. I think what we discussed is time as a fourth dimension. It's the spirit and the experience of time as a whole. Most people are moving in time, seen as a third dimension. They're growing in time. They're passing time. But an experience of whole time is seeing in a fourth dimension, not moving up or growing up or down but an experience. Smillie said that maybe we're so involved with our scientific thoughts we couldn't experience this fourth dimension. He said the Trohiander and the Wintu live in this fourth dimension. We discussed it. He used the same illustration or whatever you want to call it that I did. *(Pause.)* Walkingness—not he is walking. Seeing time as a whole.

MR. M.: Walkingness has a timeless quality, refers to essence.

D.: Yeah, walkingness. Yes, it's walkingness. The street is filled with *walkingness*. It's all walkingness. But if you say, "Those people are walking," that's motion in the present. *(Eyes light up.)* I've found a way of saying it.

MR. M.: All good things have a timeless quality.

D.: And the bad things, they're passing you know. *(Pause.)* Maybe my experience is in the fourth dimension if that's what we're going to call the timeless.

MR. M.: It's a rather exciting discovery to come to.

D.: Yeah. Wish Einstein were here so he—he doesn't think we're living in the fourth dimension and I do. I think so now, but we're so tied up with our scientific thought. And people aren't always perfect, like making atomic bombs. We're more in the third dimension. Time is passing. *(Pause.)* So I've put it in words you know. Just like I couldn't find words for it and I've got words. *(Pause.)* Will you turn the tape off just a minute so we won't waste it while I go to the bathroom? *(David returns. Period of silence.)* I have only about two weeks of school left now.

MR. M.: Now that it's coming to a close, you feel differently.

D.: I like to understand it.

MR. M.: When you began to understand, school became a comfortable place to be in.

D.: Mm-huh. Sort of a treasure hunt, discovering what he believes. After the talks we had together, he likes me. He enjoys me and I enjoy him. He's almost completely open now. What he doesn't say in words I can tell from the look on his face.

MR. M.: There's a feeling between you that sometimes makes words unnecessary. *(Period of silence.)*

D.: I said I believe that everything has a spirit, but it has its own spirit and not anything else.

MR. M.: The spirit is the final truth of matter.

D.: The spirit makes all things alive. When I was littler, I used to hold my hanky over two fingers and suck it. It seemed to me like it was alive. The things I have for a long time since I was real little, seem like old pals.

MR. M.: A spirit of communion between you and them.

D.: Mm-huh, like I was telling Smillie, if you traced matter down, down, down, to the electrons and particles of the nucleus eventually you would get stuck. They're beginning to find out it's spirit. Matter is spirit.

MR. M.: The ultimate level is spirit.

D.: That's what I think. They found that if something doesn't have motion, if the atoms aren't turning and moving, if the molecules aren't vibrating, it becomes smaller. You know what I mean. Vibrations makes them bigger. Beyond a certain point, there is no motion. I think that's spirit. *(Period of silence.)* I guess there's a lot of things you just sense. You know. For instance, when you're able to have babies. You know when it would work. I haven't been in that situation but I imagine it's like a sixth sense, you simply know, not something somebody needs to tell you. You come by it naturally I guess. For instance, the baby knows to eat without being told. He goes right to it.

MR. M.: Yes, he certainly does.

D.: When you're ready to fertilize you go about it. You don't know why.

MR. M.: Like walking and talking and sleeping.

D.: Sometimes I can sense that someone else and I are thinking the same when I'm close to them.

MR. M.: That's like a sixth sense too.

D.: Mmhuh. So when I'm ready for having babies, I'll know. It would be a strong feeling and I could judge from my feeling.

MR. M.: You'll depend on your own inner—

D.: Yeah. I don't see how else you'd know.

MR. M.: That's completely understandable. Sometimes people depend on others to tell them when they're ready for experiences, but sometimes they decide for themselves.

D.: It would be pretty awful to have to ask others every time to see if you were ready. *(Pause.)* When I first came in here, you were sitting in that chair and one of those colored books was laying over here. This was part of the design, but the keys of the typewriter seemed the main pattern. Now, as I sit here, everything in the room fits into the design. And your face, that's the main part of it. It's like the center through which everything else spirals and everything else is included. I guess it starts from your eyes or something like that, sweeping into your nose and mouth and running all over, including everything on your desk, the wall, the floor, the windows, ceiling, and bookcases. If one thing were changed like the color of the walls, the whole design would be different. *(Pause.)* I guess this will be my last time to come. I'd like my parents to hear the tapes. They sometimes think I daydream, but actually the daydreaming has been all along my life. All my life has been these feelings. You know all I've expressed to you.

MR. M.: Yes, I know, not just idle nonsense but something very special.

D.: Yeah, to me anyway.

MR. M.: Whatever arrangements you want to make with them is all right with me.

Summary

The experience with David involved two central themes: a mutual exploration of various patterns of his school life and the nature of his unique perceptions. These themes emerged within the shared experiences of child and adult. David's attempt to understand his teacher led him to formulate a philosophy of school experience and to see new meaning and patterns, new ways of living within the limited situation. School, which had been a defeating, sickening situation, became a fascinating game—David's search for the underlying basis of his teacher's behavior. The game of understanding his teacher enabled David to accept the situation and to use his talents in it. Although this gave school a positive direction which he had not known before and enabled him to be his creative self at home, the fact remains that he still sought a direct way of expressing his interests and abilities and of finding a life of substance and significance in school.

Even so, having perceived a new approach with a different meaning, school matters became rare in the discussions between child and adult. David was able to express what he felt was the true nature of perception, the seeing of unity and relatedness in all of life. He brought to poetical fruition what had been for him partial awareness of thoughts and feelings too peculiar and special to share. Thus there were meetings of two human selves who discovered a common bond of being and created new vistas of knowledge and understanding within a communal way of life.

BRUCE

There are no words to express adequately the experience with Bruce. I present it with hesitation feeling it conveys the relationship only in a limited sense. It began in a most unusual way and turned out, for me, to be a significant experience in understanding the nature of individual creativity.

My relationship with Bruce has been a turning point in my work with children. He broadened my awareness of the possibilities of therapy and gave me courage to work with "the hopeless" case, to relate with children who do not follow the usual behavioral manifestations, who do not fit into the stimulus-response process, and who cannot be labeled in any of the ordinary ways.

Bruce had been described as a bizarre and retarded child, "hopeless" and "incurable." His record of previous experiences with therapists, diagnosticians, physicians, and psychiatrists showed clearly that he was beyond the hope of therapy, that he belonged in an institution.

When I first saw Bruce, my responses to him were not really responses to *him,* since he was not there to be responded to but was there only in a communal or relational sense. Nevertheless, I tried to initiate a stimulus-response pattern in every way I could think of and imagine from my previous work with children. When this phase ended in failure, I saw two possibilities: (1) I could come to the conclusion of other specialists that he was beyond help and required institutionalization, or (2) I could decide there was nothing left but to live with Bruce like one might live with a malignant growth. Actually, there was no dilemma. I felt there was only one way open to me. I had to go ahead, to live with him, to discover for myself what a relationship with him could be. My decision to continue with Bruce in spite of the telling evidence, I thought, would be a test of my belief in the growth potentials of every child. As it turned out, however, Bruce was a person of what proved to be unlimited rather than limited potentialities. I had to learn to see in a different way in order to realize this. And rather than heading for an "imminent social death," he was always ready for a creative relationship if the other person could but relate to him in his own unique style. Fortunately for me, Bruce lived through all my "responses" and helped me to relate with him in a mutual, shared sense, helped me to relate to his individuality, his difference. When this happened, Bruce's expressions were no longer "atypical," "pathological," or "bizarre," but were "unusual patterns," "creative talents," "unique, rare, and healthy expressions." In brief, Bruce opened for me pathways of relatedness to the "creative" child and to the "incurable" one.

As I have indicated, my first attempts were aimed at giving him a sense of freedom in the playroom. (Although I did not understand this at the time, Bruce was entirely free from the first moment I saw him.)

While he explored—that is, touched, tasted, held items in the room—I followed him, naming each object. Since he spoke only rarely and in single words, I felt this technique would stimulate speech. In the psychiatric diagnosis he was described as a "little four-year, ten-month old boy who was quite unresponsive and, in general, showed little interest in people and play materials and was severely retarded in speech. He showed no curiosity in his surroundings and manipulated practically none of the play things." At the time I saw him (three months after this diagnosis), only the speech retardation seemed relevant.

Even in the first session, Bruce's talents were evident, but I was not ready to see them. He made a series of drawings of trains and of telephone poles and wires. He printed on each drawing, "Frank. All Set. O.K." In my summary of this session, I wrote "His emotional behavior is diffuse and fleeting. He tends to be repetitive in his speech and play." After the fourth session, when there was a sense of relatedness between us and I was beginning to see a connection between his perceptions and mine, I realized that Bruce's "repetitions" were not repetitious at all. With each item he chose, no matter how many times he selected it, I became aware that he was experiencing it uniquely. I could see that for him each was really a new experience and contained, within a whole perception, incomparable patterns.

When Bruce climbed the pipes and the furniture to survey the details of the room, he was perceiving his relationship to the materials from a new vantage point, just as he did when he lay on the floor looking to different places in the room. He was honoring his "house," his playroom. I sensed the different positions to be his way of perceiving the details of the place from a variety of perspectives, not looking at the same items in the same way, but seeing freshly and interweaving new sights and patterns. Also, this was his way of showing an all-inclusive respect for the items in the playroom. We saw together the various items in the room from many unusual positions. Often Bruce took my hand, leading me to the top of a cabinet. He wanted me to see the world from his many different views. What others may have seen as odd or bizarre, I was now understanding as different and thinking, "Yes, why shouldn't we experience objects from above and below as different ways of relating to them?" So when Bruce climbed the pipes to the ceiling or stood on furniture to view the place or climbed along side walls or lay on the floor, I shared these experiences with him. It became our way of including different facets or patterns of perception in an integrated view and showing respect for the place in which we lived.

Bruce was never satisfied with the visual experience of objects alone. For him, the relationship with an object could not be complete without tasting, smelling, and rubbing it against his skin. He placed materials next to his ears and seemed to be listening with complete concentration. When he took the hammer from the pegboard, he was not satisfied with the sound of the pounded peg alone. He tapped the concrete floor, the plastered walls, the cylotex ceiling, the wooden house and shelves, the plastic cars, the sand and water, and other play items, listening and watching in each of these situations. He wanted to relate the sound and sight of pounding to a variety of materials and substances. He wanted to include within his perceptual experience a holistic, unified realm of auditory and visual realities and an honoring of all things. His relatedness to objects in the playroom involved a process of forming a bond with them and from many avenues of expression of fully actualizing his potentialities. Only then did Bruce seem satisfied that the experience was complete and that he could go on to new explorations. His spontaneous drawings with their "peculiar" captions and his experience of items with all available senses constituted the two central themes which we shared in our living together. I came to see that Bruce was not influenced by others, as such, but accepted only the evidence of his own senses.

Bruce frequently expressed his unusual talent for drawing and printing. He was able to draw with both hands simultaneously, each hand completing approximately half a theme, and the drawing coming together to form an integrated whole. This was also characteristic of his printing. He started the word with his left hand and finished with his right. He wrote correctly such words as, man, attention, doctor, tomato, potato, door, arrow, and window before he was five years old. He used both hands, especially when he was in a hurry to complete his work. He was able to make a complete drawing with printed caption in approximately ten seconds.

The experience with Bruce was always exciting. I never knew what we would plunge into next. Gradually he began to want me to participate directly in his activities. We shot ping-pong rifles together, threw the darts, and played ball. These games were played in special ways which Bruce devised. For example, the ping-pong balls he soaked in a water tray and rolled in sand before loading the gun. When we pumped the gun, the sand and water sprayed out. In playing ball, sometimes he threw the ball to me and sometimes across the room, but in either case we were together.

Frequently he handed me a toy telephone and took one himself. We looked to each other, sitting there in quietude and oneness. Sometimes he would initiate a call with "hello" and finish it, some minutes later, with "bye-bye," but often we called in silence.

Bruce began to speak more often. Previously he simply pointed when he wanted to bring my attention to some aspect of his experience. His speech consisted essentially of single words and short phrases. As I came to understand his expressions, I realized that his words conveyed whole meanings rather than narrow communications. His words were generally announcements or utterances. I came to understand that "drink water" meant that he wanted me to have a drink with him, but it also meant filling paper cups with water and filling the cups to the brim. In short, it meant all the activities and gestures associated with this event. He sometimes would say, "apron on" which meant he wanted me to help him in procuring the apron. It meant his standing next to me, putting his arms through, waiting for it to be tied, i.e., a whole constellation of meanings not generally indicated in the spoken words. Occasionally he referred to the paint as, "good paint" or "wet paint," but usually he simply announced "paint," which included procuring the paint, removing the tops, placing them all together in a pile on a shelf, getting certain brushes, and the whole process of painting itself.

He did not use words which related to a self-concept, such as "I, me, or myself." On occasion when I tried to stimulate him to use his name or some other self-reference (when I tried to separate him from his surroundings), he persisted in maintaining his unified perception. One episode occurred, as follows: Bruce climbs a bench and looks into a mirror. I ask, "Who do you see in the mirror?" Bruce continues peering into the mirror. Persisting, I say, "What is his name?" There is a long pause. Then I continue, "Do you know his name?" Finally, I comment, "I see Bruce in the mirror. Do you see Bruce in the mirror?" Bruce says with a heavy sigh, "See in the mirror." He jumps from the bench and throws himself on a couch.

I concluded from this and other similar experiences that Bruce had no self-concept. Yet he was very much a self, a unique personality with central attitudes and manners of expression. Anyone who knew him must have known that Bruce was really there. I mean substantially. He had self-persistent qualities and maintained a unity of self that made him distinctly different from every other person. His self was always available as a whole and included all others and all things in his life. He never separated himself from others or differentiated his self into categories. Thus, his language was entirely expressive and conveyed whole meanings rather than concrete communications.

After the early sessions, I never felt that our experiences were anything but complete, in spite of the fact that our use of speech was limited. I never felt that his lack of a self-concept was an inadequacy, but just the reverse. I saw that Bruce did not have to struggle to be a real self (as most of us do who get self and self-concept mixed up) because he was never anything but his spontaneous, open self.

Although these episodes were rare, there were times when Bruce seemed to be centering on problems rather than growth experiences. From an early age his parents had been forced to keep him locked indoors. They had not wanted to imprison him, but they felt they had to do it. Neighbors had threatened to take action against them if Bruce did not stop "uprooting" their flowers. There was also antagonism from the police who had frequently brought Bruce home when he was "running away" or "lost." His mother could not keep him in the house any other way. She was constantly worried and afraid for his safety and deeply anxious and guilty about the harm that might come to him. In any case, his parents reported that locking him in was never entirely successful. No matter how skillful they were in securing the door and windows, Bruce devised ways of escaping.

After seeing the thorough way he explored the playroom (actually the whole counseling building, including the furnace room and basement, the classroom, offices, and lavatories), I realized that he was journeying or venturing into the territory near his home, moving into the open land, the grasses and the sky, not running away from home but going to a new world. In three different sessions he seemed to be expressing his reaction to being "imprisoned." He would heave sand into all the rooms of the dollhouse, making sure that the windows were covered. Then he would try to break the windows with a wooden hammer. He enacted this scene many times and buried the family figures in the sand repeatedly, until he seemed to have settled his score with his parents.

Another variation in the basic pattern of my relationship with Bruce occurred during our sixth months together. At the time his parents decided to enroll him in the first grade of a parochial school. He remained in the school only two weeks. Then his parents were told he could not return. In school the desks were immovable and he was forced to remain stationary all day. The emphasis was on subject matter. For the first four days he complied with the rule of remaining in his seat; although, he seemed not to attend to any of the teacher's instruction. I saw Bruce twice during this period. He was extremely tense and hyperactive. He was continually destructive. He heaved play items across the room, breaking a great many of them. He placed ping-pong balls next to the dollhouse and would turn the house over on top of the balls, crushing them. He threw sand and attempted to throw other objects down the drain. He broke all the chalk and crayons into small pieces and threw them around the room. He turned over all the tables, cabinets, benches, and shelves in the room. Every item he could reach was thrown into a heap on the floor. He screamed, made peculiar moaning sounds, and constantly ran back and forth across the room. He was completely unresponsive to the limits I set. I finally had to remove certain costly items from the room which he was attempting to break. It seemed evident to me that the outbursts were caused by the extreme restraint he felt in school. I feel, too, that the teacher's constant harping, criticism, and belittlement touched Bruce's sensitive soul. The violent attack on the playroom did not occur again in our remaining year together.

During the last year of his visits, Bruce engaged predominantly in two activities, water play and painting. In both of these he seemed to be trying to include all that was possible in the experience. One day, for example, he threw off all his clothes and started painting with a brush. He began with blue, filling the page, diluting it with water and running through a variety of shades. With each shade he used a sponge to form designs. It seemed to me that when he had experienced all that was available for him in blueness with its accompanying shades and designs, he moved on to another color. He did this with each color, laughing gaily and saying, "cheer," "joy." Yet, with all the freedom and spontaneity, it was clear that there was order, that Bruce was in control not only in the detailed way in which he worked to get the exact color or pattern but also in the fact that he did not spill a single drop of paint on the floor, in spite of all the apparent messing and free movement of the brush. Sometimes Bruce wanted to paint the walls and ceiling and other places in the room. Though I had to limit this, I could understand how, for him, it was a different painting experience; I could see its potential value. Bruce's paintings were sometimes made in quietude and with utter concentration and usually contained definite themes, such as windmills, buildings, city and country scenes, and family situations. All of his paintings contained captions like "Cobley and Other, We Serve," "Brighton Telephone Service,"

"Chlorophyl Matters," "Steam Breath," and "Hellman's Mayonnaise." Frequently, he spelled these words aloud as he printed them. The paintings contained detail, perspective, and an alive, moving quality. They showed unusual artistic talent and a sense of humor and real promise. It seemed that he had to paint and draw, not compulsively but with the "I must" of a creative talent or capacity that requires expression.

In his water play he filled up the sink until it flowed over in such a way that we were both surrounded by pools of water. Then he removed his shoes and socks and sometimes his pants and danced gaily around the room. Here, too, he seemed to be using all senses, including all that was available in the experience. Although I usually sat by during these times, once he took my hand and, saying "Always sit," insisted that I dance too. I could see how this was an experience of pure joy and fulfillment from my own direct participation.

CHANGES IN BRUCE

The behavioral changes which are discussed here were not "worked on" in the therapeutic visits. Yet therapy was the one, new major experience in Bruce's life. Why the "symptoms" and problems should have disappeared during the period of Bruce's therapy is difficult to explain, except perhaps on the basis of a year's growth and experience and the transference of qualities in the creative relationship to other relationships and situations.

The major difficulties reported by the mother in our initial interview were Bruce's refusal to accept limits, his wandering from home, urinating in the streets, picking the neighbors' flowers, and standing in the middle of the street blocking traffic. In the therapeutic relationship, he accepted all limits readily (except while he was in the parochial school). At the end of the first year, he was accepting limits at home and it was no longer necessary to lock him inside the house. On his first visits to the Mental Hygiene Clinic, because Bruce would run wildly through the building, his father had to lock him in his arms and hold him both on arrival and on leaving. When Bruce was given the opportunity to explore the building thoroughly and to his complete satisfaction, he was willing to wait quietly and leave in the same way. This transferred to other situations. When he had to be taken to a public place, the parents had full confidence that he would conform to the expected social behavior of such settings. The major difficulties described by his mother no longer were present in his behavior at home.

His sleeping habits had improved so that for the first time in his life he was sleeping through the night. He was eating better and willing to eat at regular meal times. Growth in his drawing ability, i.e., the greater detail, the perspective, the more complex themes, the inclusion of third-dimensional patterns, is immediately evident upon examination of his first drawings and his last. Thus the major changes were continued growth in drawing and painting, willingness to accept certain social limits, and willingness to participate on a regular basis in family functions. There was also some change in the amount and frequency of speech.

Follow-Up

Following the therapy experience, Bruce attended a private school for two years. Interviews with his parents, as well as follow-up sessions with Bruce, indicated clearly that the spontaneous expressions of self had largely disappeared, along with his creative work in drawing and painting, and his original story writing (a home activity that did not occur in the playroom). At the time of the follow-up, his writing was a stereotyped copy of his school work. His drawings were repetitive duplications of scenes from books and television, or they were stick figure drawings. They might have been produced by anyone, except that underneath them he had written from memory the verbatim text of nursery rhymes or excerpts from literature (e.g., a paragraph from *Twenty Thousand Leagues Under the Sea*). The sheer poetry and humor of his own style had disappeared.

He was reading at a fifth grade level and his teacher felt that the special school had no further opportunities for Bruce. When I visited the school (on two occasions) Bruce did not speak to me and did not want to see me. It came as a shock and hurt when I saw him conforming in the most exact, compulsive ways to the school rules and regulations, in a far more exaggerated manner than the school required or wished; e.g., he walked down the halls in file, marching with an erect, firm posture. The school encouraged individual freedom at many points, yet he seemed to need to do things exactly as he saw others do them. He was constantly responding to the dictates, commands, and standards of an outside social world. He had developed a self-concept, as evidenced by his use of "I," "me," "you," and other personal pronouns and proper names. Although the parents appreciated the strides he had made in social growth, they were gravely concerned with the deterioration of Bruce's creativity and originality and with his extreme conformity in school.

The following excerpts from the last of the two follow-up sessions (which occurred at the end of his second year in the private school) illustrate the difference in Bruce and the stimulus-response nature of the relationship.

> *(Bruce enters the room and shoots the ping-pong rifle. Then he throws darts for five minutes, counting his scores. He selects several books from a table and looks through them. Then he plays with a cash register.)*

BRUCE: It's money.

MR. M.: Yes.

B.: *(Takes coin from register.)* O.K. Thank you.

MR. M.: Thank you?

B.: Thank you. *(Shakes register and coins drop out.)* It dropped all out. *(Pause.)* I dropped the money all out. *(Puts coins back in register, shuts drawer.)* Keep it closed—the money. *(Tries to dump money out with drawer closed.)* Go ahead and shake up the money. *(Repeats.)* Go ahead and shake up the money. *(Money drops out again.)*

MR. M.: It came out even when closed.

B.:   Yeah, *(Pushes numbers on register.)* 92-92. Thank you 22—thank you—160—thank you.

MR. M.:   Thank you—160?

B.:   Yeah, I know these numbers. 50—thank you. No sale—thank you. I push on that and 30—thank you. Thank you. *(Pause.)* Where's the paper?

MR. M.:   Would you like to draw? *(Shows Bruce drawing paper.)*

B.:   Thank you. *(Takes crayons.)* Thank you. *(Prints words on paper.)* *(Takes horn and blows.)* Thank you. Look—that's good.

MR. M.:   Yes, that's good music.

B.:   That's good music. *(Pause.)* I want to stand in the pond. Thank you. *(Removes shoes and socks. Stands in large tray of water.)* Thank you. Keep your feet warm. *(Takes horn gives it to Mr. M.)* Hold it! Blow! Thank you. *(Dips sponge into water.)* Thank you.

MR. M.:   Bruce, we'll have to stop in a few minutes.

B.:   Thank you. *(Bruce asks help with tying shoes.)*

B.:   Thank you, thank you.

MR. M.:   Now we'll go upstairs.

Shortly after this session and a visit to his school, Bruce's parents and I together decided to find another school. The following fall, Bruce entered a public school which is known for its unusual educational approaches, its respect for the individual, and its emphasis on the significance of the personal relationship in learning. Bruce had to be accepted in the school on a special basis since his family did not live in the district. His teacher was delighted to have the opportunity to work with him. In spite of his conformity in the special school, Bruce still looked and acted differently from public school children. Yet his teacher's trust and openness of attitude, his teacher's enthusiasm and excitement in working with an unusual child, penetrated every child in the classroom. From the beginning Bruce was completely accepted and befriended by his classmates. He not only began anew to develop his special talents, but, in time, he participated in many of the activities of the educational program and showed his advanced skill in reading and spelling. This experience turned out to be a turning point in Bruce's life. It led to the return of his creativity and the change from an exact conformist to a flexible person who was able to adapt to social standards and conventions which were not inconsistent with his individuality.

BILL

Bill was eight years old when he was brought for play therapy. His parents were not satisfied with the way he was developing. They were anxious about their relationship with him. They wanted him to be an aggressive, active, outgoing boy, but he was a quiet, deliberate, and thoughtful child.

Bill was failing in school. His teacher believed he might be mentally retarded. She wanted him to do his work mechanically, rapidly, and with exact attention to her instruction, but Bill worked slowly and thoroughly, trying to understand the basis of assignments and their relationship to other knowledge. He often stopped working on the class assignment when he wished to explore a question or problem. He would sit silently thinking through the assigned task or would locate related reading materials, pursuing additional relevant lines of inquiry and going beyond the concrete task. Every problem or question he answered was correct, but he rarely completed an assignment because it represented only a fraction of his interest in learning.

Mrs. Winn visited Bill's school three times during the five months of his "therapeutic" experience and saw Bill's parents a total of six times. From these experiences, it was clear to Mrs. Winn that Bill was a problem to his teacher and to his parents but not to himself or to her. In their first meeting, he shared his special interest with Mrs. Winn. He expressed his private experiences with insects and related his utter respect and fascination for the ways of animal life. He described his method of studying and understanding the world of snakes and the *cicada*.

Mrs. Winn was prepared to help Bill overcome his school problems and find a life of fulfillment at home. But from her first moment with him, she realized that his slowness, his deliberation, his deep concentration on the single activity, were all expressions of a real self. These qualities enabled him to relate creatively with anyone who would meet him honestly as a person. Mrs. Winn found him different but realized it was this difference, this distinct way of expressing himself, that made him a unique person. With Mrs. Winn, he shared his interest in science, an interest which he had not shared with his parents or his teachers. He exclaimed: "I have a microscope home. You can see a bee's antenna through it. I want to show you a bee's antenna. I'll bring it sometime." He had never cared to show his teacher or his parents a bee's antenna. His teacher felt that Bill's interest was extracurricular, not the central purpose for his being in school. She felt it was an escape from facing school responsibilities. His parents simply considered it odd that he would rather study insects and animals than play baseball or go sledding. No wonder his parents and teacher found it difficult to "get through" to him and spoke of his "clamming up" and becoming "tight inside." They wanted him to be like the average boy his age, have similar interest and habits. They did not value and honor Bill's essence and his limitless curiosity in the world of nature. Somehow they needed another voice to reassure them that his peculiarities were healthy. They did not understand that the fulfillment of his unique potentialities was as necessary to Bill as his eating and breathing. Mrs. Winn helped his parents and teacher to accept him as a unique personality and to value his way of ordering his life. His parents began to find worth in his contemplative life and his absorption with insects and snakes. Their perceptions of Bill changed. Whereas they had once referred to him as "odd, passive, and withdrawn," they now looked upon these qualities with regard, and considered him thoughtful, serious, creative, self-dependent. His parents, in their own way, came to see that they had imposed their standards on Bill. They came to recognize his potential and his worth. In one of the last interviews with the parents, Bill's mother

said: "I've been doing all the thinking for him. I've been doing what you
could have done with us and you would have gotten exactly the same
results as we got with him. You could have told us where we went
astray with Bill and what was causing him to clam up and tighten up,
but you didn't do that. You planted an idea and we nurtured it along
and it grew within us and now it is our idea. It is part of us and what
we are doing with our children. Our standards weren't part of Bill. He
was never permitted to think anything through with us. He was never
permitted to be himself. We know now we want him to think for himself
and make his own decisions."

Bill's teacher changed too. She recognized his "need to probe into the
nature of things" and the necessity of understanding him in his own
terms. With the change in the teacher's perception and the new meaning attached to Bill's school behavior, he finished the year with good
grades and there was no trace of doubt as to his mental ability.

If Bill changed during the visits, the change was a tangential one. He
was still Bill, substantially the same person with the same curious interests. The main difference was that he no longer had to defend himself
and protect his cherished ways in his relationship with his parents.

Bill's experience with Mrs. Winn involved two central themes: sharing
play experiences and sharing his interest in science. In several sessions
he worked with fire trucks explaining to Mrs. Winn the various parts
and functions. When he found a broken item he struggled with it until
he was able to repair it. Occasionally he sought Mrs. Winn's help, but
most often he worked on his own, "cementing" buildings, constructing
tunnels and bridges, and experimenting with various shades of finger
and easel paints. There were long periods of silence, yet Bill and Mrs.
Winn shared a feeling of relatedness throughout every session. In most
of the sessions he hummed and sang as he worked. He always became
excited when he discovered a relationship between two events or when
he arrived at a new insight.

Whenever he spoke of his desire to become a scientist or of his relatedness to insects and animals, his eyes were aglow. He was filled with joy,
completely absorbed, and oblivious of everything but his central interest. Yet his expressions were not simply reports but a way of sharing
significant experiences with Mrs. Winn.

One day, after a long period of silence, he began to speak excitedly:
"You know the black widow is a spider. They make a web between two
bushes and when a bug comes on the web, they wrap it up and carry it
to their home and store it for the winter. To catch a black widow you
take a jar and its top, one in each hand, and get the black widow still in
its web. *This way it still thinks it's home.* It has something special on its
feet that other bugs don't have. *All animals have instincts that guide
them home. Snakes don't wander far from their home either.* Snakes live
in a hole in the ground. You can tell it's a snake hole if it has a round
mound of earth around it. There are two holes so I stuff up one hole and
it comes out the other. If they are in the weeds, there is a *special way to
catch them so they won't get hurt.* I fall down on them, put one hand on
the tail and pull away the weeds and follow it to its head and then just

pull it out and there's my snake. I keep it in a can until nightfall and *then I let him go.* One day we found a snake that had been run over—its tail still wriggled. That was because of the reflex action. The nerves that come from the brain were still working though the nerves had been damaged. You can see the reflex action if you stick a long pin in a frog's brain. The frog is dead but his legs still wriggle. It's not very nice to do things like this but when I grow up, I'm going to be a scientist and some of these things you have to do. I know a lot about insects and animals. *I like to keep all these things to myself. I find out these things by watching, by watching their actions. I've caught millipedes for three days and each day they have done the same act.* Millipedes are cousins to centipedes. Millipedes have a thousand legs. A centipede has a hundred legs. I usually like to keep these things to myself. Did you know that when you have a bruise—the red corpuscles turn black when they die? They turn black because they don't have any oxygen from the heart. The blood picks up the black corpuscles and little by little they are absorbed. *When I was a baby I didn't know these things. I know lots of things about insects and instincts that other kids don't know."*

He mentioned other discoveries. "I found a Canadian snail under a board. It was different from other snails because its shell was soft. It had made a path under the board. I left this snail under the board and watched it for three days. The next time I went it was gone. I also found a sparrow's nest turned over and the mother bird lying dead nearby. In the nest was one egg. Since the egg needs body heat I sat on it for a while, but it was getting near supper so I brought it home. After supper, I sat on it some more. My mother told me to throw it out but I sat on it when she didn't know. When I went to bed I put it in a jar of water. In the morning I was going to put it in some cotton but it broke when I was taking it from the jar. The egg had been fertilized because there were veins in the egg." Bill sat quietly for quite some time. Then he smeared different colors of finger paints over the paper. He remarked with closed eyes, "I love the feel of the yellow."

In one session he spoke excitedly as he entered the playroom, "Did you know that grasshoppers don't fly? For a moment I thought they did, but they don't. They hop real high and flap their wings. Do you know, I think you know, that snakes have scales just like fish and that they go in waves. Red ants bite real hard. Black ants don't. There are all kinds of spiders. The web comes out of the back of their body. The body opens like a banana peel. The place that the web comes out matches the back end. Did I tell you about the cicada? I guess I did, but did I tell you that the cicada matches the dirt or the grass depending on where they are? If their home is near the dirt, it is brown; if their home is near the grass, it is green. I caught a cicada myself. They fly with their white wings from leaf to leaf. *(Pause.)* Did you know that poison ivy is a chemical. When your hand rubs against the leaf, the chemical gets in your skin and makes it itch. You know, I use my microscope to examine insects, just now I'm examining the mosquito. Did you know that creek water is full of insects? I hold a jar up to the light and all kinds of living things are floating around it. One day I found a clam that was alive. I put it in a bucket with some sand and water to keep it alive. In the morning I learned that clams move sideways because there was a line in the sand from the place I had put him to where he was in the morning."

COMMENTS

Bill's experience with Mrs. Winn is basically an experience of sharing, of mutuality, and of oneness. Although Mrs. Winn spoke little during the meetings, her participation was direct and she expressed herself fully in every episode. There were long silences in which child and adult shared a single orbit of experience. The absence of front, of technique, and of strategy was particularly evident.

Bill's individuality and his healthy attitude are expressed in his continued integration of a variety of materials in one central theme, in his complete absorption in self-chosen activities, and in his experimental attitude. In this relationship, each person came to himself. Bill created new perceptions as he shared his "secret" interests with Mrs. Winn. Mrs. Winn, in turn, realized a new self in therapy when she saw that Bill was not one to be responded to but rather was a person to meet and to live with. There is an obvious absence of stimulus-response sequences, of child fears and hostilities, of therapist technique and interpretation, of problems and problem-centered behavior. There is a child with an unfolding potentiality which requires expression and fulfillment and an adult with a wish to share this interest and a capacity to bring to the relationship her own reverence for a child's personal world and the world of insect and animal life.

CONCLUDING COMMENT

Of what value is this recognition of the creative relationship? What evidence is there that it is a significant reality in child therapy? This chapter is simply a presentation, a pointing to a reality, a relating of an experience. It is presented as the author's inquiry into specific therapy relationships. It is not adapted to convince or change another's views or to serve as evidence, verification, or corroboration. It is presented with a feeling of responsibility to report a real experience, relatedness to another, to life, a feeling of responsibility to bring to awareness, and expression, and to understand a reality perhaps not seen or recognized by others. The creative relationship has been brought to portrayal here with the same degree of responsibility of relating an event which Dorothy Lee (2) describes in speaking of the Dakota. When the Dakota man returns from a vision quest, he brings his vision, and he is believed when he reports. He does not bring back a trophy by way of proof. I have no trophy to present as evidence or support—only the direct experience of unity, the transpersonal experience of living with a child, and the dialogue of our interhuman life. This I have tried to present in an expressive form as a personal reality and as a way of conveying the significance of the creative relationship in therapy with children.

THE REACTIVE-CREATIVE RELATIONSHIP

Although it is not possible to make the creative relationship, i.e., to direct the therapeutic situation in such a way that it becomes creative, occasionally a relationship which begins on a stimulus-response basis comes to be creative and continues long after the presenting difficulties have disappeared. This change in a relationship in child therapy is illustrated in the following example. It is not possible to present the material in any detail, since there are several hundred pages of transcribed and stenographic data from the sessions which continued for more than three years. Some of the central themes and significant episodes between the child and therapist are selected to show the nature of the experience during the stimulus-response phase and the shift to a creative relationship.

In the initial interviews, Richard's mother described him as an extremely withdrawn, passive, and bizarre child who was retarded in speech and locomotion. She stated he showed little affection or responsiveness in the family. At times, he was extremely aggressive toward his brothers and sister. Thorough medical examination revealed no physical or neurological basis for his retardation in speaking and in motor and physical development. His mother felt that his retardation was due to emotional trauma and conflict which resulted when he was left for lengthy periods in his infancy with many different strangers. His nursery school teacher indicated that his speech sounds were "like animal growls." The diagnostic examiner described him as, "an autistic, confused, disorderly child, unable to detect reality and in many ways showing symptoms of psychoticlike behavior." Institutionalization had been strongly recommended to the parents but they refused to accept this, believing that he could be helped while living at home.

RICHARD

Five major themes were evident during the first year of therapy with Richard. The first series of contacts were characterized by Richard's extremely withdrawn, anxious behavior. He rarely spoke during this period, and when he did, it often was not possible for me to understand him. He seemed to be completely oblivious to his mother, apparently autistic, not responding to her attempts to communicate with him before and after the play sessions. The second phase involved considerable expression of hostility by Richard toward family members, especially his mother and baby sister. At these times he spoke only occasionally with clear speech. The third phase involved ambivalent expressions or attitudes toward family members. Richard vacillated between attacking them and showing his feelings of love for them.

In the fourth period, there was a return to the anxious behavior accompanied by frequent episodes of strong aggressive outbursts. At this time he became deeply and overtly dependent on his mother, in contrast to his earlier indifference. During this period, it was necessary for his mother to remain with him in the playroom. His speech and social behavior improved and many of the bizarre patterns disappeared. The final theme involved Richard's constructive play and positive expressions toward family members.

In the initial session with Richard the following interaction occurred:

T.: You may play with things here in any way you wish, Richard. *(Richard stands in the center of the playroom for about four minutes, making incomprehensible, repetitive sounds. He walks to the sandbox, puts one foot into it and withdraws quickly, seemingly repelled by the sand. He then runs around the room screaming and laughing shrilly.)*

T.: You find this to be a very funny place. *(R. stops at the doll house. He picks up two doll beds and puts one on top the other. He takes a group of family figures and places them on the floor along with a number of pieces of furniture. He holds his left ear and pulls on it. He laughs shrilly and makes low guttural sounds. He takes a baby figure, starts to hand it to the therapist, then throws it at him.)*

T.: You want to hurt the baby? *(R. approaches the sandbox again. He repeats the previous anxious behavior. Finally he enters the sandbox and sits down. He feels the sand, letting it sift through his fingers.)*

T.: Feels nice and soft. *(R. rises suddenly and wipes hard against his trousers to remove the sand.)*

T.: You want to get every bit off. *(R. stoops to play in the sand but withdraws quickly.)*

T.: You don't like to touch it. *(R. laughs shrilly. Again, he sits in the sand a few minutes, gets up, and kneels while touching the sand. He rises and begins kicking the sand.)*

T.: Do you want to kick it all the way out? *(R. kicks again and laughs loudly. He gets out of the sandbox, laughs, and walks around the room. He paces back and forth several times. He takes the family figures and makes loud crying noises. He drops the figures. He takes a steam shovel and truck. He places all the family figures in the steam shovel but the baby, which he throws on a shelf. He screams, "Na, na, na, na," over and over again. He rearranges the items on a shelf while making loud sounds repeatedly, like "ga, ga, ga." He then retrieves the father figure from the steam shovel and says in a loud, clear voice, and with much feeling, "Daddy! Daddy! Daddy!" He vacillates between putting the figure into the steam shovel and taking it out.)*

T.: You're not sure whether to leave Daddy in the steam shovel or not. *(R. drops the figure and paces the room again, laughing loudly and shrilly.)*

T.: Richard, it's time for us to stop for today. *(R. runs immediately to the door, opens it, and leaves.)*

COMMENTS

This first session is similar to many which followed it—the doubt and anxiety in facing himself, in having to make choices and decisions, the fear of touching things and of getting sand on himself, the crying sounds and deep feeling whenever he touched the family figures, the angry approach to the baby figure, and the ambivalence concerning the father.

In sessions which follow, he reaches a point where he enters the sandbox freely, immersing himself in the sand completely, letting sand settle over his entire body including his face and hair. When he successfully overcomes this fear, he begins to express intense hostility, at first directed toward the animals in the room, and later the family, especially the mother and baby figures.

Episodes are selected from a number of interviews which illustrate the nature of Richard's hostility against his family and how the therapist encouraged further expression. The shrill laughing and loud guttural sounds continue throughout this period.

> *(R. paces back and forth in the room, each time looking intently at two baby figures on a table. He approaches them a number of times, finally grabbing them up and throwing them into the sandbox. He stamps on them.)*

T.:   You feel like burying them in the sand, covering them all up.
> *(R. pulls at both ears and jumps up and down, screaming and laughing shrilly. He runs to a shelf, and takes the mother figure, throws it into the sand, and starts to bury it. He stops suddenly seems extremely anxious. He pulls at his ears, paces the floor, and laughs shrilly.)*

T.:   You want to do it, to bury her, but you seem to be very much afraid.
> *(R. approaches the sandbox, repeats the previous behavior, and paces the room screaming and laughing.)*

T.:   You simply can't bring yourself to do it.
> *(R. takes two boy figures from the shelf and tosses them into the sand. Then, with his shoe he pushes the mother figure down under the sand and stamps on it repeatedly.)*

T.:   Feels good to bury her deep down, to stamp her all the way down.
> *(R. takes the iron and runs it over the mother and baby figures. He throws them into the sandbox. He runs to the dollhouse and tries to crawl into it, pulling on his ears and making crying noises and peculiar, jerky body movements.)*

> *(R. takes the mother figure and places it at the window of the doll house. With a rifle, he shoots it, saying clearly, "bang bang." Following this, he says, "Tired" and lies down in the sandbox. Later he takes the mother and baby figures and chops them with a shovel.)*

> *(R. takes all family figures from the shelf to the sandbox. He buries them one by one.)*

T.:   Just feel like burying them all. *(R. laughs shrilly.)*
T.:   It feels good to do it. *(R. laughs again and says, "Good." He continues piling sand on top of the figures.)*
T.:   You're making sure they're good and buried this time.

(R. places the baby figure in a bathtub. Then he puts it under the roof of the dollhouse and slams the roof down. He takes the mother figure and bangs it against the baby. He laughs shrilly and makes crying sound.)

T.:   Sometimes you feel so angry you want to hurt them.

(R. throws the baby figure across the room. He takes the father figure, starts to throw it into the sandbox, then changes his mind and places it on a table. He continues handling the father figure uncertainly for about four minutes.)

T.:   You're not sure what you want to do with him.

(R. throws the figure to the floor saying in an angry voice, "Daddy! Daddy!" He runs to the doll house and tries to remove the chimney. He pulls at his ears and jumps up and down, jerking his head and body.)

(R. takes the baby figure and stands it on its head. R. makes crying sounds.)

T.:   The baby is crying. She hurts.

(R. throws the figure into the sandbox. He takes a hammer and pounds the figure for approximately three minutes. He gets a shovel, digs a hole in the sand and puts the baby in it. Then he chops the figure with a shovel. The blows increase in severity; Richard seems completely involved in a state of fury.)

T.:   Smashing her harder and harder. You really want to chop her to pieces.

(R. gets out of the sandbox and seems exhausted. He takes a jar of paint for the first time and smears blotches of red paint all over the easel. Following this, he turns to the baby figure and with a rubber knife cuts the figure over and over again.)

T.:   You're cutting her all up.

R.:   Cut! Cut! Cut! *(R. makes whining, crying sounds.)*

T.:   It hurts.

(R. suddenly screams, "Oh, crazy," as he pounds the sand .)

T.:   Crazy?

R.:   Oh, Crazy! Crazy! *(He continues pounding the sand.)*

T.:   You think it's crazy to smash the sand.

R.:   Crazy!

T.:   People say you're crazy when you do funny things?

R.:   Crazy! *(R. continues pounding the sand. Then he pounds the baby figure and screams in pain, "Oh! Oh! Oh!")*

T.:   It hurts so much.

(R. pulls on the therapist and says, "Go, go." At this point R. is hysterical. He is screaming, flailing his arms, running nervously back and forth, and making strange sounds. He leaves the room, ending the session.)

(R. procures a pail of water. He gets the mother figure and throws it into the water. He throws all the family figures in. He takes the mother figure and places it in the doll house. He throws sand all

over the house and on the roof. As he does this he says clearly, "Burn it! Burn it! Oh, boy!")

T.: It's very nice to burn it all up.

R.: Up! Burn it!

T.: It's so hot there and she is burning.

R.: Burn. Ow! Ow!

T.: It hurts very much to be burning.

R.: Ow! Ow!

T.: She's burning all up.

(R. takes the father figure and buries it in the sand.)

T.: Want to be sure he's pounded right down.

R.: *(With feeling.)* Daddy! Daddy! *(R. continues pounding the figure. He puts the figure in the doll house and throws sand over it saying clearly, "Burn, burn." R. then takes the mother and baby figures and throws them in the doll house. He sprinkles sand over them.)*

T.: Burn them.

(R. takes the mother, stuffs the figure into a toy toilet. He makes crying sounds, then laughs shrilly.)

T.: She's crying.

R.: Crying. *(R. hands the figure to T. and says, "Cut it.")*

T.: I know you'd like me to, but you'll have to do it for yourself.

R.: Cut it.

T.: I won't do it for you, Richard.

(R. mixes sand and water in a cup. He puts the baby figure on the toilet and pours the mixture over it. Then he hands the cup to the T. and gestures to the T. to pour the mixture on the figure.)

T.: Richard, if you want to pour the rest on her, you'll have to do it yourself.

(R. makes loud noises and screams. Finally, he pours the sand and water over the baby figure. Later, he takes the red paint and covers the mother figure with it. Then he takes a giraffe and places it next to the baby. He says, "Bite. Bad." He steps on the figure saying, "All broken.")

Richard spent nearly every session over the next six-week period burning the house, pouring sand over the family figures, screaming "Burn! burn! burn!" and clutching and pulling his clothes and body. Following these episodes he smeared paints over everything in the room cars, trucks, shelves, walls, puppets, etc. Then the episodes of direct hostility continued.

In his fifth month of therapy Richard's anger was still at a peak. He began using an alligator hand puppet (which had a large mouth and sharp teeth) to attack the family figures. After repeatedly using the puppet to bite the figures, he takes the father doll and places its head in a vice.

T.: You're squeezing him tight—a bad daddy.

(R. takes the figure and hurls it into the sandbox. Then he gets a scissors and cuts the arms and legs.)

T.:   You want to cut him all up.

R.:   Cut.

*(R. takes the mother and baby figures and squeezes their heads in a
vise. Then he places them on a radiator, saying, "Burn! burn!")*

T.:   You want to burn them up.

R.:   Burn. *(R. places the entire family group in the sand. He stamps
their heads with a shovel. Then he pours water over them until all
the figures are completely immersed .)*

*(R. takes the baby figure and puts it into the mouth of the alligator.
He repeats this with both figures. Then he tries to bite their heads
off. He throws the father figure into a pail of water, retrieves it, and
hands it to the T. Then he takes a rubber knife and moves it across
his own neck and head. He hands the knife to the T. indicating he
wants the T. to cut him. The T. gives him back the knife. Richard
takes the baby figure and pulls its arms and legs, saying, "Baby.
Ow! ow! ow!' He pounds the head of the figure on the floor.)*

T.:   It hurts. You want to smash her all up.

R.:   All broke.

COMMENTS

Richard's hostility did not begin in a relatively mild manner and reach
a peak of intensity before tapering off. Although there was a change in
the frequency and duration of hostility, the severity or intensity remained the same. Every episode contained a fullness of unbounded
angry feelings.

Richard bit, tore, burned, drowned, cut, chopped, trampled, buried,
painted, strangled, and attacked the family figures consistently and repeatedly over the first seven months. The sand was his most frequently
used material. In the first few sessions, the sand had greatly disturbed
him, but during the hostile episodes he used it freely. The sand was not
merely a symbol of fire; with his whole being he experienced it as fire.
His entire body shook when he used it to burn and torture his victims.
His chief phrases, "Burning in there," "Burn," and "Ow!" were spoken
clearly in nearly every session.

Richard expressed considerable hostility toward the therapist and,
along with it, much dependency. These attitudes appeared in the third
month of therapy and continued through the seventh month. Among
other things, he tried to cut the therapist, painted him, threw water at
him, and frequently "burned" him with sand. In contrast he sought the
therapist's help in opening jars of paint (although he could do this himself), in cutting paper, in drawing and pasting, in painting—all activities
which he could do on his own. He also wanted the therapist to repeat certain things after him—for example, drink from the nursing bottle and
burn the baby and mother figures— so that he would not have to face the
full responsibility for his regressive and hostile acts. While the hostile attacks on the therapist occurred in almost every session between the third
and seventh months, there were three brief episodes in which Richard

called the therapist, "Daddy." One time he asked the therapist to blow up some balloons, saying "Daddy, Daddy" each time the therapist inflated one. Another time he was feeding the baby doll with a small nursing bottle. He handed the bottle to the therapist, saying "Daddy." He repeated this three times and insisted that the therapist feed the baby, finally taking the therapist's arm and forcing the feeding.

The hostility was not only directed against the family figures and the therapist. Sometimes it was of a general nature, when he threw the materials around the room, pounded the furniture, broke every item he could, tore up paper and threw it around the room, chewed crayons to pieces, kicked and bit the furniture and play materials. And sometimes it was directed against himself as he cut and burned and bit himself and pulled at his ears. He often chewed his fingers and clothing.

Following each of the hostile episodes, Richard became extremely bizarre—pulling on his ears, clothing, jumping up and down, laughing shrilly, shaking, flailing arms and legs, pacing nervously around the room, and making loud piercing screams, crying sounds, and animal-like noises. There was a great deal of self-punishment and self-attack.

The stimulus-response nature of the relationship over this hostile phase was evident in the various interaction sequences. Richard's hostility served as a stimulation for the therapist. The therapist followed Richard's leads, putting into words what Richard seemed to be expressing with deep feeling. The therapist responded by listening, reflecting feelings, and encouraging further expression, and by selecting and interpreting the essence of the hostile expression at its most intense and severe level. In brief, the therapist's responses served as an encouragement to Richard to continue to express himself openly and freely, to face his underlying hostility and to express it ultimately, completely. Only occasionally did the therapist set limits with Richard during this period, even when the attacks on the therapist were somewhat severe.

Richard's hostility toward his family was the central theme of his play and dominated every session between the second and seventh month. There were brief periods in some sessions however (most frequent in the seventh month), when he used the play materials in a constructive fashion. At these times, he carried on telephone conversations (primarily with gestures) with the therapist. He put tinker toys together, making objects that moved on wheels and geometric figures. He traced a number of play items, and made silhouettes of his family and colored them. He played with trucks and cars, moving them in and out of a garage which he built with blocks. In two sessions in the seventh month he cut and pasted for about fifteen minutes each time. Often during these activities Richard sang or hummed popular melodies.

A PERIOD OF AMBIVALENCE

Another attitude evident in Richard's play, particularly in the sixth and seventh months, was his ambivalence toward members of his family. He vacillated between expression of love and hatred. These episodes were generally centered on mealtimes and sleep. He prepared meals or tenderly placed figures in bed, expressing his affection and wanting each member to enjoy his food and to sleep comfortably. References were made especially toward his father, mother, and baby sister. He usually attacked them and "burned" them before the meal scene was finished, however. Only once in the many brief episodes which occurred did he carry through the activity in a wholly positive manner.

Brief excerpts have been selected to illustrate the ambivalent expressions and the therapist's responses to them.

R.: *(Richard takes the father figure.)* Daddy! Daddy! *(He throws the figure on the floor.)*

T.: Really slammed him down.

(R. runs to the doll house and kicks it. He then picks up the father figure and places it gently in a large bed. He takes the baby figure and places it in a crib next to the father.)

T.: Night, night for baby too.

R.: Oh, baby. *(R. takes the baby figure out of the crib and pounds its head on the floor.)*

T.: Now you feel like pounding the baby.

(R. puts the figure into a soft chair, then into bed. He takes each of the family figures and, holding them gently, puts them in separate beds all in one room.)

T.: Night, night for all of them—you want them to have a good sleep.

(R. takes the figures and drops them one by one down the stairs, saying "Ow! Ow!" as each falls.)

(R. takes table, chairs, plates and utensils. He prepares a meal. First he feeds the baby.)

R.: Dinner. Dinner.

T.: You've made the baby a nice dinner.

R.: *(R. takes each of the family members and puts "food" at each place.)* Dinner. Dinner.

T.: All of you are eating dinner now.

(R. takes the mother figure and throws it into the sandbox. He buries it in the sand.)

T.: No dinner for her.

(R. retrieves the figure and places it at the table again. He sits next to the figures for about a minute. Then, screaming, he takes the mother and baby figures and throws them into the house, saying, "Burn in there.")

(R. takes the father figure and places it on a large chair.)

R.: Daddy. Good.

T.: You love Daddy.

(R. takes the figure and buries it. He retrieves the figure and places it at a table. He makes food and says to the figure, "Eat it.")

T.: You want Daddy to have good food.

R.: Daddy eat. *(R. then places the figure in bed saying, "Good night." R. kisses the figure. Then he takes it and throws sand over it saying, "Burn!")*

T.:   Sometimes you love him and sometimes you feel like burning him.

(R. places the family figures around a table. He prepares a "birthday cake," humming "Happy Birthday to you," while doing this.)

R.:   Happy birthday.

T.:   Happy birthday.

R.:   Happy birthday to you. *(R. sings the song while serving the cake. He plays through this event, expressing only positive feelings.)*

RETURN OF THE ANXIETY

At the beginning of the eighth month, Richard's direct hostility stopped abruptly and did not appear again in any concentrated form during the next two years. With the cessation of the hostile episodes, Richard's main expression was a severe anxiety centered on dirt. His anxiety in connection with dirt began with an extreme fear of touching the sand and spread to everything in the playroom. The fear became so magnified that he refused to touch anything. When he accidentally touched something he shook himself completely. He begged and demanded the therapist to pick up the items he wanted, to make outlines for him, and to cut and paste for him. The therapist insisted that if he wanted to do these things he would have to do them himself. Torn between his desire to work and his extreme fear, he paced the room nervously, approaching the materials and moving away from them many times. He would rub his hands frequently and thrust them into his pockets. After about one month of this tortured behavior, following one especially frenzied session in which he shook and pulled himself mercilessly, made strange animal-like sounds, and hid behind shelves and under the easel to escape the challenge of the situation, Richard walked out of the playroom. The following time, he refused to enter without his mother but he also refused to go home. He insisted that his mother accompany him. It was during this month of intense anxiety that Richard became deeply attached to his mother and for the first time in his life related to her in a significant way. This dependency reached a climax about the same time that he refused to enter the playroom alone. He would not let her out of his sight and would pull at her continuously until she did what he wanted. His mother accompanied him to the playroom for the next seven sessions. The fury which he had directed toward the family figures in his play was now unleashed directly toward his mother. Along with his hostility he attempted to control and limit her. He required her to do everything for him and to be where he wanted her to be. During the play sessions the therapist related with mother and child on a similar basis, responding to each with empathy and acceptance and encouraging them to face the hostility—dependency struggle and to live through it.

SESSIONS WITH RICHARD AND HIS MOTHER

Since this was a unique aspect of Richard's therapy, numerous verbatim excerpts are presented:

Richard, his mother, and the therapist enter the playroom. Richard takes his mother by the hand, leads her to a chair, and indicates she is to sit. He points to a jar of paint.

R.:   Open that. *(M. picks it up and turns the top.)*
M.:   It's stuck, Richard.
R.:   Open it. *(R. pulls on his mother's arm. M. works with the jar and finally opens it. R. takes it and puts it back on the easel stand. R. then takes his M.'s hand and leads her to the sandbox. He gestures for her to take the shovel and dig in the sand.)*
T.:   You like to tell Mommy just what to do.

From the sand, Richard takes his mother to a table with paper, scissors, and crayons. He insists that she trace, cut, color, and paste a number of different shapes and figures. Then he has her make a cut-out of each member of the family. As she completes them he names the member, takes the scissors, and cuts the figure to pieces. At his mother's slightest reluctance to work he pushes and shoves her. When she finishes cutting out the mother figure, Richard says, "Cut Mommy." His mother hesitates but proceeds to cut up the figure. He insists that she make another and has her cut it up. He repeats three times. On the fourth repetition, she refuses; Richard screams and pulls at her. He shouts, "Cut Mommy." His mother begins again, her face flushed with anger. She hurriedly cuts across the figure and right over Richard's finger which is nearby. Richard's reaction is violent. He screams and shouts at her. He kicks and bites her. The cut on his finger is small, but he will not be comforted. His cries and screams become louder and sharper. He attacks her repeatedly, punching and kicking her and yelling, "Bad Mommy." Though she is thoroughly angry, she tries to comfort him saying, "It will be all right." Whenever she speaks he screams louder and wails harder to drown out her sounds. Finally, he pulls his mother from the chair and literally shoves and kicks her out of the room. He screams repeatedly, "Bad Mommy." This continues all the way up the stairs, out of the building and down the street to their car.

Fortunately for all concerned, Richard's fury subsided and he never attacked his mother in quite the same fashion again. It was a significant experience for his mother because she realized that she could no longer avoid facing Richard and his hostility or her own intense feelings. These attitudes and insights she examined in the relationship with her own therapist.

In the next two sessions, Richard again had his mother make cut-outs, each of which he identified as a member of his family. At first he insisted that she cut them up, but in the third session he cut all the figures himself. Gradually, Richard's mother set limits with him and insisted that he be responsible for his own activities. She no longer seemed afraid to meet him and to express her own convictions and feelings. She was willing to help but, for the most part, she insisted that he work on his own. Richard accepted these limits and began to play independently of his mother. Two months after his mother's first visit

Richard again was coming by himself, although at first he did so with some hesitation and uncertainty. His speech had improved and many of the strange and bizarre patterns disappeared.

THE POSITIVE EPISODES

Following the above sequence of interviews, Richard became quiet. He began digging holes in the sand and making caves and bridges. He used the sand equipment and other materials in carrying out different themes. Occasionally he put family figures in a landslide or cave-in, but for the most part he seemed to play for the sheer enjoyment in the activity. His work was thoughtful and concentrated. He often remained with the same activity the entire period. Even when he mixed sand and water and put his hands in it, he remained calm using the material without any disturbance. When he failed to achieve a task, he would remain with it a long time. After repeated failure he still remained calm and patient and continued to concentrate on the problem. After many trials, he sometimes would find a method of solution which satisfied him or he would give up and go on to do something else. During this time he sang as he worked. The words often came out clearly and the melody was accurately presented.

In one session he took the baby figure and handed it to the therapist. He took it from the therapist's hand and placed it against his cheek. The following interaction occurred which illustrates his positive feelings toward the baby during this period.

T.: You want me to love the baby?
R.: Baby. *(R. hands T. a bathing suit.)* Bathing suit on.
T.: You'd like me to put it on, but you can do it yourself. *(R. puts the bathing suit on the baby and hums "Rock-a-bye Baby.")*
T.: When the wind—
R.: Blows the cradle will rock—Rock-a-bye baby on the tree top. Night night. All night, night. *(R. hugs the baby.)*
T.: Nice to hug the baby.
R.: All kiss. *(He kisses the baby figure.)*

RICHARD'S SPEECH

This type of socially constructive play continued for the next year. Richard was becoming completely silent in the playroom. Since there had been definite improvement in his social behavior and social responsiveness and in his willingness to accept limits at home, but little change in speech, the therapist decided to try to influence Richard's speech development. While Richard made his caves and bridges in the sand the therapist verbalized every detail of his overt behavior. The comments were made in the form of questions. After approximately one-half hour of this, Richard began to respond. He would describe what he was doing in single words or brief phrases. The therapist stimulated Richard in this manner for two months. Although he talked more in these sessions, the therapist decided to discontinue the pressure on Richard to talk. The speech was forced and contrived, not at all spontaneous or meaningful. Also, the therapist's stimulation kept Richard stationary and forced him to explain and talk about what he was doing. It prevented him from enjoying his projects and moving ahead in his own way. The therapist became more and more unhappy about this manipulation and the way it affected Richard. He decided finally to stop his efforts to improve Richard's speech.

Richard had moved from an extremely anxious and hostile child to a person who became deeply engrossed in construction activities in the sand. The situation had changed from an obviously therapeutic experience to one that appeared to have no immediate therapeutic value. The therapist had been concerned that he was no longer being a therapist. Thus he had searched for ways of helping Richard to overcome his bizarre behavior, to improve his speech, and to become fully socialized. He attempted for a while to maintain the stimulus-response relationship which had led to the alleviation of tensions and the resolution of the anxiety and hostility patterns. He attempted to continue something which no longer was of any value. Only on minor occasions during the second year of therapy did Richard express intense anger or fear, and at these times the feeling seemed to be situational, i.e., aroused by something painful and frustrating which had recently occurred in his life. The therapist had a choice to make, to continue the sessions on a different basis or to terminate. Since Richard wished to continue and looked forward with much excitement and enthusiasm to the visits, the therapist decided not to end the sessions.

During the next year, Richard and his therapist met as two persons related in the experience of creating a life for themselves in the setting of the playroom. Richard's sessions took on a consistent form, very much like the pattern which evolves in family living. Regular events took form which recurred in each session. These were not experiences that were compulsively repeated, but rather they were valued as living events. Within them the relationship became personal. When Richard and his therapist were together there was satisfaction in the activities they shared, but there was also a sense of communality, of personal exchange, and of mutual love which makes any personal encounter an alive experience. The final experience between Richard and his therapist could only have occurred when two persons shared a life. A pattern or guide was established, a bond in the setting of the playroom and only in this connection, within this exact pattern, did the experience have any meaning. Everything that took place during this time occurred in this personal context and had significance only in this personal pattern.

From an external point of view most sessions between Richard and his therapist might appear like every other session. Richard would enter the playroom, remove his left sock and shoe, and run his foot through the sand. It appeared that he made the same kind of figures and patterns each time. Then he would leave the sandbox, get a pile of books, and hand them to the therapist. He always secured the entire pile, although he knew the therapist would select the same two books.

Richard would take colored paper, crayons, and scissors and make his live figures and cut-outs. Then he would rinse his foot, dry it, replace the sock and shoe, and leave. The time limit was rarely mentioned, since Richard seemed to have his own way of knowing just when the fifty-minute session would end. An observer might easily see and identify the rituals and recurrent patterns. Yet an observer would miss the significant dimension which cemented the relationship and made everything within it attain a unique and alive meaning. The therapist's being there as a person and sharing with Richard every aspect of every experience within the emotional climate of the playroom meant that Richard was not involved in repetitive acts but in a unique experience; each experience contained its own pattern and its distinctive qualities. Richard was always completely present and wholly absorbed. The relationship became a way of life for these two people, a timeless and changeless experience which maintained its significance because it remained personal and because it maintained a communal continuity. Apart from the story reading, many, many months passed when neither child nor therapist spoke, yet they thought together, contemplated together, and lived together. It was a quiet and quieting experience, an hour of respite and absorption, calm and unhurried, a time for thinking and being alone, which refreshed and strengthened these two persons and enabled them to grow although there was never any concern about growth.

THE CHANGED RICHARD

How did Richard appear to others after three years of therapy? He was still somewhat bizarre in his behavior. He spoke little and communicated mainly through gestures. He disliked being told what to do and rebelled strongly when he was forced to participate in formal learning situations. He occasionally yelled and screamed at his parents and siblings when they tried to change his way of life or interfered with what he wanted. When left alone he was willing to work and to learn but what he learned was generally not recognized by others as important. He worked over his constructions, his cutting, pasting, and drawings, but he refused to read or write just as he refused to talk.

A TEACHER'S REPORT

At the end of the three-year period, a report was obtained from his teacher. Brief excerpts are presented.

When Richard first entered the school he was noisy and extremely active. He moved aimlessly around the room. He often emitted sounds and humming noises. He made no effort to speak to the other children or with me. Sometimes he 'attacked' me or other children by hitting and pinching. All this was accompanied by much finger biting. He was restless and paced nervously. He refused to settle down. He seemed to have no need for the group. However, he responded very well to commands such as, "No, Richard come back. We can't go out of the room today."

I thought maybe he behaved this way because he was in a strange place with people he didn't know. Therefore patience was employed and the pressure to do things was lessened, although he was encouraged to do anything that interested him. His span of attention was very short.

As time passed, he became less active and worked for fairly long periods of time. He was less noisy and sang while he worked. He began to show more interest in the group. Instead of working by himself he would move his work to a spot where other children were gathered. We sometimes talked together and often he joined in a game. There were many times when he acted as he felt. If he felt restricted, he would lie down. If he felt peppy he would bounce and run, regardless of other situations in the room. . . .

He had to learn to share his materials with other children. This was difficult. He wanted to grab the color of paint he wanted. He was made to wait his turn, though I made certain the wait was not too long. He practiced working with other children and helped to clean the room. He made many friends. Other children took an interest in him and admired his dexterity and rapidity in working puzzles. When he was late or absent, there was always the question, "Where's Richard?"

He was encouraged to print his first name in capital letters. Twice this was accomplished. Most of the time he would rebel shortly after he began. He did better when he felt he was not being observed.

All sorts of methods were employed to teach him arithmetic, but he seemed uninterested. He did count to six and then refused to go higher. The results in reading were the same. He generally refused to participate. I tried a number of things to stimulate him and familiarize him with the common words, hoping this would improve his speech also. Books were interesting to him, but he preferred to take them and use them alone in his own way.

Richard has a good sense of rhythm when he wishes to display it. He enjoys singing and often sings the words better than he is able to speak them. He has excellent pitch and musical potentiality.

He spends much of his time in school coloring and painting. He likes to cut pictures from magazines and work with construction paper.

All in all he has made progress in coming into the 'real' world.

CONCLUDING COMMENT

There is no doubt that Richard's peculiarities make him a difficult child for most people to live with. Yet his mind is generally untroubled and his emotional expressions reflect a positive orientation to others. He wants to love and be loved, to honor and be honored, to express himself fully in an atmosphere of friendship and acceptance and to enable others to enjoy this same freedom of self. But he is finding this a struggle. His differences, his peculiarities, and his nonconforming ways are too obvious. In our culture his kind of uniqueness is easier to separate, to isolate, and to consider queer than to share and cherish.

There are occasions when he wakes up screaming and crying, but no therapy can heal these social hurts and wounds. The remedy lies in the human beings he meets in his daily life who try to shear him of his self-possessions, who treat him as a thing or object apart from life, who deal with his peculiarities by restricting and ordering his behavior, and who would be more comfortable and less threatened if he looked more like other people.

The urge to maintain his selfhood is strong. Richard always returns to face others and to try to meet them as persons with all their human frailties and potentialities. Somehow he is able to let others be. The problem is with us who lead our lives on the basis of appearances, who see the unordinary only with a shrewd and jaundiced eye. We find it difficult to let him be. We're too accustomed to the usual ways to be able to recognize his difference as a value. It seems strange that our sights are set on a binding international understanding and friendship, on a single world where human beings live together when we have yet to learn to live with Richard, to stretch and strain our human resources and our potentialities to include him, to recognize him as a human being of intrinsic and incomparable worth. We have yet to find a way to nourish him to his own self-fulfillment. Our tendency is still to separate the obviously peculiar one, to impede and stunt his growth, to force him to struggle to keep from seeing himself as some kind of freak, as a subhuman creature who has a very limited life of inner freedom and self-development.

REFERENCES

1. Buber, Martin. *I and Thou.* Tr. by Ronald G. Smith. Edinburgh: T. & T. Clark, 1937.
2. Lee, Dorothy. Responsibility Among the Dakota. Mimeographed Paper, Merrill-Palmer School, 1957.
3. Levy, David. Capacity and Motivation. *Amer. J. Orthopsychiat.*, 27, 1-8, 1957.

6

Play Therapy with the Handicapped Child

CHILDREN referred for psychotherapy sometimes must live with physical or mental handicaps, neurological and constitutional "limitations," as well as with severe emotional problems. Cowen (1), making a critical review of psychotherapy with exceptional children, observed, with some reservations, that there are reports of successful psychotherapy in almost all areas of disability. In a survey of studies of mentally retarded children compiled and edited by Stacey and DeMartino (2) the consistent conclusion was that psychotherapy was of value in releasing the capacities of these children.

The handicapped child faces multiple difficulties. He must learn to live with a handicap which is perceived by others as a defect rather than a difference. He must work through intense feelings of anger and fear which result from frequent belittlement and rejection. In his relations with others, he often is made to feel less than a whole person. He must accept the fact that he lives in a culture which compares him unfavorably and offers him limited opportunities.

Psychotherapy with the handicapped child always involves a unique process. The only meaningful readiness of the therapist is a flexibility and a willingness to meet the child as he is, and a belief in him as a whole person of immeasurable potential.

Many handicapped children will not respond to the usual therapeutic procedures. New ones must be devised which have meaning for the particular child. The child who cannot walk must be carried to the playroom. He is dependent on the therapist from their first moment together. The child who is blind sometimes needs the therapist's help in locating materials and in using them. The child who is deaf requires the therapist to develop a new language. In many instances, important as it is that the child feel self-dependent and autonomous, the therapist must do things for the child and allow the child to lean on him. The relationship with the exceptional child differs in other ways. The child's expressions are sometimes peculiar. His words have special meanings which the therapist must take time to understand. In many instances the therapist's words are wasted. The brain-injured child or the child with lim-

146

ited word comprehension often will not listen even to brief comments. Movements and gestures must be devised if the therapist is to have a relationship with the child. The relationship comes to have meaning through the therapist's listening and feeling with the child. It is a matter of *being* with the child as he expresses his anxiety and hostility, as he lives through aspects of self-hatred and self-contempt, or as he explores the resources available to him in the playroom.

These children may be so limited at home and in the community that it is necessary to expand the boundaries of the playroom. They need an experience of extended freedom to be able to sense and accept the rules which define or structure a situation. Sometimes the therapist's active participation in the child's play is essential to the relationship.

The basic principles of child therapy—being with the child, sharing the experience, encouraging the child to express and explore his feelings, accepting the child's expressions, listening fully to the child, perceiving the essence of his expressions, and relating with respect and empathy—are also principles of therapeutic work with exceptional children. It is sometimes exceedingly difficult to take the cues from the exceptional child and to permit him to follow through on his own decisions when they seem to be detrimental, but the child's perception of himself, and of his situation, is the best guide.

When the handicap itself is not a center of difficulty, when the emotional conflict is the sole motivating factor, play therapy with the exceptional child does not differ basically from play therapy with the non-handicapped child.

ILLUSTRATION OF PLAY THERAPY WITH THE HANDICAPPED CHILD

FIRST SESSION, JERRY

Jerry, three years old, was unable to approach the playroom without help. He could walk but could not go up or down stairs. The therapist carried him to the door of the playroom. He stood outside the door, very much frightened and lost. The therapist stood by him. He put his arm around Jerry, kneeled down, and said, "This is a big room. I know you're afraid being here. But it will be all right." Jerry did not respond at first. He stood stiffly for several minutes. Then he walked into the room. When he saw the toys, he leaned his face against a corner wall and covered his eyes. During the next twelve minutes, he stood against the wall. Occasionally he glanced at the therapist with a frightened expression. He began to tap against the wall with his fingers. He turned and took a step toward the therapist, who sat nearby. He seemed to be experiencing a severe state of anxiety. He felt safe only in the confined area of a corner wall. When he moved away from it, his entire body trembled. After several moves toward the center of the room, Jerry, who had become increasingly anxious, began to whine. He walked to the door, opened it, and walked out into the hallway. He explored the many doors in the hall and tried to open them. From time to time he whined. He seemed to be trying to find his way back to his mother. The therapist asked, "Is it that you want Mommy?" Jerry did not respond. After a few more minutes in the hall, he began to cry. He was extremely disturbed and distraught. His cries soon became loud wails. The therapist asked, "Would you like to leave? We can go now if you wish." Jerry continued crying. When the therapist saw that Jerry was becoming more and more disorganized and uncontrolled, he carried Jerry up the stairs. Jerry saw his mother but turned away from her and wandered into an office. His mother approached him and asked if he had had a good time. There was no response from Jerry. His mother took his hand and led him out the door.

SECOND SESSION, JERRY

(When Jerry was placed outside the playroom he began to cry. The therapist approached him.)

T.: You don't like it here, do you Jerry? *(Pause.)*

T.: This place is big and it scares you. *(Long period of silence. J. continues to cry.)*

T.: Are you afraid of me, Jerry?

(J. puts his thumb in his mouth. He walks to a corner of the playroom. He stops crying momentarily. He walks back to the door but is unable to open it. He begins crying again.)

T.: We will stay just a while longer today. Then we can go up. *(J. stops crying. He stands by the door a few moments. He goes to a corner of the room, puts his face against a wall and begins crying again. The crying becomes louder. He goes to the door and pounds it.)*

T.: You're angry with me now because I don't let you leave. *(J. stops crying. He sucks his thumb for a few minutes and then begins crying again. The therapist gets a fire truck and rolls it to him. He stops crying. He examines the truck.)*

T.: And here's another one.

(When the therapist rolls the second truck to J., he rolls the first one back. J. walks to a group of trucks about ten feet from the door. He makes verbal sounds. He kneels near the trucks. He takes a steam shovel and chews on the end of it. He then pushes a truck to the therapist who rolls it back. This continues for six minutes.)

T.: It's fun to push the truck back and forth.

(J. surveys the room. He crawls to a tray of water, puts his hands in it and crawls quickly back to the therapist.)

T.: Afraid to touch the water?

(J. crawls to the easel. He takes several jars of paint and throws them on the floor. He heaves a jar across the room. It breaks and the paint splatters. J. begins to cry.)

T.: It's all right, Jerry.

(J. walks toward the door. He falls, and cries louder. He puts his face against the wall. He kicks the wall and screams loudly. He throws a car at the therapist. Then suddenly he stops crying. The therapist wipes the tears from his face.)

T.: Do you want to leave now?

(J. smiles and they go upstairs.)

THIRD SESSION, JERRY

Jerry refuses to go to the playroom without his mother. He enters the room ahead of the two adults. His behavior shifts from the intense diffused anxiety to a pattern of generalized hostility. Almost immediately he throws the crayons around the room. He throws the telephone toward his mother and pushes all the drawing paper onto the floor. He takes the baby figure and baby bottle and throws these across the room. He takes a gun, puts it in his mouth, and throws it across the room. He does this with clay and darts. He then puts a rubber ball in his mouth and throws it in the direction of his mother. He kicks a number of trucks and the steam shovel. He picks up two crayons, chews on them, and throws the broken pieces around the room. He throws a jar of paints on the floor. He puts numerous items, such as soldier figures and rubber cars, in his mouth and then throws them across the room. He approaches his mother, puts his mouth on her arm, and tries to bite her. Then he goes back to a shelf of toys and tosses some items to the floor. He returns to his mother, raises her dress, and tries to bite her arm. He returns to the toys and throws more of them across the room. He walks to the therapist and reaches for his glasses. He puts his head in his mother's lap and sucks his thumb for about ten minutes. He moves to the sandbox and puts sand in his mouth. He spits it out. He wipes his tongue with his shirt. He pushes his head up and down against his mother's arm. He tries opening the door.

T.: You want to leave now?
(J. walks away from the door. He throws several more items to the floor and empties the tray of water. He takes the cash register and sits on the floor for about two minutes playing with it.)
T.: It's time to leave now Jerry.
(He ignores the therapist and continues playing with the register. His mother approaches the door. J. looks at her. Taking her hand, they leave together.)

FOURTH SESSION, JERRY

(J. enters the play room with his mother and the therapist.)
T.: We'll be here together again today.
J.: Ah, ah, ah,. *(He hums.)*
T.: Rather nice now, hum?
J.: Ah, ah, ah.
(J. sits on the floor. He plays with trucks and the steam shovel. He sighs "Ah, ah, ah," repeatedly. He pulls at the chain of the steam shovel.)
T.: The chain. When you pull it, see how it raises the shovel.
(J. works it up and down.)
T.: You can push it up and down. You know how to make it work.
(J. continues raising and lowering the shovel. He picks it up and carries it toward a table. He drops it. He finds it difficult to carry.

He becomes irritated. The therapist goes over to help him. J. becomes angry. He pushes everything on the table across the room.)

T.: You're angry that you can't lift the steam shovel, so you throw everything down.
(J. continues throwing items. He picks up the receiver of the telephone and says, "Ah, ah, ah.")

J.: Ah, ah, ah. *(He replaces it.)*

T.: You couldn't carry the steam shovel but you do know how to use the telephone.
(J. begins humming and continues playing with the telephone. He lifts the receiver and replaces it.)

T.: You see how it works. You know how to do it.
(J. leaves the telephone. He turns the handle of the vise.)

T.: When you turn it that way the vise opens, see.
(J. looks at the therapist and says something that sounds like "Hi.")

T.: Hi, Jerry, Hi.
(J. continues turning the vise for about seven minutes. He sucks his thumb during this time. He plays with the phone again, humming into the receiver. He takes several baby figures from a shelf and throws them onto the floor. He rolls a ball to the therapist. The therapist rolls it back. This activity continues for about six minutes. Then Jerry throws it.)

T.: Oh, you want to throw it now.
(J. approaches the therapist, touches his arm and squeals with delight. He takes the cash register again and plays with it for five minutes, until the end of the session.)

FIFTH AND SIXTH SESSIONS, JERRY

In these sessions Jerry's play is similar to the preceding ones. There are moments of concentration and positive play, although no clear theme is established. He continues expressing aggression in a diffused manner, throwing items across the room. He uses most items by sucking, biting, and manipulating them. He frequently attacks his mother, pushing, biting, and kicking her. He seems frightened whenever he approaches Bobo, the comeback clown toy. The therapist makes a tower with blocks. Although Jerry duplicates it with success, he seems angry and resents being "tested." There is considerable humming and singing of "Ah, ah, ah" during these sessions.

SEVENTH SESSION, JERRY

(J. comes to the playroom without his mother. He is carried down the stairs by the therapist. He seems happy as he enters. He hums and sings. He goes to the floor drain and examines it.)

T.: The drain.

J.: Ah, ah, ah. *(J. plays with the cash register. He makes other sounds for the first time, "Da, da, da, buh, buh, buh, mmm, ma." The therapist repeats these sounds. J. takes an apron.)*

J.:   (*With much feeling.*) Ah, ah, ah.
      (*When the therapist repeats these verbalizations, J. smiles. He looks directly toward the therapist.*)

T.:   Hi, Jerry, Hi.
      (*J. plays with the apron. The therapist touches it and says, 'Apron, apron." J. replaces the apron and takes several plastic spoons.*)

T.:   Many spoons. Spoons.
      (*J. gets the apron again. He throws it on the floor and steps on it many times. Then he goes to the door. He puts his thumb in his mouth. He looks at the therapist and says, "Ah, ah, ah." He stands by the door and seems to be listening intently.*)

T.:   It's quiet in here. Not a sound anywhere.
      (*J. goes to the sandbox and throws sand on the floor. He then throws two jars of paints on the floor, the last of which breaks.*)

T.:   It broke into many pieces.
      (*J. tries to break another jar. The therapist explains that he cannot permit him to break any more. J. begins to pick up the broken pieces. The therapist stops him.*)

T.:   The pieces are sharp. Let me sweep them away.
      (*J. watches the therapist as he works. He points to a box of Kleenex. The therapist hands him the Kleenex; J. wipes up paint from the floor.*)

T.:   You want to help too.
      (*After wiping the paint, J. throws another jar across the room. It does not break. The therapist removes the remaining jars.*)

T.:   I'll have to take them out now. You keep wanting to break them.
      (*J. goes to the door.*)

T.:   We can go now if you wish, but there's still time left to play.
      (*J. plays with the steam shovel until the end of the session.*)

EIGHTH SESSION, JERRY

In this session, Jerry has a delightful time throwing sand. He sprinkles it everywhere in the room. He gets it on his shoes, clothing, and hair. Following his play with sand, he seems physically relaxed for the first time. Up to this point his body has always been tense and his muscles rigid. Toward the end of the session he approaches Bobo without fear. At first he pushes the figure gently, but then he punches and slaps with vigor. He indicates he wants the therapist to hit Bobo too. When the therapist does this, Jerry laughs loudly. The therapist comments, "You like to see him punched."

Jerry and the therapist take turns punching Bobo. When the session ends Jerry leaves the room smiling. He laughs all the way up the stairs.

NINTH SESSION, JERRY

In this session, Jerry repeats much of his previous activity with the steam shovel and cash register. One new element occurs. Jerry approaches the baby figures a number of times but does not touch them.

The therapist comments, "You want to take the baby?" Jerry attacks the baby figures. He bites them, steps on them, and chews at their bodies.

Jerry often is frustrated when he attempts to do something and fails. He becomes angry, makes crying noises, and sometimes chews at his fingers. He masturbates and sucks his thumb violently.

At the end of the ninth session, he decides he is going to take a truck home. The therapist briefly explains that all the toys have to remain in the playroom. Jerry ignores this limit. When the therapist repeats the limit, Jerry gives it up but begins to cry and scream. He flails his arms and legs. The therapist picks him up to carry him upstairs. Jerry kicks and bites him. He is still upset when they meet Jerry's mother. The therapist explains the difficulty. Jerry's mother offers several alternatives. Each time she speaks, Jerry screams at her and attacks her. She seems upset. Jerry refuses to leave the building. His mother asks the therapist if she can borrow the truck. The therapist realizes that the long-standing rule of not letting the items be taken home will have to be broken. He hesitates, but Jerry's need is overwhelming. The therapist gets the truck and hands it to Jerry, saying, "This belongs to the school. Bring it back when you come next week."

COMMENTS

The therapist decided that adhering to the rule is a mistake when it ignores the intense need of a child who cannot understand the limit. Maintaining the limit in the light of Jerry's extreme reaction would have seriously impaired the relationship and might have forced Jerry to return to a dependent relationship with his mother.

Although the therapist's gesture came late, Jerry accepted the truck and left on his own volition. He returned the truck the following week.

TALK WITH JERRY'S MOTHER

Jerry's mother requested a talk with the therapist. She wanted a brief summary of Jerry's progress. She had recently taken him to a neurologist who had diagnosed his condition as "severe mental retardation with progressive deterioration." He recommended institutionalization. Mrs. Line was extremely upset with this report. She felt that Jerry's behavior indicated more hope for his future life. The neurologist referred her to a psychologist who confirmed the diagnosis. On the basis of the Cattell Infant Scale, an I.Q. of 50 was determined. Mrs. Line was told that there was no possibility of improvement and that there would be a gradual deterioration of mental functions.

It was at this point that she asked the therapist for his report. He told her that Jerry had come to enjoy his experiences in the playroom. He was gradually relating to the therapist. He became extremely frustrated when he failed in a task. There seemed to be a great deal of underlying tension and accumulated hostile feelings as well as a sense of anxiety and self-destructive tendencies. Most of his play was erratic, without any integrating theme or purpose. He had not spoken at all. In short, it was difficult to say what value, if any, the therapeutic experience offered him, except that he enjoyed coming. There seemed to be a combination of mental, emotional, and neurological factors involved. He was unable to solve most problems which arose in his play. He was socially unresponsive. His motor coordination and muscle strength were not adequate to deal with most of the developmental tasks he faced. In spite of this gloomy picture, the therapist indicated he would like to continue if the parents decided to keep him home.

The therapist felt that there were some positive signs. He was beginning to relate. He occasionally struggled with a problem which he could solve. He had been making decisions in his play. There were a few glimpses of release following the expression of diffused hostile feelings. There was therapeutic value in the direct expressions of hostility he expressed against the baby. Most important of all, there was an obvious change in his physical appearance. The muscle rigidity and body tension had definitely lessened. There were times when he was physically quiet and relaxed.

Following this presentation of hopeful signs, Mrs. Line began to cry. She knew that Jerry was not as retarded as the diagnosis indicated. She said, "The last thing in the world I would consider right now would be to put him in an institution." She believed it was possible that he could have a satisfactory life at home. She asked how she might go about starting an educational program at home. A list of references were given her which described home programs and activities for the mentally retarded child. The therapist suggested that she consider joining the parent association in the community dedicated to finding educational opportunities for the mentally retarded child. He suggested the possibility of a second examination and recommended a neuropsychiatrist who was sympathetic with parents who wanted to work with their handicapped children at home.

Eleventh Session, Jerry

This was a day of great excitement—the day that Jerry spoke his first words. As the session opened, he picked up the phone, dialed several numbers.

T.: Hear the ring?
      (*J. continues dialing and seems pleased with the results.*)
T.: You know how to make it ring?
      (*J. goes on dialing.*)
T.: See how the numbers are?
      (*J. then approaches some animal figures.*)
T.: Lots of different animals there. See the animals.
      (*J. picks up a father figure.*)
T.: It's the daddy. See the daddy.
J.: No.
T.: No?
J.: No.

T.: All right. No.
     (J. begins tossing items on a shelf. Then he takes a number of cups and plates and puts them on a table.)
T.: Cups and plates.
     (The therapist puts a cup on a saucer. J. does this with the remaining ones. Then he procures more dishes from a shelf. He brings a chair to the table and holds a cup near his mouth a few seconds. Then he sweeps everything onto the floor. He plays with the steam shovel a few seconds and then kicks it. He listens intently to sounds in another room.)
T.: Hear that?
J.: No.
T.: No.
     (J. Looks at his hand.)
T.: Hand. See your hand.
J.: No. *(J. stumbles.)*
T.: You tripped on your shoe lace.
J.: Shoe.
T.: Yes, yes, shoe.
     (J. Looks at his shoe.)
T.: Let me tie it for you.
     (The therapist ties J.'s shoe. J. hands a jar of paint to the therapist.)
T.: You want me to open it?
     (J. does not respond.)
T.: You want me to open it?
J.: Open.
     (The therapist opens and closes the jar. He hands it to J. J. tries to open it. He becomes angry and throws it across the room, breaking it. He takes the therapist's hand and pulls him to leave the room.)

TWELFTH SESSION, JERRY

After the eleventh session Jerry uses the word "No" frequently both in the playroom and at home. In the twelfth session, he breaks another jar of paint. The therapist explains the limit again and removes the jars. Jerry says, "No! No!" He picks up the baby figure and chews it. He hums, "Ah, ah, ah." The therapist repeats these sounds. Jerry responds with "No! No! 'No!" He takes the father figure and chews on it. The therapist comments, "Daddy." Jerry screams "No" six times. Jerry stacks the dishes on a table. The therapist remarks, "Play with the dishes." Again Jerry screams "No!" several times. Then he hands the therapist a dish and a spoon. The therapist asks, "Do you want me to eat?" Jerry tosses all the dishes to the floor and shouts, "No! No!" The therapist says, "Now you've thrown them all down." Jerry again says, "No!" He takes the baby figure and throws it onto the floor. He repeats "No! No!" again and again. This pattern of play with the dishes and baby continues throughout most of the session.

THIRTEENTH THROUGH SEVENTEENTH SESSIONS, JERRY

These sessions are similar to the preceding one. Jerry uses a number of new words, however, including "cup," "book," "see," "push," "hello," and "shut." The use of "no" is infrequent. He plays with the telephone, sand, baby and father figures, the dishes, and the animal figures. He makes numerous lines with crayons on pieces of paper. When he hands the crayon to the therapist and the therapist makes similar marks, however, he becomes angry. He throws all the crayons around the room. At another point, he asks the therapist to throw a rubber ring over a peg. The therapist explains he would like to play the game with Jerry. He takes Jerry's arm and helps him throw two rings. After this, Jerry throws them himself and enjoys the game. In another episode, Jerry takes a large sheet of drawing paper. The therapist asks him to mark on it. This is the first verbal suggestion that Jerry shows he understands. He marks the paper vigorously with several different colors. Then he takes chalk and marks the slate. There is little aggression in these sessions, although he punches Bobo a number of times and repeats the word "push" when the therapist says "You like to push it." He plays constructively and for much longer periods of time.

EIGHTEENTH SESSION, JERRY

Jerry enters the playroom eagerly. He spends most of the session playing with dishes, cups and silverware. The therapist asks Jerry to bring him a dish and a knife. Jerry responds immediately to the suggestions, showing not only that he comprehends but also that the relationship means something to him. He now wants to please the therapist. He repeats a number of words he has used before.

NINETEENTH SESSION, JERRY

Jerry enters the room and closes the door after the therapist.

J.:   Shut.
T.:   Yes, this time you shut the door.
      (J. begins punching Bobo.)
T.:   You like to hit him.
J.:   No.
      (J. looks at the nursing bottle. He holds it.)
T.:   I think you want to drink from the bottle.
J.:   Okay.
T.:   Okay. Then you drink from it.
J.:   Taste.
T.:   Does it *taste* funny?
      (J. drops the bottle to the floor. He examines an Indian figure on a horse.)

J.: Go.
T.: The Indian will go if you move it.
(J. picks up a truck.)
T.: It's the truck you like.
J.: Kucks.
T.: Truck
J.: *(J. listens to sounds in the hall. He goes to the door.)*
Door sut, okay.
T.: Yes, it's tightly shut.
(J. dials the telephone.)
T.: Hear the telephone ring.
J.: Hello.
T.: Hello.
J.: Okay.
T.: Okay.
(J. picks up darts.)
T.: Some children like to throw the darts. Like this.
(J. listens.)
T.: Hear sounds.
J.: Sone.
T.: Sound.
J.: Okay. *(Continues listening.)*
T.: Hear the sound.
J.: Sound. *(J. picks up a toy chair and shows it to the therapist.)*
T.: See the chair.
(J. takes a nursing bottle to the therapist.)
J.: See.
T.: Yes, I see the bottle.
(J. plays with the cash register. He tries to open the drawer.)
T.: You push down on this button.
(J. tries unsuccessfully.)
T.: You have to push harder.
(J. tries again without success.)
T.: Would you like me to open it?
J.: Okay. *(He takes out the paper money and coins. He drops them and goes to the shelves to play with cups and spoons. He moves a spoon back and forth in a cup.)*
T.: Are you stirring something?
(J. approaches the sandbox. He stands staring into it.)
T.: Do you want to play in the sand, Jerry?
(J. takes handfuls of sand and watches as the sand sifts through his fingers. He takes the nursing bottle and sings "La, la, la, la, la." He removes the nipple and puts his fingers in the water. He puts a spoon in the bottle. He becomes frustrated after several attempts to remove the spoon. He shouts at the therapist.)
J.: Get it out.
T.: *(The therapist tries to remove it.)* It's stuck, I can't get it out either.
J.: Stuck.
T.: There are more spoons on the shelf.

(J. takes another spoon. He puts it into another bottle and again is unable to get it out. He becomes angry.)

T.: Maybe if you put more water in the bottle you could get the spoon out.

(J. begins sucking his thumb.)

T.: Would you like me to do it?

J.: Okay.

(The therapist fills the bottles. Then J. removes the spoons.)

J.: Mommy. Mommy.

T.: You want to go to Mommy now?

(J. goes to the door.)

TWENTIETH SESSION, JERRY

(J. insists that his mother accompany him to the playroom. He pulls at the therapist to shut the door.)

J.: Shut.

T.: You want to be sure you have Mommy inside this time.

(J. walks to Bobo and pushes it over. He pushes it against the therapist who returns it. J. steps away from the Bobo and begins playing with a truck. He pushes it across the room to a table. As he moves along, he touches the dart board. He takes apart a ring toss game. He tries to screw it together but needs the therapist's help. Then he places the rings over the peg. J. takes the therapist's hand and stares at it.)

J.: Hand.

T.: Yes, Hand.

J.: Money.

T.: You think I have the money. It is still in the cash register.

J.: *(J. gets the register.)* Open.

T.: Remember, you can do it yourself.

(J. pushes the button.)

T.: You must press harder to open it.

(J. succeeds in opening the drawer. He plays with the money. Then he pushes several numbers.)

T.: See, when you push these down, the numbers come up here.

J.: Down.

T.: When you push down, the number comes up.

J.: Up.

T.: Yes.

J.: Close.

T.: I think you can push the drawer in and close it yourself.

(J. pushes the drawer but has difficulty closing it.)

T.: You must push harder.

J.: *(J. pushes harder and is successful this time. He picks up a telephone.)* Telephone.

T.: Telephone.

(J. takes cups and saucers and sets them up appropriately.)

T.: Cups and saucers.

(J. takes scissors.)

T.:   Would you like to cut up some paper?
(J. drops the scissors and returns to the cash register. He puts the therapist's hand on the keys of the register.)
T.:   You want me to push the numbers now?
J.:   Push.
(J. plays with the register a few more minutes.)
T.:   It's about time for us to leave now.
J.:   *(Jerry goes to the door.)* Open.

TWENTY-FIRST THROUGH TWENTY-FIFTH SESSIONS, JERRY

During this period, Jerry's play is similar to preceding sessions. The cash register, cups and saucers, Bobo, and a small kitty puppet are the most used items. His use of these materials is manipulative, although occasionally he develops a theme. He generally insists that his mother accompany him, but in the playroom he ignores her entirely. His vocabulary increases with each session. The most notable change is his more frequent use of phrases and short sentences. He is now definitely interested in language and in conveying his thoughts and feelings verbally. In the twenty-fifth session he recognizes and uses his own name.

TWENTY-SIXTH SESSION, JERRY

(J. decides to go to the playroom without his mother. For the first time he walks down the steps on his own. His mother reports that he has been practicing for three days since he first discovered he was able to climb steps. J. enters the room and hands scissors to the therapist.)
T.:   You want me to cut?
J.:   Cut.
T.:   You cut too. *(The therapist hands J. scissors and paper. Together they cut small bits of paper. J. has considerable difficulty in using the scissors. He becomes frustrated and pulls at the paper. Finally, he throws the scissors down. J. looks at a new toy in the room.)*
J.:   Don't touch.
T.:   Is that what Mommy says, "Don't touch"? In here, you can touch whatever you wish.
J.:   Don't knock it over.
T.:   Sometimes you knock things over at home and Mommy doesn't like it.
(J. plays with the toy. Then he takes apart a tower made of blocks. He puts it together again. When he realizes he can do this, he becomes excited and jumps up and down. An angry expression crosses his face. He starts to destroy the tower. Then he changes his mind.)
T.:   You wanted to break it but something inside you says "No."
J.:   *(J. hesitates a few moments. He tosses the tower into the sand. He takes a nursing bottle and drinks from it. He puts several spoons and forks into the bottle. He tries to get them out.)* Stuck.
T.:   Remember how we got them out last time?
(J. fills the bottle with water and removes the spoons and forks.)

T.:   Now you have it.

J.:   *(J. stares at drops of water that have spilled on the floor and speaks with disgust in his voice.)* Oh Jerry!

T.:   They don't like it when you spill water at home but in here it's all right if you want to do it.

J.:   *(J. shakes the bottle and more water spills out. Again with disgust.)* Oh Jerry!

T.:   Oh, Jerry! That's what they say.

J.:   Let's go. Let's go.

T.:   We can if you want to but there's more time to play.
      (J. Looks at the water and repeats "Oh, Jerry!" He screws the top on the bottle. He looks at the therapist.)

J.:   Hi.

T.:   Hi, Jerry.

J.:   Hello! Hello, Jerry. Where's Daddy?

T.:   Where is Daddy?

J.:   Daddy work. Sing. Sing anything.

T.:   All right. What shall we sing?

J.:   *(J. drinks from the bottle. He again spills water.)* Oh, Jerry! Oh, Jerry! *(He spills more water.)* Oh, Jerry! *(He tips the bottle and empties the remaining water.)* Oh, Jerry!

T.:   You like to spill it all over no matter what they say.

J.:   *(Puts his hands in the water on the floor. He splashes it and spreads it around. He stands up suddenly.)* Oh, Jerry! *(He walks to the door.)* Come. Out.

T.:   Oh, Jerry. It's all right here.

J.:   Come, Come on.

T.:   Okay.

TWENTY-SEVENTH THROUGH TWENTY-NINTH SESSIONS, JERRY

Jerry has developed a great fascination for bottles. He now begins each session by gathering all the bottles in the room. He puts varying amounts of water in the bottles. He stares inside them, drinks from them, and empties the water onto the floor. He fills the bottles with sand and paint. He speaks as often with brief phrases as single words. He uses the following expressions: "Open it," "Down goes," "That's bottle," "Where's cup," "Come on out," "Where's Mommy," "Fix it," "Another cup," "Let's walk, Jerry," "This door opens," "Open the door," and "Oh, Jerry! Don't touch the cake." There is little hostility or anxiety in his behavior. He seems completely absorbed and satisfied in experimenting by putting various solutions in bottles. His spilling of water on the floor is clearly a protest against the restriction at home. On one occasion he tries to open a paint jar. He becomes extremely angry. He throws items across the room. This occurs whenever he becomes frustrated and particularly after unsuccessful attempts to solve problems in the use of play materials.

Thirtieth Session, Jerry

(J. does not want to come to the playroom today but his mother insists. He enters the room angrily. He begins immediately to heave toys across the room. The therapist hands him a gun.)

T.: Maybe you feel like shooting.
(J. begins to laugh. Then he starts crying.)

T.: Mommy made you come.
(J. approaches the therapist. He puts his arms out. The therapist holds him on his lap. He sits quietly for approximately five minutes. He runs across the room to the cash register.)

J.: Money. Down it goes. *(He shakes the register and the coins spill to the floor. He stamps his feet and knocks over chairs and tables.)*

T.: You're getting even with mommy by making a mess here.

J.: *(He spills water on the floor. He sits in a corner of the room sucking his thumb. He takes money from the cash register and hands it to the therapist. He closes the drawer.)* Open it.

T.: You know how to push the key and open it.

J.: *(He spills some coins out.)* Put the money back.

T.: You'll have to do it yourself.
(J. tries to open the register. This time it sticks and he throws it on the floor.)

T.: You seem to get angry when you can't work it.

J.: Open it.

T.: No, Jerry. I know you can do it.

J.: *(Picks up the register and tries again. This time he succeeds.)* Where's the bottle?

T.: On the shelf.

J.: *(He gets the bottle.)* Open it.

T.: You always want me to do things for you. You can open it for yourself.
(J. removes the nipple and drinks from the bottle. He spends the next ten minutes drinking and spilling the water. He approaches the sandbox, then hesitates.)

T.: You can put sand in the bottle if you wish.

J.: Where the cap go?

T.: You dropped it by the table.

J.: *(He fills the bottle with sand.)* Oh, Jerry!

T.: Oh, Jerry! Is that what Mommy says when you mess?

J.: What did you do? Oh, Jerry! Jerry! Jerry! *(He tips the bottle.)* Oh, Jerry!

T.: You sometimes spill from the bottle.

J.: More water.

T.: Okay. You want me to go with you.
(J. drops the bottle. It breaks. He sucks his thumb vigorously.)

T.: You didn't mean to break it, did you?

J.: *(J. gets a rubber knife. He drops it. The therapist picks it up.)* Don't touch.

T.: This knife is rubber. See?
J.: Don't cut.
T.: No, I won't cut. I'll put it on the table.
J.: *(Hands the therapist a box of crayons and several jars of paints. He seems fascinated with the opening of the paint jars. He takes a container of finger paints.)* Open this. Polish.
T.: You call it polish?
J.: Wash it.
T.: You show me how.
J.: *(He drops the jar.)* Go home now.
T.: We still have time but if you want we can leave now.
J.: Go home now.
T.: Okay.

THIRTY-FIRST SESSION, JERRY

(J. enters the playroom reluctantly.)
J.: I want to go see mama.
T.: After a while, Jerry, but now that we're here, let's stay.
J.: I want to go home now.
T.: I know you want to leave, but your mother brought you a long way and she wants you to stay.
J.: *(Takes chalk and crushes it with his foot.)* Don't crush it. Pick it up, Jerry.
T.: Now that you've made that mess, you think you ought to pick it up.
J.: *(J. takes the cash register and plays with it for about ten minutes. Pointing to wall.)* Clock. Let's go open the door.
T.: It's not time to leave yet, Jerry.
J.: *(J. goes out, examines the hallway and other rooms. He returns with a cup of water. He pours it into the sand. He continues this procedure for the next fifteen minutes. Then, he points to the floor.)* Is that the drain?
T.: Yes
J.: More water.
T.: You can get all you want.
J.: *(He fills a pail of water and dumps it into the sandbox.)* Go home.
T.: You keep saying "Go home" yet you like it here.
J.: Go see Mommy.
T.: We have a short while to play here. Then we can leave.
J.: Go upstairs now *(He pushes over toys.)*
T.: Now you're really angry because I insist you stay.
J.: Go home now.
T.: Just a few minutes more.
J.: Go home now. Go up now. Go up now.
T.: You want to go up right now. Okay, but you have not stayed the full time.

THIRTY-SECOND SESSION, JERRY

Jerry enters and becomes immediately absorbed in play. He speaks often and in complete sentences, but his language is made up of stereotyped statements he hears at home. He expresses in threatening tones, "Don't touch the Roman Cleanser, Jerry," "Don't touch the bottle," etc. More often he struggles with a problem until he solves it himself, but he still frequently becomes upset and screams or cries until the therapist helps him. When the time is up he does not want to leave.

THIRTY-THIRD THROUGH FORTY-FOURTH SESSIONS, JERRY

In these sessions, Jerry's continued improvement in speech is the most notable gain. He speaks in terms of immediate situations rather than in repetitions of commands and conversations which occur at home. He selects a book in each session and asks questions about the pictures in it, such as, "What is this?" and "What are they doing?"

He is sensitive to the therapist's attitude. The slightest irritation in the therapist's voice is detected and Jerry becomes upset. On the other hand, he is now willing to accept limits if they are stated simply and in a positive manner.

In the thirty-sixth session he uses up all the paints and asks the therapist to get more. The therapist leaves the room to refill the jars. During this time, Jerry plays quietly in the sand. He seems comfortable while alone. When the therapist returns after about five minutes, Jerry gives him a warm greeting. This seems a significant step in the development of an independent attitude. It is the first time Jerry has been willing to remain alone in the room. He seems more willing to be by himself and play without the direct support of an adult.

THIRTY-SEVENTH THROUGH FORTY-FOURTH SESSIONS, JERRY

The major developments in language expression and in independent play continue over this period. Jerry's language now involves consistent use of complete sentences. He makes frequent effort to communicate and to answer questions. His play is largely on an independent basis. He seeks help only after repeated efforts to manage on his own.

Jerry expresses an increasing interest in books. He wants to know more about the content of pictures and the words on labels. He asks many questions about the use of tools in cleaning, washing, and caring for a home. When he is given information, such as, "The vacuum sweeper is used for getting dirt and lint off rugs," he repeats it over and over again. He seems to be thrilled with the words and says them softly and with much feeling. He talks mostly in terms of immediate situations. He plays in a lengthy, concentrated fashion. There is generally one simple theme in each play activity.

Summary of Personality Changes and Functional Limitations

The changes in Jerry's behavior are presented to point to the differences which appeared during the period of his therapy, not to imply that these were the result of the therapeutic experience.

When Jerry first began the therapy sessions he did not walk or talk. Two years later he could walk with ease, climb up and down stairs, and accomplish many of the developmental skills of five-year-old children. He was speaking fluently, using complete sentences and able to converse with other persons. He could communicate his ideas and interests. His attention span and ability to concentrate on a project improved steadily so that he was able to express his interests in themes and carry out his plans. He learned to focus on an activity and to solve problems which arose in his play.

In his first sessions, he was inconsistent and unsteady. He had frequent and sudden outbursts of temper. He attempted to destroy materials and hurt himself. He frequently expressed intense, hostile feelings. Later, he began to express positive feelings which conveyed a direct relationship between the way he felt and the immediate situation. Though he still became angry and resisted suggestions, he was not completely disorganized and uncontrolled.

In the beginning when other children joined him in the playroom he remained unresponsive, unaware, and relatively isolated from them. He learned to play beside other children in an imitative fashion and sometimes initiated cooperative play with one or two others. He was able to participate in organized group activities. Although he still preferred to have periods of time by himself and to explore his environment alone, he responded to warm, sympathetic encouragement and interrupted his solitary play to enter a group.

When he first arrived, Jerry showed no interest in the play materials and equipment. For the most part, he simply sat in a corner of the room or touched one or two items. He developed interest in paints and crayons, scissors, sand and shovels, water, trucks, cars, airplanes, balloons, and many other materials.

Perhaps the most significant change is the development of Jerry's trust in others and his acceptance of others. When he is related to as a whole person and not in terms of his handicap, he responds immediately, expresses his potentialities and participates in a cooperative manner.

Certain problems persist in Jerry's behavior. He occasionally lapses into hostile and destructive behavior or becomes totally dependent. He sometimes confuses fantasy and reality. Occasionally he confuses past and present so that it is difficult to know whether his expression is relevant to the immediate situation or whether it has only a historical significance.

INTELLIGENCE TEST RESULTS

In order to complete the requirements of admission to a special educational program in a public school, it was necessary to have an intelligence test administered to Jerry. The report of the psychologist follows:

Jerry came in to Merrill-Palmer for two testing interviews. When I first met him he came over to me and took my hand. He seemed ready to go upstairs to the testing room. Jerry asked where we were going and seemed curious to explore new places, although he had usually gone to the playroom in the basement. While his mother stayed in an adjoining room, I started to introduce paper and pencil to Jerry and, later, test items. Jerry responded readily to limitations which I set, staying within the test room, looking at the materials which I presented, etc. However, repeated attempts to get him to follow my directions and to respond to the test material in a given way failed to elicit a complete performance on any one item. When I asked him to name different pictures (Picture Vocabulary, Stanford-Binet) he responded only to the first picture with "That shoe's broken," but would not name other pictures. With the introduction of tests in other areas such as the Binet Form Board and the Seguin Form Board, Jerry made an initial approach to the material, handling one or two of the forms, but then quickly losing interest and turning to other objects in the room. As I continued to present material with the attempt to relate it to his on-going play, he became less interested and more excited, asking, "Go home now," or "Go to the playroom." For a while I held Jerry on my lap where he was content to sit as long as I didn't ask him to try any more of the tests. Soon he said, "No more puzzles, no more puzzles," and rather than continue in what seemed to be an increasingly frustrating situation, he went down to the playroom.

Jerry seemed pleased to see me on his second visit and readily left his mother to come upstairs and "do things" with me. This time I suggested very simple tasks such as drawing a vertical line (Gesell Schedule) and test items that had an element of a game (Naming Objects from Memory, Stanford-Binet.) Again, Jerry made an initial approach to the test, scribbling with the pencil and trying to lift the cardboard box covering the hidden object, but he did not enter into the task enough to make a formal assessment of his abilities. After about fifteen or twenty minutes of repeated attempts to introduce test material in an appealing way, we again left the test room for the playroom.

From my own experience with Jerry it does not seem possible to obtain an accurate assessment of his intelligence to get a quantitative score from an intelligence test, at this time. It was clear that Jerry was refusing items rather than failing them and that at his present level of functioning he has the ability to utilize intellectual functions and to learn.

A qualitative analysis of Jerry's intellectual ability must take into account some of the following factors:

1. Jerry is able to talk in complete sentences and to express his interests. He indicated an interest in the playroom, asked the examiner to help him move a bookcase, expressed a desire to feel some pipes. At other times, however, he talks in an incoherent way or uses disconnected phrases which are not understandable to me. His functional use of language is, however, well below the level of the usual six-year-old.

2. Jerry is able to comprehend and respond to simple limits and requests from others. While I was not able to get Jerry to follow through on the test

items which I presented, he responded to my directions and limits when these did not involve a sustained effort on his part. As far as I could tell, his functioning comprehension also was well below that of the average six-year-old.

3. Jerry shows a general ability to relate to people, objects and locations in an adequate if somewhat immature manner. He responded to me in a friendly way and on the second visit recognized me and was willing to leave his mother to do the puzzles. He recognized and named a bottle of ammonia and a can of Ajax cleaning powder on our way to the playroom. As he left after the second visit he said that it was time to see "Gramma."

It should be remembered that this report of Jerry's intellectual functioning represents a relatively brief contact with him at the present time and does not take into account the progress and development that he has shown in the past several years.

In summary, it does not seem possible to obtain a test score of I.Q. for Jerry at the present time. He did not show enough sustained interest or concentration on any of the items presented to be able to credit him with either a passing or failing score. A qualitative analysis of Jerry's functioning intelligence indicates that he has abilities in language, comprehension, memory, and general orientation which are well below his chronological age level but which would allow him to profit from a special educational program. I feel that Jerry functions most adequately intellectually when he is allowed the freedom to explore without external demands and suggestions but with firm and kindly controls over his excitability. A situation which would provide warmth and care and encouragement as well as definite limits would probably be the most conducive to Jerry's continued growth and development.

On the basis of this report, Jerry was admitted to a special program for retarded children in a public school.

School Visits

The therapist visited Jerry's school regularly. He found it necessary to support the teacher in what she was doing and helped her to see that, although there were no outstanding improvements, Jerry was making gradual progress. In the beginning the therapist visited the school once a week. The teacher seemed to need a great deal of support. Jerry was not adjusting to the group easily.

The first week of school was exceedingly difficult both for Jerry and his teacher. On the third day, the therapist received a call from the school principal, who doubted that Jerry would be permitted to remain. The therapist spent the morning in the classroom. Jerry was responding in much the way he had in his first experiences with the therapist. There were frequent outbursts of crying and screaming. The therapist related his experience to the teacher and urged her to give Jerry time to feel safe in the group. He also suggested that she allow him to play on his own and to enter the group on a gradual basis. He pointed out that his anger and attacks were consistently connected with her attempts to force him into group situations. Jerry needed time to be by himself.

By the fifth day of school, Jerry felt safe and confident. Being allowed to set his own pace, Jerry gradually became interested in other children and spontaneously joined group activities.

At first, he was permitted to attend school for only two hours a day. His schedule was gradually increased so that by the end of the year he was attending four hours a day. Each time it was on the therapist's suggestion that the teacher extended Jerry's time in school. His teacher approached the question with mixed feelings until she saw that Jerry was able to function in a cooperative way for longer periods.

It was often necessary for the therapist to encourage the teacher to allow Jerry to use all the resources of the classroom. Her tendency was to restrict him to a few materials. It was only after many long discussions with the teacher that she approached the problem experimentally. Gradually, she offered him an enriched environment and began to view him as a child with potentialities and abilities. Then she did not see only his limitations but became concerned with what he could do and what he could learn to do.

At the end of Jerry's first year in school his teacher doubted that Jerry could remain permanently in a public school program, but, having seen his possibilities, she also doubted that institutionalization was the best solution.

FOLLOW-UP

The therapist did not see Jerry for the next two years. His family had moved to a distant state. When the family returned, four follow-up sessions were held with him. At the time, he could speak in a fluent and comprehensible manner. In the playroom, Jerry reported a number of recent family experiences. The most notable growth was his ability to communicate in a meaningful way, his use of an extended vocabulary, his ability to answer questions, and the further development of clarity and consistency in his play. Jerry still exhibited nervous mannerisms and his language contained many bizarre and unconnected expressions which were meaningful only to individuals who really understood him. The therapist met with the parents and helped form a plan for Jerry's education. He is currently enrolled in a private day school for exceptional children and attends both morning and afternoon sessions.

CONCLUDING COMMENTS

Play therapy, although an important resource for the disturbed, handicapped child, cannot resolve the social and educational problems which this child faces. In the American culture handicapped children are not fully accepted and opportunities for their growth and development are sometimes severely limited. Their handicaps are not recognized as differences or unique aspects of self but seen as inadequacies. These children are generally segregated and isolated in schools. They are often given inferior equipment, materials, and space. It is often difficult to find any adequate educational program in the community for them.

Only the unusual school and the unusual teacher considers these children of value, sees them as unique persons. Only the rare teacher recognizes their differences as an opportunity to learn, and to relate and to grow with human beings in the broad sense.

Most teachers are as unwilling to work with these children as most persons in our society are unwilling to accept and live with them. Because his difference is obvious, the handicapped child faces rejection at every turn. He often has few resources for defending himself. Most people take it for granted that his difference is a limitation and that he needs less opportunity for growth and development. This minimizing of him by the culture, this isolation and rejection are something psychotherapy cannot change. It is something with which the handicapped child must live, being of the human world but not in it. We still pity the blind, the crippled, the mentally retarded, and the deaf rather than pity ourselves for not being able to relate with them and share the wonder and presence, the unique person each is. Without resources and defenses, without ways of maintaining their individuality, of valuing and sharing their uniqueness, these children even after a positive experience in therapy must live as less-than-whole persons in a culture which restricts them.

Because of the limitations in the culture, the child therapist has a much greater responsibility and a more complex function. He must work to open opportunities for these children where none exist, to encourage individuals who are in key positions to allow these children opportunities and resources which are generally closed to them. He must work closely with school personnel especially during the initial enrollment of the child, helping individuals face problems that arise, helping them to discover creative, positive solutions. It is too easy to reject these children on the basis of the program's lack of value for them. The therapist must often help change the program to make it a valuable one for the handicapped child. It is much healthier for all concerned to modify a program than to remove a child. The therapist often must work intensively to help others recognize that the handicapped child is a person with potentialities and abilities who needs an atmosphere of adequate resources and positive human values. An essential part of the work of the therapist is his relations in the community, particularly with the authorities and resource persons who can help to bring about the full growth of children with physical or mental handicaps. The therapist points to a way, offers a possibility and makes tentative suggestions. He attempts to bring about a mutual exploration, an experiment which hopefully will lead to a new trend in educational thinking or to a new attitude. It is important that the therapist follow through by keeping in close touch with the persons concerned whenever a new educational resource has been created for the child. The therapist who works with the handicapped child realizes the significance of active community participation in helping the child to live in a single orbit of humanity without qualifications, divisions, or separations.

REFERENCES

1. Cowen, Emory L. Psychotherapy and Play Techniques with the Exceptional Child and Youth. In Cruickshank, William M. (Ed.). *Psychology of Exceptional Children and Youth*. New York: Prentice-Hall, 1955.
2. Stacey, Chalmers L. and Manfred F. DeMartino (Eds.). *Counseling and Psychotherapy with the Mentally Retarded*. Glencoe, Illinois: Free Press, 1957.

7

Counseling with Parents

RARELY do children enter an experience in psychotherapy without their parents. Although many children have benefited from therapy without concurrent parent counseling, it is often necessary that at least one parent be involved in regular interviews. From a study of child guidance clinics, Newell (4) reported that, "We get our best results when someone interviews a parent every time the therapist sees the child." The alleviation of the child's psychological tensions, the resolution of his problems, the perception of himself as a worthwhile, lovable person are goals which are achieved more completely when parents participate in the counseling experience.

In general, parents realize the significance of their own participation and are eager to explore their relationship with the child, to express their interest and concerns, and to discover new ways of approaching him. Parents cannot be blamed for the emotional difficulties of the child. The problems which are created arise in living, in relations. They grow out of experiences in the family. It is important that the therapist approach the parent with the attitude that the parent has done his best to make a good life for himself and his child.

Every parent who brings his child for counseling is expressing a basic concern and an underlying love. It is true that other motivating factors may be present, such as the alleviation of guilt and anxiety by taking a positive step, or the recognition that they can no longer bear to face the child, or the wish to have someone else take over their responsibility. Recognizing that other motives may exist, it is rare to find a parent who is not struggling and groping, who is not searching to discover a healthy basis for relating to the child. It is rare that the parent does not express a deep concern for the child's fullest development and growth, rare to find a parent who feels only rejection and hatred, who feels no relatedness or responsibility. Nearly every parent relates himself to the child's difficulty, recognizes his own part in it, and wants to help, wants to be involved in the process of the child's experience in therapy. Although parents want to help they often seem uncertain, confused, and bewildered as to what to do. They often feel that everything they have attempted has failed. They do not understand their child and do not know how to approach him any more. Sometimes they feel the child hates them. Sometimes they cannot be with the child long without feeling some repulsion and disgust. Often they would rather be given suggestions and advice, told what to do and what not to do. It is difficult for them to face themselves, explore the nature of their experiences, discover new approaches to the child, and arrive at solutions as the result of their own self-examination and self-insight. Parents need to be encouraged to verbalize their frustrations, their feelings of deprivation, and their resentments and fears (2). They need to feel free to elaborate current and earlier relationships with the significant people in their lives.

SCHEDULING THE APPOINTMENT

A number of factors must be considered in scheduling the first appointment with parents. It is important to indicate to the parent that the procedure for the initial interview is to see the parent alone. Since it is the child who has been referred for treatment, many parents assume the child will be seen on the first visit. Therefore, it is necessary to state the purpose of the first meeting as that of discussing the nature of the problem and making arrangements and plans to begin work with the child or to refer him to another person or agency.

The request for service usually does not indicate whether the father, mother, or both wish to be involved in the counseling experience. Since it is important to leave the decision of participation with the parents, the initial call or letter scheduling the first appointment must be open enough to enable parents to decide on their own. Some counselors believe it is necessary and fruitful to see both parents at least once and on the basis of this interview to single out one parent for further counseling or to see both parents throughout (1). Other counselors prefer to leave this decision with parents. When both parents decide to come for the initial interview, it is a problem to know whether to see them individually or together. Since the parents may know how they want to participate, it is generally an effective procedure to accept whatever decision they make.

THE FIRST INTERVIEW

Although formal questions initiated by the counselor often interfere with the development of a therapeutic relationship with parents, it is sometimes necessary to raise such items as fees, scheduling the child's hours of appointment, making arrangements for parents to participate if they wish to do so, getting permission to procure reports of medical examinations and previous diagnostic and therapeutic contacts, and discussing visits to the school. It is often wise to leave these questions to the end of the interview unless they are brought up spontaneously by the parents.

The first interview is often opened by the counselor with a statement which leaves the parent free to begin in his own way. A statement such as, "I wish you would feel free to begin wherever you'd like," or "I'd be interested in whatever you'd care to talk about," generally provides the necessary freedom. In most instances it may be unnecessary for the counselor to say anything. The parent often begins expressing his concerns if the counselor waits a few moments.

In this first interview the counselor conveys attitudes of acceptance, respect, concern, and trust. He believes in the parent's potentialities for self-exploration and growth. He listens with complete attention and accepts the parent's expressions exactly as given. He attempts to see with the parent the child's behavior and experience. He follows step-by-step the parent's views, feelings, and thoughts. He cares how the parent feels. He cares that the parent is suffering, is angry or frightened, that the parent feels defeated, wronged, helpless. He wants to share a process with the parent which will lead to a healthy relationship between the parent and the child. He listens fully to every expression of the parent. He reacts in such a way that the parent is encouraged, is free to continue expressing his feelings without guilt or reserve.

The parent is not pressured to come for therapeutic help for himself. It is important, however, for the therapist to indicate his interest and willingness to meet regularly with the parent in therapeutic sessions. An attitude such as the following is sometimes expressed: "If you'd like to come in to discuss further your experiences and relationships, I would be very much interested in exploring them with you."

If the parent sees no value in a counseling experience for himself, the counselor indicates that he would like to see the parent occasionally in order to discuss the nature of the child's experience in therapy and to learn of new developments in the family. This is an important aspect of child therapy. When parents do not participate of their own accord, the counselor must have some way of maintaining a continuous relationship with them not only to present some of the major trends in the therapy sessions and to be aware of the current significant events in the child's life but also to help the parent feel that he is participating in the work with the child. This procedure allows the counselor to keep relations with parents open and alive. A way of stating this to the parent is as follows: "Although I can understand that you see no real need in having regular counseling experiences for yourself, it would help me if I could see you from time to time to discuss the important trends in the therapy sessions and also to learn from you of some of the significant happenings in Bill's life. It will probably be three or four weeks before I have come to some understanding of Bill's behavior. I'll call you when I have something definite to report. In the meantime, feel free to call if there is anything you wish to discuss with me." Even when the interviews are centered on the child's difficulties, through direct participation in occasional discussions with the counselor the parent becomes related to the child in an experience that may have far-reaching consequences.

In making arrangements for the child's experience, it is necessary to secure the parent's permission to record the sessions if recordings are to be made. The one-way vision mirror in the playroom is explained to the parent, as well as the fact that a person who records the interviews and sometimes students in training are in the observation room. Sometimes parents ask to observe their child from behind the mirror. Here a limit is set. A simple statement is made that it is contrary to the philosophy and purpose of play therapy to permit parents to observe. If the parent persists, a brief explanation is offered that the child's world of private feelings is his own. He must be free to express his deepest feelings toward the significant figures in his life without any fear of being observed by them. The ultimate purpose of the counselor is to help the parent live with the child in a person-to-person relationship, not to promote a plan for the parent to study the child or analyze his behavior.

The setting of fees sometimes challenges the counselor's basic attitudes and premises. When fees are arranged on a sliding scale, it is an expression of trust in the client to permit him to decide the fee in terms of the published scale. Usually the parent makes a decision which accurately and honestly reflects what the family is able to pay. Occasionally there is an obvious contradiction between the amount decided upon and the family income. If this is the case, it is the parent's problem and can have meaning in the therapeutic relationship only when the parent is ready to face it. Sometimes the parent selects a fee that is apparently too high. Even so, this is accepted, but the counselor may state that if the fee becomes a hardship on the family it can be lowered. When the parent indicates he cannot decide upon a fee, the counselor suggests that the parent think the matter over and make a decision the following week. It is important in arriving at a fee to recognize the parent's anxiety, conflict, or hostility and to discuss these feelings with him.

When the child is having difficulties in school, it is usually necessary for the counselor to plan to make regular visits to the school. In the first interview, the counselor indicates this plan to the parent. Through talks with parents, principals, and teachers the counselor works toward a placement for the child which will facilitate a happy, self-fulfilling school life. He also works toward helping the parent to perceive the school in terms of its potential and promise, in spite of previous negative experiences.

Sometimes parents want to be told how to explain to the child the reason for his therapy visits. The parent is encouraged to formulate his own statement. Through discussion with the counselor, the parent usually is able to make a decision. In some situations, the parent decides to give a direct explanation, for example, that the child is coming to get help in solving his problems. In others, he is told he is coming to a special school to play. Which approach is best depends on the family situation. If pressed, the counselor may indicate possible approaches, but he leaves the parent with the responsibility of deciding what to say to the child.

Parents occasionally request a definition of play therapy. They sometimes want to have an idea of what it is. Usually, only a brief statement is required. One way of stating it is that "Play therapy is a relationship between the child and therapist in the setting of a playroom, where the child is encouraged to express himself freely, to release pent-up emotions and repressed feelings, and to work through his fear and anger so that he comes to be himself and functions in terms of his real potentials and abilities." If the parent wishes a more detailed explanation, the counselor may give specific illustrations or suggest a list of readings.

A verbatim initial interview with a parent is presented below to illustrate the first meeting and the way in which the relationship between the parent and counselor was evolved.

First Interview, Mrs. Dyne

MRS. D.: I seem to be in a very bad state of confusion. And when I say that I don't know what is best anymore.

MR. M.: Right now you're feeling more mixed up than ever?

MRS. D.: Yes—absolutely. I have tried to figure out whether it's best to leave with the child or whether to leave the child with my husband who has never been responsible for his children. . . . He does not talk to him or explain things or play with him or do anything. We are both guilty. I do certain things because it's necessary. But to actually sit down and play games with him or do anything, even I shun being near him. And I think Don is a bright little boy and I think he understands what his parents are doing to him, I really do. And yet this being hurt is what bothers me very much. I can't understand why I should have to hurt him. I understand one thing, that he likes it, and that's what I'm worried about.

MR. M.: Does he know that you don't like what you're doing to him?

MRS. D.: Yes, he knows that I don't. Yes! Yes! I've talked to him about being sent away. He says, "Well send me away." Now here is a child who's not even nine years old. If you talk to a fifteen-year-old and he says, "Send me away," I could understand it but this is a little boy and it really is—I'm not happy about it.

MR. M.: He doesn't seem to care whether he stays home or goes away.

MRS. D.: Frankly I think he still would like to stay with us because if he didn't he would try in every way not to be near me. *(Pause.)*

MR. M.: It isn't so much that you want him to go, it's that you don't know how much longer—

MRS. D.: I don't know how to cope with him.

MR. M.: And perhaps how much longer you can hold on.

MRS. D.: Well, probably not too long. Here it is after all these years where it should be easier, you know, a little bit, it's harder on me now than it was when I was younger. I could take it then, you know, fight with them and come back. I just can't do it much longer.

MR. M.: Well, I can see that things have gotten to such a state you're wondering whether there's any opening, any way out or any kind of change that can ever come about, for the better.

MRS. D.: That's true, that's exactly what I'm trying to say, yes. I don't know now what is the best way. When the other boy came home from school, I asked him to do something. He was in bed, and he wouldn't. Well, I ignored him the whole day and just wouldn't bother getting him his dinner or his lunch. I mean, as far as he's concerned, Mother didn't exist. At least he hoped that she didn't exist. . . . My husband hasn't made a place for his children in his business. Here is another thing that he has done and we have a little bit of property and he's pushed it on me and I've done it very badly, I mean taking care of the little bit of rent or something. We've discussed it and still he blames me and he says you must do it. Now I have done it, I will say that. He accuses me of being lazy. I say maybe I am lazy but the fact that he never took it off my shoulders and allowed me to continue to be like this. This is what I'm getting at, all these years I've been allowed to do as I please, more or less. We'd fight and everything but nothing came of it. The same thing is happening now. We fight and nothing comes of it. I've said, "Well why do you allow me to do these things? If you don't want them, your food or whatever it is, don't let me do it." There are other men who say you can't do it and they see that their wives don't do it, that's all. Either they're not home or they just don't bother, I mean, but there's no two ways. Do you know what I'm trying to explain? It's got to be one way or the other.

MR. M.:   When you do something you want him to accept it or else drop the whole thing.

MRS. D.:   That's right. That's right. Well, we aren't doing that. That's what I'm getting at. It's got to a point now where I know if I don't do it it won't be done and it won't matter because eventually we're going to get together and it won't mean anything and pretty soon it will be something else that we'll quarrel about or we'll be mad about—and that's exactly the way we've been living. So Don lives that way too. One minute you do it this way and one minute you do it that way. So actually we're all in a turmoil, our home is continuously in a turmoil. There's no happy medium in our home.

MR. M.:   And there's no consistent behavior.

MRS. D.:   No, No, nothing at all. No! And I've realized and talked to my husband and told him, I said, "You run your business that way, you did it from the beginning, you haven't changed in any way. You want to be consistent and at home you are inconsistent." And it's true. And that's what I've begun to realize, that we're both inconsistent and yet we both want to be consistent. . . . And we don't go out. We haven't been invited, oh, for a long time. No one asks us, I mean, you know where you say you have friends. We don't have friends; we have people that we know. It is frightening to come to a point late in your life where you have no one who really cares. And that's exactly what it's come to. I don't know whether it's our mental attitude to people that is repellent or what and I am really concerned because it all comes back to our child. This child is going to be a big, big problem if something isn't done and done soon. But what to do about it is the thing. Where do we go from here with him and with ourselves? I have seriously thought of taking him away. However, I don't know if I'm capable.

MR. M.:   Whether you could really live with him alone.

MRS. D.:   That's right. I don't know my capabilities anymore. At one time I could say "Yes, I can do this, or I can do that," but I can't anymore.

MR. M.:   You don't seem to know who you are anymore.

MRS. D.: Well I would say that I've been quite strong willed. If I hadn't been I probably wouldn't be here *(laughs)* right now in this place. I think if I had some help somewhere I could do it. I mean, I more or less need someone to, let's say, give me support.

MR. M.: You think then you could discover again where you are capable and—

MRS. D.: Yes, that's right, yes. . . .

MR. M.: Perhaps if we discuss these incidents as they come up in your life and examine them, you may see clarity or a direction and be able—

MRS. D.: Yes, you're right because that's the only way I can go on in this home the way it is, with someone, as you say, pointing to a direction and showing me how I can get along with Don.

MR. M.: Yes. Well, we can make weekly appointments for you and me to talk together and also for Don.

MRS. D.: All right.

MR. M.: I would see Don myself.

MRS. D.: You mean you'd see both of us.

MR. M.: Yes, if you can make two visits.

MRS. D.: That's all right, I'll make room for it because it's important.

MR. M.: Uh-huh. I'd like to suggest three o'clock on Friday. Would it be possible to bring Don at that time?

MRS. D.: I'll make it a point to bring him then, absolutely.

MR. M.: And could we meet on Tuesday at two o'clock?

MRS. D.: Uh-huh.

MR. M.: That would be regularly, each week.

MRS. D.: All right.

MR. M.: You seem to have some doubts about my seeing both of you.

MRS. D.: Will Don be happy about that? I mean, your talking to both of us. Will he understand? Would it be better for him if he was with someone else instead of you?

MR. M.: Well, if this comes up as a problem then he and I will just have to face it.

MRS. D.: I see. Well, I'll be very frank with you. I am willing to do anything.

MR. M.: You understand that when he and I are together, what happens is just between us.

MRS. D.: Yes, I understand.

MR. M.: And when you and I are together, that's our own experience.

MRS. D.: Yes, yes, I understand that.

MR. M.: I can understand your hesitation.

MRS. D.: Yes, that was it. In our talks, you know, he might sense something and that's what I was worried about. *(Pause.)* Well, here's one thing I would like to ask you about. People that feel that way about parents, not, say, caring for them, what makes them want to be with those parents?

MR. M.: People who don't care for them?

MRS. D.: Yes. Or act as if they don't care. What makes them want to stay? Now a lot of children want to be away from their parents, want to lose all connection. Do you know what I'm trying to say? What is it about me that they want to be continuously near me— what is it?

MR. M.: Perhaps underneath they really do care.

MRS. D.: Even my husband, now you would think that a person that if he didn't want to—do you understand what I'm talking about? I would avoid those people that would be making me unhappy. I would stay out of their way. And yet I find even my husband instead of wanting to be away from me, continuously he'll be home. I'm wondering why doesn't the man who is unhappy in his marriage make any effort to find happiness somewhere else?

MR. M.: You don't believe he feels there's any hope there, is that it?

MRS. D.: I don't know whether it's hope or what. I mean, why do people want to be unhappy.

MR. M.: Why do they stay in a miserable situation when they have other opportunities?

MRS. D.: Yes. Actually my husband is in the position where he could leave me and go to a hotel, go somewhere and live. He doesn't have to. And if he's not happy with his food or anything else he could go to a restaurant, my heavens, and eat there. And avoid me. I mean, avoid the situation. What makes him come home every night to the same miserable deal that he feels he has? Why does he want to come back every time?

MR. M.: It seems like very odd behavior to you.

MRS. D.: Wouldn't you—that's why I'm wondering how sane am I, actually maybe I'm not. I'm very bewildered. Frankly, I'm very bewildered.

MR. M.: Are you afraid you are losing your sense of reality?

MRS. D.: More or less. Yes, I would say more or less. I don't think that I'm as sane. I'm wondering how long I can go on like this without somewhere losing my balance.

MR. M.: You seem to have some hope that maybe things will get better.

MRS. D.: No, I don't, that isn't what I come here exactly for. I don't see any change in our situation, because as far as the marriage is concerned—

MR. M.: It's hopeless.

MRS. D.: Well, it's never been (laughs) a marriage. No!

MR. M.: I see.

MRS. D.: Or if it has been a marriage it hasn't been anything that you can say, well, look back and say, at least one year out of my life I've been happy. . . . I'm of Jewish origin and my husband comes from a very orthodox family. My parents did not bring me up in that way. I knew I was Jewish and that was all. Mother observed holidays but not in the orthodox way of life. I mean, not in that particular way. The last few years I've taken courses with our Rabbi and found that I could, that God doesn't stricken you just because you believe in this or believe in that. You can take or leave—so that now when my husband says well, that brought this on you, I don't have to accept that. I can accept the fact that I've tried to live a decent life. I've tried to raise my children as best I can, and to the best of my ability. To a certain degree I have done, I should say, a fairly good job. With all the incapabilities that I had when I was a child. With all the ways, with the way I was brought up, is what I'm trying to say. And with all the, everything else that has come into my life, I think on the whole I've handled it pretty good. Even my mother who has always been against me in the sense of, well, you're lazy or just no good or anything, even she in the last year said "You are, people like you don't exist, able to take what you're taking." And mother says it's partly, it is partly my fault but not to the degree when I have to live the way I do. It's not necessary anymore. We have no problems about money. We have a lovely home. We have everything to make us, we should have everything to make us happy and yet we have no friends. Even the family has stopped coming to our house. They'll come if they're invited but actually they don't—

MR. M.:   Spontaneously.

MRS. D.:   No, they never drop in. No one drops in on us. Yes, you're right.

MR. M.:   Well, we're going to have to stop for this time. Would you consult this chart and decide upon a fee.

MRS. D.:   Yes. It would be $5.00 for me and $2.50 for Don.

MR. M.:   All right. I'll see you on Friday.

COMMENTS

Mrs. Dyne states the central problems as a difficulty in relating to her son in a positive manner, a breakdown in her belief in herself and her abilities, and a growing anxiety in dealing with her son's aggression and destructiveness. She realizes she needs a pattern to guide her and emotional support from the therapist. Although she described the serious conflicts with her husband, she does not raise the marriage as a problem of concern because she feels it is a hopeless union. In addition to the increased severity of breakdown in the relation with her son, she doubts her own sanity and validity of her perceptions. She has become separated from herself, no longer understands herself or what she can do and wants to do. She no longer knows her abilities and is unable to take a direct course of action.

During the hour she spoke hurriedly in loud, uneven tones and seemed afraid the counselor would interrupt her. For this reason, the counselor made brief comments only when Mrs. Dyne paused or asked a question. Although Mrs. Dyne was discussing an important aspect of the marital relationship, the counselor held to the time limit and brought the interview to a close.

INTERVIEWS WITH PARENTS

As talks with parents continue, it is often necessary to present a brief picture of the significant themes in the child's play. The counselor presents only as much of the picture as will be meaningful and helpful to the parent. Although the stated purpose of the interview may call for the counselor to make a report, the parent frequently begins discussing his own experience with the child. Or in the middle of the report the parent may start to talk. The counselor stops his presentation, listens to the parent, and encourages the parent to continue to express his feelings and thoughts. Thus in these meetings the counselor may respond primarily to the parent's feelings and experiences. He may offer a brief picture of the child's attitudes and behavior in play therapy. He may give child development information, or simply support the parent's efforts to achieve a positive relation with the child. In short, the therapist responds in terms of the requirements of the immediate situation.

Frequently the parent begins the interview wishing to elaborate on the child's symptoms and how they are affecting members of the family, or wanting to discuss the child's school experiences. Following these initial statements, the parent often expresses his own concerns, interests, family background, and current significant relationships.

The counseling experience seems particularly worthwhile when the parent describes the situations which are causing anxiety and emotional conflict, when the parent's problems are focused in himself and when he wants to obtain help for himself. Occasionally, however, parents do not see the child's difficulties as related to their own feelings and attitudes, or if they do, their perceptions are vague or purely intellectual. These parents see the problem as the child's, not their own. Moreover, they come to the counselor with the expressed purpose of obtaining specific, authoritative advice about the "right way" to manage their child, often in specific situations such as eating, sleeping, toileting, and cleanliness. Or they seek an explanation of how and why they have failed. Often these parents come to the counselor as a last resort and are intent on obtaining definite guidance from him. Sometimes they come with an aggressive dependency motivated by desperation and anxiety. Since they come with definite attitudes and goals related to their *children,* the counselor's response to *their* feelings may be perceived by parents as inadequate and frustrating. Such parents continue to demand direct advice, and when it is not given to them they terminate the contact because they feel their real needs are not being met. To avoid these problems in counseling it is important for the counselor to keep the focus of the problem in the child, if this is where the parent places it, and to discuss directly with the parent incidents of the child's behavior and ways in which the parent may handle problems. He may give information or suggest possibilities for action, leaving the parent free to make the final choice and to judge the adequacy of the counselor's thinking in a particular situation. The counselor may offer the parent views which the parent has not considered. In every case, however, the counselor accepts the parent's conclusions and decisions. Such a flexible approach of meeting the parent where he is at the moment and responding in terms of the parent's expectations, wishes, and expressed needs seems to be a necessary part of effective counseling. On the other hand, when the parent approaches counseling with a desire to examine his own experiences, it is important to allow this to be the focus of the coun-

seling process rather than the child's experience in therapy or his difficulties at home or school.

When the parent does not wish to examine his own personal experiences, it is sometimes necessary for the counselor to present his own
ideas. Some excerpts taken from interviews with different parents illustrate one way in which the counselor may approach these relationships
(3). The first is an example of an interview in which the counselor failed
to respond to the parent's questions.

Mr. J. came to see the therapist about his five-year-old son Ernest, who
was a withdrawn, sensitive child, afraid of new situations and easily
upset. For the first twenty minutes Mr. J. related incidents of Ernest's
behavior, expecting the therapist to give a diagnosis on the basis of the
described behavior and offer definite suggestions for handling the child,
or at least a definite therapy plan. When he discovered that only his feelings were being responded to, he began to pressure the therapist.

C.:* I'm not worried, but I'd like to know about certain things we're
doing, whether they're right or wrong, and should we attempt to
change them.

T.: I can see that that is of a great concern to you. *(Pause.)*

C.: Specifically, his lack of a desire to make any decision at all. He has
a fear of new friends and new situations. That's my main concern.
He's very quiet. He's a poor sport, too. Should we always give in to
him, or should we let him know that he must lose at things sometimes? That's what I want to know.

T.: You see those aspects as problems and feel very unsure about what
to do, is that it?

C.: I don't know if we're really seeing anything. Would you like to ask
me some questions now, or what?

T.: You don't feel as if we're really getting anywhere this way?
*(After a long pause the client then related more instances of the
child's troubling behavior and the therapist reflected the feelings involved. Again they came to an impasse.)*

C.: One of the things I want to ask your advice on is should we let him
go his own way or should we correct him? . . . Well, am I supposed
to ask you now what to do, or do we just go on like this? What do we
do in a situation like the one I told you about?

T.: There are really no right or wrong answers to these things—we can
just explore your feelings about the situation and perhaps work out
some solutions together. *(Pause.)* I gather that you feel, at this
point, that you can't handle it alone anymore, that you're very unsure about your next move. *(Again there was a period when the father illustrated the child's behavior with still more incidents, stress-
ing the seriousness of the problem and his need for expert guidance.)*

C.: I don't know whether you have a picture of the child or not. We
would like to know whether we should bring him out more, make
him more of a social being to live in the world, or let him remain as
introverted as he is.

* C., client; T., therapist.

T.:   You feel there might be something that should be done to change him, that if he were more outgoing life might be easier for him.

C.:   Oh, he could live fairly happily the way he's going. . . . But should we force him to meet new situations, or shouldn't we? That's the question. It's just a problem of how to attack this—I don't know! For instance, should we try to force him to go to nursery school when he gets all dressed up for it and then refuses to get on the bus? Or should we just let him go his own way? My wife feels we shouldn't coerce him, and I've always deferred to her—but we want your opinion. Which is better to do?

T.:   Evidently you feel it might be better to coerce him?

C.:   I do feel that, but maybe my professional training is influencing me, because in my job you often do have to be firm. But I would like you to tell me what is really right to do. For instance, when I try to play with both children, each wants to do different kinds of things, so it usually ends up with one of them mad. Now how would one handle that?

T.:   It is important to you to satisfy both of them and have them both happy, is that it?

C.:   Yes, and we would like some suggestions.

T.:   I know you would like me to be able to give you some definite answers and tell you what to do, but I can't really do that. We can continue to look at the problem in all its aspects and perhaps work out something.

C.:   Well, I don't know as you've said anything yet. Are we expecting too much of him? Can't you give us an answer? Specifically, shall we defer to him in competitive games? Shall we let him win in order to give him confidence, or what?

Near the end of the interview the therapist explained the possibility of play therapy for the child. Here again Mr. J. wanted an opinion as to whether or not play therapy would definitely help Ernest and whether he and his wife would be helped by any further interviews. He left without making any decision and did not return for further interviews. He expressed the opinion that he had wasted his time in coming to the service. Obviously the kind of counseling offered was not meeting his needs in any way.

In the following two examples a different approach was used.

Mrs. L. had spent most of the hour up to this point describing her son's hyperactivity and disobedience.

C.:   He'll get worse and worse. He needs to be set right. How he got wrong, I don't know. We didn't do it intentionally. I think we must have made some mistakes and he is on the wrong road and we can't reach him and help him.

T.:   The biggest problem then is trying to set him in the right direction. I see that our time is about up. Would you like to make another appointment?

C.:   No, I don't think so. Not if this is the way we are going to operate. I can see no point in coming here and just telling you all the things he has done unless you are willing to discuss them with me. For instance, we insist that he tie his own shoes when he asks us to do it. Other children his age tie their shoes. What I would like you to do is tell me whether that is right or wrong and how we should change.

T.:   Yes, I understand it would be much easier if I could tell you what was right and wrong in your relations with Fred, but I don't have any specific answers.

C.:   But you could tell me what you think. What about the shoe business?

T.:   Well, I don't believe that in itself it is either right or wrong to insist that he tie them. I would rather look at it in a different way. For instance, perhaps Fred is trying to reach you and your husband in some way so that the shoe business is really an expression of some other need.

C.:   You mean he might be asking for something else?

T.:   He might be reaching out for some sort of security in his relationship with you.

C.:   Then how could I help understand that better?

T.:   Well, one way you might do that is by trying to respond more to his feeling about things, trying to show him that you understand how he feels inside.

C.:   You mean that when he asks us to tie his shoes we could try to discover what is behind it. Well, he sometimes says, "Oh, I don't want to do it, it's too much trouble." Do you mean it would be better to say to him, "It is a very hard thing to tie your own shoes"?

T.:   That is one thing you might say.

C.:   Then he would expect us to tie them all the time.

T.:   Since you feel that you shouldn't tie them, perhaps you could still respond to his feelings in some way, but insist that this was one of the things that he ought to do for himself.

C.:   Well, I know that the time is up. I would like to come in again. These last few minutes have been more helpful to me than *anything* you have said. My husband feels that way too. We think it would be more helpful to us if we could talk about things in just this way with you.

T.:   Something like this was what you really wanted, and it has been much more satisfying to you.

C.:   Yes, it definitely has.

Just how did the therapist approach the parent at the end of this interview? He maintained the basic attitudes of counseling; he reflected and clarified her feelings. He did not attempt to persuade. He did not interpret the child's behavior or the mother's feeling about it according to some external system of psychological concepts. He did not diagnose or attempt to deal with "resistances" and "defenses." He kept the focus of the problem where the parent placed it—in the child. He did, however, discuss with the mother incidents of the child's behavior which she wanted to know how to handle. He did give some information about children's behavior and offered possibilities for action which the parent was completely free to evaluate in her own way. He widened the parent's perceptual field by offering views other than those she had seen, but he accepted any decision she made or any feeling she had about them.

At the beginning of the interview, Mrs. F. indicated the kind of help she needed.

C.: Before I start talking to you about Ronald, there are a few things I'm concerned with. The person I talked with before was passive and made me feel insecure. Every time I asked her something she'd just go back to the way I felt about it. Well, I came here to get some help and when I asked questions I wanted some explanation from her, some of *her* thinking. I realize it might be helpful to have someone who's objective listen, but I want more than that. I don't expect to be given flat answers to questions, but I do expect some ideas to be offered to me. *(She then proceeded to describe Ronald's difficulties. The therapist responded here to the feelings she expressed. Following this Mrs. F. raised some questions).*

C.: There are two things we would like to know. First, is his speech normal, or should I take him to a speech clinic? We're unable to reach him completely, for some reason. Maybe he's been hurt at some time. He's sensitive and insecure. How can we help him? Can you answer these questions?

T.: I really can't say whether Ronald should go to a speech clinic or not. There are a number of possible explanations for speech retardation. There may be maturational factors involved. You have mentioned that he's advanced in other areas, and it may be that in time he'll catch up in his speech without any special help. Another possibility is that he may be bothered by some troubling feelings and ideas and that these are blocking his speech development. A third possibility might be that he has insufficient experience in listening and talking to people. Another possibility might be that he is pretty much operating at his potential level of performance.

C.: Well, that is helpful, to look at it in those different ways. I don't think it's his level, because he's so much brighter than that in solving puzzles and understanding stories.

T.: You're pretty sure then it's not that?

C.: Yes, I think so. It also couldn't be that he's had insufficient practice because we talk to him a lot at home and give him plenty of opportunity to express himself. I'm not sure which of the other two it is. It may be a little of both. I've noticed that he's very afraid of new situations and new people, so that there may be some emotional factors that are not too clear to us. What about those?

T.: We could explore some possibilities. It's true that some infants from a very early age show certain qualities that seem to continue in spite of experience.

C.: Well, I've always noticed that Ronald has been more sensitive than most other children. I've always wanted him to be outgoing, so maybe I've pushed him that way. Maybe he's just not an extroverted type of child. I should accept him as he is. Maybe that's the reason he's insecure—because he can't accept himself as that kind of child.

T.: That is another possibility—that he might be insecure because there are certain things about himself that he has not accepted, or perhaps doesn't understand.

C.: You know, I had almost decided not to come to this place any more. I'm glad I did, because this has been most worthwhile. As for Ronald, I think I will just bring him down for play therapy to see if anything can be done. If it doesn't change him, well, it's all right anyway.

T.: You feel that you might be able to accept him as he is if he should remain essentially the same.

C.: Yes, looking at it that way.

It is clear that this parent saw the therapist as a helpful person with whom she could discuss things, and that she gained some insight into the rejecting nature of her relationship with her son. There are many occasions in counseling with parents when it is important to respond directly to parents' questions about the child's progress or to reassure them. The individual parent and his problems must determine the exact process required.

A Complete Case in Parent Counseling

Since the work with Mrs. Barry was terminated after four interviews it is possible to present a verbatim account of each talk. When Mrs. Barry applied for counseling she was in her eighth month of pregnancy. In her initial call to the service she stated that she had been a total failure in matters of discipline and needed to learn how to limit her children.

She realized that she had only about one month to plunge into the problems she faced and to explore the basis for her extreme anxiety. The time reality was undoubtedly a factor in making each interview a meaningful, significant experience. From the beginning Mrs. Barry entered into a direct examination of her family situation. She searched within herself to discover a better way of life.

First Interview, Mrs. Barry

MRS. BARRY: The reason I called was that I used to be in nurses training. We had visited The Merrill-Palmer School, and I knew that they had a child guidance service.

COUNSELOR: Yes.

MRS. B: It seems to be in the matter of disciplining them mostly, I guess.

C.: Sort of upsetting to tell them what they can and can't do and not have them respond to you.

MRS. B.: Yes, that's it. He gives me quite a bit of trouble. He's a very active child, extremely, compared to other youngsters I've seen. He seems to be quite high strung and always on the go. It just seems that he's always getting into things and when I try to discipline him—I've tried just about everything and nothing seems to work with him. I've tried isolation and I've tried spanking and ignoring and what others have suggested but it just doesn't seem to work.

C.: It's awfully hard to know just what is right when everything you do fails.

MRS. B.: It is, especially. *(Pause.)* Another thing, he's always been a child who clings to a blanket. Have you ever heard that?

C.: Mmhuh. Many times.

MRS. B.: Since he was a small baby. For a while I was worried because I thought it was taking the place of me. Whenever he gets into any trouble, he goes into a panic if he doesn't have his blanket. He clings to it and he has to have it every place he goes. And the other day I was going Christmas shopping and I wanted him to get out and walk and he wouldn't because he didn't have his blanket. He just threw a regular fit right there in the street.

C.: Mmhuh.

MRS. B.: And I just don't know exactly how to handle him. For awhile I thought about taking it away completely, but the pediatrician said that he would outgrow it. He also sucks his fingers. The pediatrician said he would outgrow that too. He's only two years old. But I don't know; it has me worried. Now the other youngster, you know, sees his older brother do it so he has to have his blanket too.

C.: Mmhuh, sort of copying, learning something you don't approve of.

MRS. B.: Mmhuh. Although, I'm trying to do better with the younger one. Well, you know, before with the oldest boy I imagine he was spoiled a bit. Then there was jealousy when the other one came along, so I'm trying to correct some of the things I did with Tommy.

C.: Mmhuh, I see.

MRS. B.: Before Jeff starts them too. *(Pause.)* With Tommy when he would do things and I wouldn't keep after him, you know, to make him stop. I'd just let it go because I get tired of being like a Gestapo and following him around the house, telling him he can't do this and he can't do that, so I would just let him go most of the time. But with Jeff I'm trying to make him see that when I say something I mean it, although I'm not very—

C.: Forceful about it.

MRS. B.: No, not like his dad. I'm afraid his father is the opposite way. He wants to help me in his own way, but I'm afraid he's making the kids afraid of him because they both, you know, follow his every word. They do what he says.

C.: When he says something he—

MRS. B.: Yeah, it's just the opposite with me. They know that they can get away with things with me.

C.: They've discovered that when you tell them something you don't always see it through.

MRS. B.: I guess. I try, at least I have tried. I don't know where I fell down, but I must have made a big mistake.

C.: Mmhuh. As you look back on it you feel it's something you—

MRS. B.: It must be. It's the only thing I can see because they—*(Long period of silence.)*

C.: Now, the problem you see as most significant is your relationship with Tommy.

MRS. B.: Yes.

C.: And his refusal to accept any limits.

MRS. B.: Yes, that's my biggest problem. *(Long period of silence.)*

C.: Was it your hope to explore some of your own attitudes and background as a way of understanding why this difficulty exists?

MRS. B.: Either that or I don't know if it's entirely my fault, you know. Maybe he needs the help.

C.: I see. *(Long period of silence.)* Well, he's young for direct help from the service.

MRS. B.: Yes. *(Long period of silence.)*

C.: Today, we might discuss further your relationship with Tommy so—

MRS. B.: Mmhuh I better point out he seems to be an aggressive child, too. He doesn't—of course, I realize that he's too young to get along with other children, but he's always been—He likes other children, but he fights it seems all the time and I thought, myself, that if I considered nursery school for him, part time, perhaps two days a week, that would help. But my husband very violently objects to it. He feels that it's my duty to raise them and if I can't do it, I shouldn't put the responsibility on other people. But I really thought that that was what he needed, contact with others his own age and real supervision in his play.

C.: Mmhuh.

MRS. B.: Maybe he'd learn to get along a little. It's out of the question now but I have thought of this.

C.: Mmhuh.

MRS. B.: Someone else to guide his play other than myself.

C.: I see.

MRS. B.: I wanted to see, you know, how he would react and get along.

C.: Mmhuh.

MRS. B.: With someone else there, but I don't know. Everybody says, my in-laws, even my folks, say that if they had him for a month they could, you know, cure him. *(Pause.)* It seems like they think it's all me.

C.: They think that you should be able to do a better job.

MRS. B.: I don t know.

C.: They feel that you should be able to do it yourself?

MRS. B.: Mmhuh.

C.: So you feel you've got to do something about it or—

MRS. B.: Else it will go on.

C.: Mmhuh.

MRS. B.: *(Whispering.)* I don't want that.

C.:   Do you feel this urgency because of the way other people are reacting to you?

MRS. B.:   I suppose that's partly it. *(Period of silence.)*

C.:   I guess it must be pretty painful when so many seem to be against
you.

MRS. B.:   *(Begins crying. Cries silently for about six minutes.)* I'm sorry.

C.:   You can feel perfectly comfortable in crying here. It's really quite all
right. *(Pause.)* I can understand how hard it is when you've tried so—

MRS. B.:   I've tried, and everybody says that with my background in
nursing surely I should be able to handle one child. They make me
feel like such a failure. *(Cries loudly with heavy sighs for about
three minutes.)*

C.:   It can be a terribly defeating experience.

MRS. B.:   You know I've even got afraid of my own feelings lately. It
just seems as though at times when Tommy's at his worst I just
have such strong feelings of hatred toward him. I'm afraid because
I don't want to hurt him. I know I never would.

C.:   Mmhuh. But you can have strong feelings against him when you
feel that he is preventing you from being what other people consider a good mother.

MRS. B.:   *(Begins crying again. In tears.)* I guess that's it.

C.:   Somehow they blame you for his behavior.

MRS. B.:   I guess so. Particularly bad are Barney's feelings. He thinks
that I should be able to discipline them and make them see what's
right and what's wrong.

C.:   He thinks it ought to be a pretty easy job.

MRS. B.:   Well, he doesn't think it's easy. But he can't understand why,
when he's only such a short time with the children, he can make them
behave. You know he gets along very well with them and they both
love him. It's just that when he makes them behave they're, I believe,
afraid of him because they really follow his directions to the letter.

C.:   Mmhuh, pretty hard when he does so well, to feel you do so poorly
yourself.

MRS. B.:   Yes. *(Pause.)* He's only two years old, but he's always in it. My
husband and I never argued before the children came, very much,
but it seems that whenever we argue now it's always over the children and the way they should be brought up, and things like that. I
guess it's been bothering me since— *(Long period of silence.)*

C.:   Your husband thinks you should be firm and strict?

MRS. B.:   Yes.

C.:   And yet you, yourself, can't be—

MRS. B.:   Well, I've tried, but when I find myself spanking them, you
know, I think I'm spanking them too hard and that's when I have
these feelings that I may hurt them—

C.:   Afraid of what you might do.

MRS. B.:   *(Sobbing painfully.)* Because sometimes I really do spank
him hard! I have used a belt on him.

C.:   Mmhuh.

MRS. B.:   I don't like that. I just don't like it.

C.:   So what it comes to is that you can't continue doing—

MRS. B.:   I guess not.

C.:   And still live with yourself.

MRS. B.:   I guess not. I don't know why, but it just seems like all our friends and relatives and people that we know have children that are mild.

C.:   Mmhuh.

MRS. B.:   They don't have the same problems that I do. My kids, it seems, dream up things that other people's kids never do.

C.:   Sort of unique in that respect.

MRS. B.:   (With slight smile.) It seems to me it's 'cause they're both boys and you know, as I said, both active. Golly, Tommy is the type that would rather have a hammer or a screwdriver than anything else. He wants to know how things are put together. He's just always—He seems to be advanced or ahead for his age. I don't exactly know. Other kids are satisfied with their toys. I didn't realize that they get into things—drawers and pots and pans and things like that.

C.:   Mmhuh.

MRS. B.:   But, golly, he's got to be taking a radio apart or something like that or he's not happy. And I've even given him a portable radio that wasn't much good. I let him have it. My husband thinks that anything in the house I'll give Tommy, just to keep him quiet.

C.:   Mmhuh.

MRS. B.:   And that's not true. I think that he should be encouraged in things that he's interested in. (Pause.) I don't even have him toilet trained and he's two years old. I should have done that. I should have that done too.

C.:   You think you've been pretty much a failure in some of these matters.

MRS. B.:   I certainly do. (Period of silence.)

C.:   It's hard to continue to believe that you are worthy when—

MRS. B.:   (Begins crying again.) I always thought raising kids was not easy—but nothing like this. I thought (sobbing) that every woman was capable of raising children.

C.:   And at bottom that's the thing that troubles you, isn't it? A feeling that you're not capable. (Pause.)

MRS. B.:   (Cries silently for several minutes.) Here I am in a month to have three and I can't handle one. I keep waiting for the day when Tommy will grow up. And you should actually enjoy your kids because they grow so fast. You really don't have them very long. And I certainly don't enjoy them.

C.:   Pretty much a painful existence rather than something wonderful and happy. . (Pause.) You must wonder whether there are any joys at all in raising children.

MRS. B.:   Oh, yes, 'cause it doesn't seem like we have any now. (Pause.)

C.:   I understand how depressing it can be to go on day in and day out without any change.

MRS. B.:   That's about what it is, I guess. (Long period of silence.)

C.:   Is it possible for you to come in until the baby is due to arrive?

MRS. B.:   Does it do any good for one member to come? I wonder, in my family it's more a matter of both?

C.:   You mean your husband?

MRS. B.:   Yes.

C.:   Well of course, I'd be happy to talk with him if he would be interested.

MRS. B.:   That's it. You have to be willing.

C.:   Yes. There wouldn't be any value unless he was willing and wanted to come in. He would have to take the initiative.

MRS. B.:   Mmhuh. Would it be like interviewing?

C.:   It's pretty much like what we've been doing here. *(Pause.)* Sometimes it's hard to see how you can grow by just talking over your experiences, but we find that when people feel free to express themselves and get to the core of their feeling, it really helps. It's a way to understanding your feelings and accepting yourself.

MRS. B.:   I see. Well, I would like to. But as I said, my husband is quite militaristic as far as the children are concerned and he wasn't even a great deal in favor of my coming down today.

C.:   I see.

MRS. B.:   So I just made up my mind that I wasn't going to let him talk me out of this. So I would like to if it's at all possible. *(Pause.)*

C.:   There is a fee based on the income of the family. *(Hands Mrs. Barry the fee chart. Mrs. Barry is reluctant to state an amount.)* If you'd like, you can take the chart with you and think about the fee.

MRS. B.:   O.K. I'll show it to my husband. Mmhuh.

C.:   Then, in talking it over with your husband, if he decides that he wants to discuss his own feelings and experiences, if he would call me, I will make the arrangements with him,

MRS. B.:   Mmhuh. *(Long period of silence.)*

C.:   The approach I use is pretty much like our experience today. I'm interested in whatever you think is important in your life either from the present or the past. If you can feel free to talk with me there is a possibility that you can come to terms with the problems you mentioned.

MRS. B.:   Huhhuh.

C.:   What I'm trying to do is to understand your experience rather than analyze your behavior. Somehow if you can reach a point where you feel able to face these problems perhaps they won't seem so unsolvable.

MRS. B.:   I know that I would like to come. It's mainly the problem, you know, of having someone stay with the children, and having my husband agree on the money. That's what I have to find out about. *(Long period of silence.)* There's one thing—when I was in nurses' training, we went up to the State Mental Hospital, for three months. I think that's a big mistake. It, you know, they gave us courses in abnormal psychology. I think they scared me for one thing. They told us that neuroses are formed early in childhood and about all the different things that mothers can do to their children. And I don't know, it just kind of scared me. I don't want—I'm always worried about—I just don't want to do anything that would affect them in their—it seems like I'm always worried about giving them a psychosis or something like that. That's one reason why I never tried to force Tommy with his bowel training because it seems as though they stress that so much, you know—

C.: Mmhuh.

MRS. B.: How many things could come from rigid bowel training in childhood. That was a poor thing for me to study—

C.: It took all the naturalness out—

MRS. B.: Yes.

C.: Makes it hard to be yourself and act with confidence.

MRS. B.: Yes. The way I guess I would normally do, but now I'm afraid.

C.: It prevents you from being yourself. *(Pause. Mrs. Barry begins to cry.)* I gather the thing that hurts most is that you may be ruining your children. *(Long pause.)*

MRS. B.: *(Cries silently.)* I don't want that to happen.

C.: It's a terrifying thought.

MRS. B.: Oh God forgive me. . . . *(Puts her head on the desk and sobs with painful, heavy sighs. Then there is a long period of silence.)* Do you mind if I smoke?

C.: No, not at all. *(Period of silence, Mrs. Barry continues crying and breathing deeply.)* It's not necessary to say anything. Sometimes it helps just to sit and cry.

MRS. B.: Thanks very much. Whatever it is that's bothering me it's making me very nervous. I guess you can see that. I blame it on the children I guess, but I bite my nails and smoke more than I used to. I've changed a great deal. At least I think I have.

C.: Become more worried and nervous.

MRS. B.: I also feel that I'm wasting my life. I feel like I'm not accomplishing anything. It just seems like all day long I take care of the house and the children. At night all we do is watch television or something like that. I'm the kind of person, I'm used to being, you know, outgoing, and I like parties and people and things like that and I like to accomplish something, to do something. I don't know, I just feel like I'm wasting a lot of time and I should be doing something that I'm interested in.

C.: Mmhuh.

MRS. B.: And I can't seem to get up the ambition or whatever it is—

C.: Somehow you've lost the enthusiasm and excitement of—

MRS. B.: Mmhuh. It seems like it. All of a sudden, you're just shut in the house. It's kind of hard to adjust to it. *(Pause.)* If I just had a happier home situation, I wouldn't mind it at all.

C.: It's really not having one or the other, not being able to accomplish what you want and yet not having any happiness—

MRS. B.: At home, no. *(Pause.)* It's funny, you just automatically put the blame on the kids whenever there's any kind of trouble. Everybody tells me I should be thankful I have two healthy, active youngsters. I truly am very grateful. But I don't know, it seems that there's always something to take away from it. If your kids are healthy, then. . . .

C.:   Mmhuh. *(Pause.)* I see that our time is just about up for today.

MRS. B.:   I'll call you about the fee and my appointments.

COMMENTS

In this interview Mrs. Barry begins with an exploration of her difficulty in the managing of her children, particularly her two-year-old son. She expresses anxiety over the fact that her son from an early age preferred the comfort and warmth of a blanket to being held by his mother. The real source of her anxiety emerges, however, as she begins to examine her relationship with her husband. Mrs. Barry describes with much feeling his criticism of her. She tells how friends and relatives have made her feel inadequate as a mother. The major conflict is reflected in her struggle to maintain her faith in herself in the light of mounting external evidence that she is a failure.

In addition to her sense of inadequacy as a mother, Mrs. Barry is deeply afraid of the harm she might do the children in forcing them to adhere to social standards and in punishing them. She feels that a course in abnormal psychology which emphasized the damage parents do to children has made it impossible for her to act spontaneously. She realizes too that much of her behavior is in reaction to the criticisms of her husband. As she speaks of her relation with her husband, she sees that their central dispute is in disciplining the children. Although she has been influenced by him in becoming firmer and harsher, she does not believe that his approach is a healthy one. She concludes that her method of disciplining the children is inconsistent and contradictory but that her husband's is cruel and authoritarian.

At several points during the interview she sobs uncontrollably, with heavy sighs, for long periods of time. The two thoughts which disturb her most are the perception of herself as a failure and her fear that harsh treatment of the children will cause them to become neurotic.

Toward the end of the interview she considers the possibility that the static nature of her life, the empty, monotonous, and unsatisfying existence, is at the root of her difficulty. She feels she has become separated and isolated from important relationships with other adults and that she has stopped growing and developing as an individual. She seems to conclude that the uncreative, wasted nature of her life has made her feel inadequate and worthless. During the interview, the counselor conveys an understanding and acceptance of Mrs. Barry's feelings. He encourages her to explore her experiences fully. He asks questions and makes comments at points where she seems vague or incomplete in her examination. He interrupts the long silences and suggests ways of proceeding because she seems blocked and unable to explore the problems further on her own initiative. He senses her deepest feelings and supports her when she seems embarrassed and ashamed. On several occasions he relates the nature of the counseling process to her, the potential value in open expression of feeling, and the function of the counselor. He helps Mrs. Barry see that through a process of self-conscious examination of the significant aspects of her life she can come to an awareness and acceptance that will make it possible for her to face the conflicts and dilemmas she feels are overwhelming.

Second Interview, Mrs. Barry

(Mrs. B. waits for the counselor to speak.)

C.: How has everything been going since your last visit?

MRS. B.: Pretty good. *(Long period of silence.)* Was there anything in particular you wanted me to talk about?

C.: No. Just whatever comes to your mind that you wish to—

MRS. B.: He was quite agreeable to my coming here. He didn't seem to mind at all.

C.: You had kind of expected that—

MRS. B.: In a way I didn't know how he would react, but he didn't seem to—he thought it would help me. But he didn't want to come himself. I didn't want him to be against me again.

C.: It would have made it hard for you to come.

MRS. B.: Yes. I had made up my mind to come, but I would rather have him agreeable to the idea.

C.: Mmhuh. *(Long period of silence.)*

MRS. B.: I was going to ask you, does this sort of thing occur very often? Are there many cases like this, you know?

C.: Where somebody—

MRS. B.: Where mothers are broken up over their children, I mean completely overcome by them.

C.: Mothers who are so upset that—

MRS. B.: They feel that they can't or don't know how to handle them.

C.: Mmhuh. Well there are many mothers, especially with two small children, who have similar difficulties. *(Pause.)* Is it consoling to know that you're not the only mother who—

MRS. B.: To know that I wasn't a weird case or anything like that. You know, none of our friends have this trouble. It doesn't seem like they do.

C.: You seem to be the only one who—

MRS. B.: Yes.

C.: Mmhuh. *(Long period of silence.)*

MRS. B.: Sort of makes you feel foolish, knowing that there are a lot of people around and you're the only one who can't control your kids.

C.: Mmhuh. You mean they make you feel inadequate?

MRS. B.: Oh, I don't know, it just makes me feel like, you know like people talking behind your back or something.

C.: People are apt to judge you and react to what you're doing as a mother.

MRS. B.: Yes.

C.: You feel they do talk about you.

MRS. B.: Yes. That's the impression—that's how it makes me feel, you know I can't—Mine are sort of wild and everybody else's are so well behaved.

C.: Mmhuh.

MRS. B.: Right now we have a problem. My husband's mother gave Tommy a small-sized victrola for Christmas and he's only two years old. I didn't say anything when she suggested getting him that. I didn't want to hurt her feelings. Now it seems like—I don't know how much they gave for it—but it looks like a pretty expensive instrument, you know. It's in a portable case and he's always wanting to carry it. You know, naturally, and play it himself. Now I'm afraid—

C.: Mmhuh.

MRS. B.: And put the records on and I'm so afraid he'll drop it and ruin the mechanism or break the arm off or something like that. I don't know whether I should put it away until he knows how to handle it or whether I should just try to supervise him when he's playing with it. It seems like when he does play with it, I just have to sit right there and tell him "Don't pick it up." "Don't move the arm." And show him how to put the records on. I don't know what to do with the darn thing.

C.: I can see it's quite a worry.

MRS. B.: Yes. I like to let him do it his way. It seems like he's destructive, at least my husband thinks that. He doesn't seem to realize, you know realize.

C.: But you think he's just sort of investigating and learning about how it operates.

MRS. B.: Sure. It's only natural. When they gave it to him, they told him it was his so he doesn't see why he shouldn't have it his way.

C.: But you're so afraid that your husband would be quite upset and angry if he—

MRS. B.: If he breaks it, yes. I know he will be. *(Pause.)*

C.: I can see it makes for a difficult situation.

MRS. B.: Yes. So I guess I'm just going to put it away, but he keeps asking for it because he knows that it's his. If he forgets about it, I thought maybe—I'm talking too much. *(Lengthy period of silence.)*

C.: Pretty hard to know what to turn to.

MRS. B.: I guess so. *(Long silence.)* Another thing that bothers me. . . . There are so many little things. They're all little things that I don't do right or that he doesn't really like. I don't know. It seems like.

C.: Sometimes those little things can hurt a lot.

MRS. B.: Well, there's so many, and you know everybody has their faults. It seems like they add up and add up.

C.: Are you coming to feel that anything you do—

MRS. B.: Is wrong. You get discouraged from trying to do things right. You just let them all go. You get disgusted.

C.: He keeps after you with a lot of little things.

MRS. B.: Yes he does. It seems to me that he's trying to make me over or change me from what I am. All those little things that you never think of before you're married, you know.

C.: Mmhuh.

MRS. B.: You just don't know each other on small matters. It just seems like he's forever trying to change me.

C.: Mmhuh. Makes you feel that to satisfy him you have to change yourself a great deal.

MRS. B.: Yeah. Sometimes he makes me wonder just what good qualities I did have. I ask myself, "Am I really so lucky he married me?"

C.: Mmhuh. That seems to be the only conclusion you can come to. *(Pause.)*

MRS. B.: I don't have any particular talents. I don't. I can't do anything exceptionally well. *(Period of silence.)* One thing he's been after me about since we got married, he thinks I should take up sewing. I don't know why but he wants me to be as good as everybody else's wife in everything.

C.: Mmhuh.

MRS. B.: And to me, why should I be like other people? I hate sewing in the first place. I took it when I was in school and I don't have the patience for it. He's been after me and after me to get me a sewing machine, to take lessons. He thinks it would be good for me.

C.: He wants you to be like other wives.

MRS. B.: He wants me to have all their good qualities.

C.: But sewing, that's something you aren't very much interested in.

MRS. B.: That's right. It's something I just hate. I can't help it.

C.: It's hard to learn to do something you dislike so strongly.

MRS. B.: Yeah, it is. It seems to me like, you know, I don't pick at him. It doesn't seem to me like I find faults with everything he does. He does some things I don't like, but I just keep them to myself and—

C.: Recognize that—

MRS. B.: It's just him.

C.: You overlook his weaknesses.

MRS. B.: Well, I try to. I don't know. It doesn't seem as though I find faults like he does. It just seems to me like he picks and it's just—

C.: Mmhuh. That he wants you to do everything exactly his way.

MRS. B.: Yeah. He wants things done perfectly.

C.: You mean his way.

MRS. B.: Yes.

C.: And that makes you feel you have to be on guard.

MRS. B.: Yes. I feel sometimes as though I have to do certain things before he gets home if I want to avoid an argument.

C.: Mmhuh. *(Period of silence.)*

MRS. B.: I don't know how many routine jobs there are to do—the doors and things like that. But he never wants to do them. His father never did much at home. He was, you know, just a businessman. When he got home, he would flop. She more or less had to do all the things around the house herself. I come, you know, from a different type of family; my father was always working around the house for all of us. I guess he feels that I should do the things his mother does, but I feel they are more or less his job, you know.

C.: Mmhuh.

MRS., B.: He thinks that if his mother could do it I should do it too. He thinks that I shouldn't have help from him with washing walls or some big job like that. He doesn't take into consideration that people's circumstances are different. His mother had two children but they were farther apart. I don't know, you know, there are a lot of things that change.

C.: Mmhuh.

MRS. B.: The circumstance, the situation is different. He doesn't understand that.

C.: Your life is quite different from hers and you're a different person.

MRS. B.: Yes. But he doesn't seem to see that at all. Of course, he does a lot around the house, he takes care of the babies and things like that. But he thinks I should do more than I do.

C.: Mmhuh. Whereas it's your feeling that the heavy jobs are his responsibility.

MRS. B.: Yes. And I think—I don't see why he shouldn't help me with some things, because they're just babies, two small kids, and pretty soon I'll have another one. I don't know, there's so much that I can't do with the kids around.

C.: Mmhuh.

MRS. B.: It's hard.

C.: A full-time job just looking after the children.

MRS. B.: Yeah, as I told my—during the day if I try to do some big job like cleaning the Venetian blinds it takes a lot of my time. Then it takes me the rest of the day to clean up the mess the kids make while I'm working.

C.: Mmhuh.

MRS. B.: But if I have someone to help me, you know, it makes things a lot easier but—

C.: He doesn't see it that way.

MRS. B.: No. It seems that I should be able to do both.

C.: He thinks you are failing to be a good wife and mother.

MRS. B.: Yes. He thinks that the children should be under my control enough that they shouldn't get in the way when I'm busy. He thinks they should play like little angels. It kind of seems to me that whenever they do something wrong that in the back of his mind he blames me for it. Because I should have, you know, taught them better.

C.: So in the end he puts the blame on you.

MRS. B.: That's the feeling I get. I don't know if it's right or not. I think he expects too much from the youngsters. I mean he treats them and expects them to act much older than they really are.

C.: Mmhuh.

MRS. B.: He forgets they're babies. He didn't have much contact with children before he was married. He loves the kids, I know, but the only child he ever had contact with was his nephew and he always considered him a brat. So from the very beginning he wasn't going to have a brat. His child wasn't going to be spoiled. That's why he's overstrict; he's so afraid that the kids are going to be brats and—

C.:   Mmhuh. And that would be the worst thing that could happen.

MRS. B.:   Because there were so many things that his little nephew did, you know. He tells me about the things he used to do. He thought it was terrible. He thinks it was the parents' fault because they didn't teach him better.

C.:   Mmhuh. He wants to be sure your children don't turn out to be spoiled brats.

MRS. B.:   Yeah. I think that's his worst fear.

C.:   But that's not something you worry about.

MRS. B.:   Well, no, because I know—anyway, his nephew is older now and he's a perfectly respectable boy. It's just things that they go through.

C.:   It's the nature of boys to—

MRS. B.:   That's right. They don't know how to behave like adults and I don't think you should expect it all the time.

C.:   So your standards are different—

MRS.: B.: Yes, and that's something we never discussed before we were married. I guess you just don't sit down nowadays and discuss your ideas and methods of raising children. And in the first place I don't think he had any ideas until we actually had children.

C.:   Mmhuh.

MRS. B.:   And I realize that there are different problems that you have to face as children are growing.

C.:   It's pretty hard to see your attitudes ahead of—

MRS. B.:   What you do. That's right! You don't know until you have to face it yourself. And it upsets your whole life when you're constantly at odds, you know, when all your ideas are different about raising children. And things that he does just upset me so that I feel that I can't stay there and watch him do them to the kids. He insists, you know, on certain things. Like, Tommy doesn't eat well at all. He hasn't since he was a year old. I worry about it and I take him to the doctor. There's nothing you can do about his appetite, you know. He tells me and I've read it in books. They tell you not to force the child to eat. For a while he let it go, you know, accepted that you shouldn't force the child. Now he's getting so every time Tommy is irritable it's because he doesn't eat. Everything because he doesn't eat.

C.:   Mmhuh.

MRS. B.:   The other night he made Tommy sit at the table until he had finished what was on his plate. I just, I don't know, it sort of goes against me. I just can't stand to see him make Tommy sit there by himself in the kitchen and eat. The way he ate, you know, he takes a little mouthful and then gulps it to force it down.

C.:   Mmhuh.

MRS. B.:   I just couldn't stay to watch him do that because—

C.:   It's too painful an experience.

MRS. B.:   To me it is. It seems kind of silly but it just goes against me. I just can't stand to see him do that to him.

C.:   Seeing him suffer that much.

MRS. B.:   I don't know if he's suffering, but I am. I don't know.

C.:   Sort of put yourself in his place.

MRS. B.:   It seems that way. That's the way he eats now and it bothers me. He sits there until whatever it is gets cold. Then he tells him he must eat it and he'll take two or three mouthfuls and swallow them down with milk.

C.:   Mmhuh.

MRS. B.:   He'll never enjoy eating if he goes on like that.

C.:   That will only—

MRS. B.:   Make it worse. He doesn't seem to eat enough to keep him alive but he doesn't seem to suffer physically from it. *(Pause.)*

C.:   I guess if you had your way you'd let him eat what he wanted even if it seemed inadequate to you.

MRS. B.:   Yes. I don't know what else to do. I've tried tonics.

C.:   And it's your husband's feeling that he should be forced to eat.

MRS. B.:   Yeah. He has to sit there until he eats.

C.:   He's more concerned with getting the food in.

MRS. B.:   Well, he's worried that it's making, you know, him sick. He's underweight. It's not that he does it to be mean. He wants Tommy to be well and strong.

C.:   But you're really afraid that if he keeps that up, Tommy will learn to hate eating, is that it?

MRS. B.:   Yes! No! I don't know! Maybe it isn't hurting him. But it bothers me so much that I just can't stand it. I've been trying to toilet train him. I guess I don't do it right in the first place. Now, the other night, he did a bowel movement in his pants. He made him sit on the chair for an hour because he did that. He's been after the child, that's hard for him to do. He forces him to do it. And that bothers me too. I don't know if it bothers Tommy, but it bothers me. I don't know why it should.

C.:   You don't like what your husband is doing—

MRS. B.:   No, I think that he's overstern. *(Pause.)* He just did it because, you know, to help me. He wants to teach him that he should go to the toilet properly. *(Pause.)* One thing, I think he talked to the men at work and it seems like they're mostly older men who have been in the factory and they have kids, maybe eight or nine, and they tell him how they discipline their children, you know. We just can't—it just isn't the same thing. Kids are all different and different things work differently.

C.:   Mmhuh.

MRS. B.:   And besides they're older and they understand more.

C.:   And so you think he's doing what other people tell him to do rather than—

MRS. B: Yes, I think that's it. He gets his ideas from other people and you know he should try his own thinking on Tommy.

C.:   Mmhuh. *(Pause.)*

MRS. B.:   I know that a lot of it is my fault because I should have toilet trained him by this time.

C.:   You feel you've failed in this respect.

MRS. B.: Yeah. *(Pause.)* I guess I'm more easygoing. I just let things go and they take care of themselves, like eating and things like that instead of forcing.

C.: In your own mind eventually his eating and other things will more or less work out.

MRS. B.: Mmhuh.

C.: But when things have to be done on a schedule it kind of shatters your own faith in yourself, is that it?

MRS. B.: I guess that's it. *(Period of silence.)* I guess I can't stand his criticisms. It seems as though it's bothering me and I don't know why it should because while I was in nurses' training, you know how it is, there's always somebody on your neck and I never lost any sleep over it.

C.: But now it's different somehow.

MRS. B.: It seems as though I just don't like to be told. That's what he says and I guess he's right.

C.: When you're criticized it makes you feel so unworthy.

MRS. B.: I guess so. *(Period of silence.)* I guess the reason it didn't bother me when I was in training was because that's something you expect and everybody else is getting it too. You expect your supervisor to watch you and find fault. But you don't expect it from someone you love.

C.: Mmhuh. *(Pause.)* Quite a difference when it's from somebody that you love. *(Pause.)*

MRS. B.: I guess I never had much criticism from my family. At home I was the only girl with two brothers. I never got into much trouble, you know. It was always the boys who were getting it.

C.: So now it makes it hard suddenly to—

MRS. B.: I guess to have it all of a sudden. *(Pause.)*

C.: I see that our time is up for today.

COMMENTS

In this session, Mrs. Barry explores further the nature of her relationship with her husband. She realizes that their basic conflict is in child-rearing beliefs and practices. In addition, he expects her to be capable in areas which are of little interest to her. His criticisms are particularly painful and make her feel unworthy. She does not understand how someone who loves her can be so critical of her. Although during much of the hour she examines the painful nature of the relationship with her husband, she occasionally expresses confidence in herself and a belief that her way is healthier. Her husband holds her responsible for the children's negative acts but his stern and strict way causes them to rebel when he is out of sight. Throughout the session, Mrs. Barry is more controlled and organized. She seems more secure and states with more conviction her belief that children need to develop their own pace and in their own way.

The counselor worked toward sharpening the issues while leaving Mrs. Barry free to come to her own conclusions. He encouraged her to face the situation openly, to examine her feelings and attitudes, and to come to see the validity of her own thoughts.

THIRD INTERVIEW, MRS. BARRY

MRS. B.:   I don't know exactly what to talk about this time. *(Pause.)* It seems like I've been trying to realize the situation and do something about it, but I don't know how well it's working.

C.:   You've made an effort to—

MRS. B.:   Well, I try to stop and think you know and I say to myself, "Take it easy." But I don't know. It just doesn't seem to work.

C.:   Maybe you aren't the sort of person who can talk yourself into feeling calm and relaxed.

MRS. B.:   I guess so. *(Period of silence.)* My husband is working afternoons. He just started. Of course, he's home most of the day. I can see the change that comes over the house when he walks out the door. Even this morning he knew that his dad was home, that he was sleeping late. Tommy had one of his temper tantrums. It was really a doozy. When he woke up I asked him if he heard it and he said, "No."

C.:   Tommy really let loose.

MRS. B.:   But he wouldn't even think of it when his dad is watching. He's so different then.

C.:   He's one child when his father is physically present and quite different when he's not.

MRS. B.:   Mmhuh. He's more submissive, you know, when his dad's around. He doesn't show his strong will as much. In a way I wish the kids could always be like my husband says—because in a way they don't seem to mind it at all, his discipline.

C.:   They accept it.

MRS. B.:   Uhhuh—a lot of times they prefer him to me.

C.:   So it's not so much a matter of the discipline itself.

MRS. B.:   That's it. I don't know what it is. Why I can't handle them like that, and even the little one, he's beginning to catch on too, because at first I made up my mind I was going to be different with him. So as soon as he started climbing up on tables and things like that I kept after him. I'd keep putting him down and I wouldn't let it go on. But he just ignores me when I tell him to get off and when I put him down he's right back up even if I swop him. But with his father all he has to do is speak to him a couple of times and he stops.

C.:   Mmhuh.

MRS. B.:   I don't know what it is I lack.

C.:   You'd like to be a much stronger person, is that what you mean?

MRS. B.:   I'd like to have them, you know, obey me more, listen to me. I don't know they just treat me as if I weren't even there most of the time except when they want something.

C.:   They discount—

MRS. B.:   As if they didn't hear. *(Period of silence.)* As far as thinking about Tommy—as far as the right thing to do with him. I've been having trouble at night too getting him to go to bed. He'll get up and he'll get up and I'll keep putting him back in bed and spanking him and it doesn't do any good. He just gets up again. And he used to— some nights even with his dad he'd get up a couple of times. But he used to go to bed real good. *(Period of silence.)* Do you think it's because I'm an immature person myself that I can't handle the kids?

C.: I gather that's something you've considered.

MRS. B.: I've thought about everything I guess.

C.: As to why you aren't able to handle them.

MRS. B.: Mmhuh.

C.: Do you think somehow you'd become more mature if you could control your feelings better?

MRS. B.: I'm willing to try anything. *(Period of silence.)*

C.: You've looked at it so many different ways but it's hard to see any new possibilities.

MRS. B.: Yes, you kind of give up. I think that's where I am right now.

C.: Perhaps the only thing to do is to live with it. *(Period of silence.)*

MRS. B.: My husband starts after them on a number of things. I don't approve of the way he does it.

C.: He makes the situation worse?

MRS. B.: I keep telling him that eventually they'll grow out of it, but if they don't, then where will I be. *(Long period of silence.)* I just don't think that anything needs to be done about the eating.

C.: Just let him develop in his own way.

MRS. B.: Yes.

C.: But it puts you in a position where you have to disagree with your husband.

MRS. B.: Yes, he doesn't agree with me. I don't consider them problems right now. I think that by the time he goes to school, even before that he'll give it up. *(Period of silence.)* It seems as though I'm so unsure of myself. And when I do something I like to know its right. I do discipline Tommy, but I don't know if what I do is right. *(Long period of silence.)* It just seems as though I've lost the feeling of being an individual.

C.: You've lost your individual identity.

MRS. B.: It seems as though I'm fighting for it.

C.: You get caught in all these heavy feelings, in marriage and children, and sometimes you get lost in the process of living.

MRS. B.: Yes. *(Period of silence.)*

C.: Quite important being able to maintain your own individuality and your own beliefs.

MRS. B.: There's so much in one day, it takes you apart from yourself. *(Period of silence.)*

C.: I see it's time to stop.

COMMENTS

In this session there are many long periods of silence, but they seem to be times when Mrs. Barry is examining and struggling within herself, really thinking through basic family and personal issues. Again, she explores her relationships with the children. She indicates more uncertainty about her own beliefs than in the previous session. Also, she seems to be in a state of continual depression. At the end of the session, she expresses the feeling that she is fighting to maintain her own identity as a person but her problems are sometimes so overwhelming that they set her apart from herself. On the positive side, she seems to be increasingly aware of herself and recognizes the value of her own beliefs. She feels that in time the children will become more self-dependent and cooperative. Though there is still doubt, she seems to maintain some confidence in her own convictions regarding the nature of child growth and development.

Final Interview, Mrs. Barry

MRS. B.: I don't know if I'm getting used to the way Tommy acts or whether I'm just now learning how to take care of him when he has those temper tantrums, but it doesn't seem to bother me as much as it used to.

C.: Mmhuh. You're able to manage him better.

MRS. B.: At home. It's still quite difficult when we're out in front of other people. I can't do as good a job then it seems, but at home it doesn't bother me like it used to. I used to get awfully upset when he—in fact, I'd get more upset than he did, but now it doesn't bother me as it used to.

C.: Now it's easier for you.

MRS. B.: Yeah. Of course, I guess you never enjoy anything like that, but you learn to live with it and you know he will outgrow it. (Pause.) I was thinking about it before I came down but a lot of it, you know, was because I was just always afraid in the back of my mind of the harm I might do. I don't know, but it doesn't bother me as much, but, you know, afraid that whatever I did would affect the children.

C.: Mmhuh.

MRS. B.: And their habits and what they would become when they got older. I guess I was always afraid—

C.: You'd harm them.

MRS. B.: I guess so. I don't know why it bothered me so much.

C.: Fears like that can persist even though you know they're unreasonable.

MRS. B.: Yes, you're afraid to do anything almost, you know, because you think what great affect it might have on the child.

C.: You feel that everything you do is of the utmost significance. (Pause.)

MRS. B.: What I can't figure out is why it still bothers me when my husband tries to discipline the kids. Maybe when it comes down to it, if I do it, it's all right, but I don't want anybody else to discipline them, I guess. I guess I'm afraid if he really gets angry he might be too severe.

C.: That's something you can't come to terms with.

MRS. B.: Yes. *(Period of silence.)* I guess in most of the families the fathers do most of the disciplining.

C.: You don't quite agree with that practice.

MRS. B.: I don't know if I do or not. Actually, I have nothing against it. I had a very mild father myself and I never got any whippings or anything. All he'd have to do was just talk to me and I'd break down and cry and everything. He never had to spank me. I don't think he even spanked me once.

C.: So that if they're like your father it's all right for fathers to discipline.

MRS. B.: Yes, I believe it is. I don't think they should take it over entirely.

C.: But you think they often can help.

MRS. B.: Yes. In fact, I even call upon him to take a hand with the children. Still, sometimes it bothers me, you know, certain ways that he has of doing it. I just feel I guess that he gets too strict and when he gets mad you know, I'm afraid he'll spank him too hard or something like that.

C.: Sort of feeling for the children.

MRS. B.: Yes. I guess so. I turn around and ask him to take care of them and then I take their side.

C.: Sometimes it's hard to know what you want.

MRS. B.: Yes. *(Pause.)* Sometimes he'll sit down if he's not mad and talk with them. That's wonderful. You know, he has a very quick temper. When he gets mad he does things in a flash. I think he's sorry for them later and tries to make it up. When he's not mad he'll take Tommy and sit down and explain to him and talk to him and that's the way I think—

C.: It should be.

MRS. B.: Yes. If he really gets mad and does something, oh, I don't know, that I didn't approve of, like making him stay in the room for a long time or something like that.

C.: Then you can't stand to see the children suffer.

MRS. B.: I guess not, bothers me, I guess. *(Long period of silence.)* A lot of my trouble is the fact that I get upset too easily and I can't understand why. You know, I have everything and things shouldn't bother me I guess.

C.: What people say—

MRS. B.: No, things that happen when the kids do something.

C.: You react pretty completely.

MRS. B.: It seems that way. It seems like somebody is always telling me not to let it bother me but I guess it just seems to—

C.: Mmhuh. Sometimes it's hard to know why you let yourself feel that way.

MRS. B.: Yes, it is. Well, my husband and mother particularly are the ones I'm speaking of. *(Pause.)* I think that the children must sense that they can get me upset and therefore they do it.

C.: Mmhuh. They know you're an easy person to—

MRS. B.:   I think they must know it because they don't try to get away with as much with other people as they do with me.

C.:   Sort of a feeling that they can push you around.

MRS. B.:   Mmhuh. That's the feeling I get lots of times.

C.:   That you're helpless, that they can push you the way they want.

MRS. B.:   I have that feeling a lot. I just don't know what to do in certain situations.

C.:   That can be very depressing.

MRS. B.:   I guess that's just the feeling I get. *(Pause.)* And it seems to me that I was never like that before— before I was married and had children. I just accepted things as they came along, as I said before I was easy going.

C.:   You were confident in what you were doing.

MRS. B.:   Yes, it seems to me I was. I went into nurses' training as soon as I finished high school. In about six months I hurt my back, then I had to quit and go to bed for about a month or so and nothing, you know, seemed to really upset me. I went to work and back to training. Some kids used to, you know, make practical jokes and things like that and I don't think it bothered me. I can't remember ever arguing with friends.

C.:   You used to take things in your stride.

MRS. B.:   Yes, and things never used to bother me before. Just all of a sudden, that's the way it seems, every little thing.

C.:   And all this has happened to you since you've been married.

MRS. B.:   Huhha, seems that way. Of course we had, you know, the first child right away. My husband and I never had a chance to actually get accustomed to each other before Tommy was born. Then we had another child to get used to.

C.:   So there was a double adjustment.

MRS. B.:   Yes. *(Long period of silence.)* I guess all my troubles boil down to one thing, being able to control my feelings.

C.:   You think that that's at the root of the difficulty.

MRS. B.:   Yes, you know, because when he does something to the kids I get upset.

C.:   If you could control your feelings better you think you could discuss it with him.

MRS. B.:   I guess so. I think that's what I mean, control my feelings. I guess it's something inside of me but I don't want to be that way. I want to be able to talk out these problems with my husband.

C.:   Mmhuh.

MRS. B.:   But I guess I learned from experience that I can't win, so I just gave up and I quit talking. I guess I decided that it didn't do any good, you know. He always had a better argument. I just learned to keep quiet.

C.:   You let these feelings build up inside yourself. *(Period of silence.)*

MRS. B.:   It just seems that he won't listen to anything I have to say.

C.:   He doesn't consider what you say worth listening to, is that it?

MRS. B.:   I don't know whether it's just—no, I don't think that's the reason. But it seems every suggestion I make he thinks is silly. You know like I told you my solution, part of it, is to send Tommy to nursery school. He wouldn't even let me present an argument or tell him why or anything about it.

C.: Mmhuh.

MRS. B.: He just wouldn't listen. He preferred me to keep quiet. I didn't try to explain it to him.

C.: He makes up his mind and won't—

MRS. B.: Yes, I guess he thinks that a lot of the ideas I have are just silly or something—just stupid. I don't know if he feels that way because I have always felt—I don't know if he has an inferiority complex because he never even finished high school and he has to make himself feel smarter than me. I'm not saying that I am or anything because I don't feel that I am, you know.

C.: But you feel that has something—

MRS. B.: I think so. Because I know that all of my ideas are not silly.

C.: In your own mind you're pretty sure they make sense.

MRS. B.: Yes. I think we should talk about things naturally and state our own opinions. We should consider each idea and talk about it until the best solution is reached.

C.: Mmhuh. You'd like to discuss things together and work out a joint—

MRS. B.: Yes, I would. *(Period of silence.)*

C.: I see that the time is up today.

MRS. B.: Thank you for the help you have given me. This will be the last time I am able to come.

C.: Yes, I know. I'd like to say that it has been good to have had this opportunity to work with you.

COMMENTS

In the last interview, Mrs. Barry indicates that she is better able to face problems in the family and manage the children. She no longer experiences intense feelings of defeat and failure. Although many problems continue to exist, there has been a definite change in her attitude. She is learning to live with the difficulties and to react differently. She realizes that the lack of spontaneity and sureness in the relations with the children is based on a fear of damaging them.

She continues examining the different facets of her relationship with her husband and comes to the conclusion that their differences of opinion and their arguments could be resolved if they could respect each other and each other's ideas. She feels that, through a process of discussion, a joint plan of action could be determined.

The counselor's approach was to encourage Mrs. Barry to continue examining her feelings and relations as a way to a deeper understanding of the difficulties and to new ways of approaching them.

With the termination of the experience, it was apparent that Mrs. Barry had arrived at many personal insights. She felt more confident and relaxed. She saw real possibilities for resolving the conflicts with her husband and for the first time felt that harmony in the family could be achieved.

PRINCIPLES IN COUNSELING WITH PARENTS

The following principles are important considerations in counseling experiences with parents:

1. When the parent is concerned with his own self and his emotional background, when he wishes to express and explore his own personal experiences, the counselor allows this to be the focus of the counseling process. He listens in a complete, concentrated way as the parent relates the significant episodes in his life. Through his verbal comments he encourages the parent to consider aspects of the experience and the relationships which seem vague or hidden. He accepts the parent's perceptions. He expresses an interest and concern, and experiences some of the parent's suffering and pain. He shows that he cares. He experiences with the parent the depth of feeling involved, and the struggle to find pathways of relatedness to others. He believes in the parent's potentialities for growing himself and developing into a fully self-actualizing person. Counseling becomes an experience where two individuals work together to evolve an understanding of self and others and to come to recognize and bring to awareness certain relevant personal insights.

2. When the parent focuses the interview on the child and seeks advice in the management of the child and on the resolution of certain specific difficulties, the counselor discusses these concerns with the parent. He may present child development information to show behavioral patterns of average children, or in answer to direct questions when the parent is trying to see how deviant the child is from the norm. Sometimes the counselor offers a tentative explanation based on his experiences with the child in therapy, if this seems significant to the parent. Occasionally he supports the parent's view if this seems to be the only way for the parent to continue to relate to the child. When he discusses a problem with the parent he offers many possibilities and encourages the parent to explore them in the light of his own particular situation. In every case, the information is presented tentatively rather than authoritatively. No value judgments are made. Every comment is related to the parent's expression and made in the framework of the parent's thoughts and feelings. Thus, throughout the interview the counselor remains close to the parent's perception and understanding.

3. All decisions are left to the parent. The counselor may give information or even offer a number of alternatives for approaching a problem but he maintains his belief in the parent's capacity for self-dependent thoughts and actions. He struggles and lives with the parent as the parent searches for a way to come to terms with himself and to discover new meanings and patterns in his personal relationships but he insists that the parent arrive at his own choices, decisions, and conclusions.

REFERENCES

1. Fraiberg, Selma. Counseling for the Parents of the Very Young Child. *Soc. Casewrk.,* 35: 47-57, 1954.
2. Langford, William S. and Emma Olson. Clinical Work with Parents of Child Patients. *Quart. J. Child Behavior,* 8: 24-249, 1951.
3. Moustakas, Clark E. and Greta Makowsky. Client-Centered Therapy with Parents. *J. Consult. Psychol.,* 16: 338-342, 1952.
4. Newell, H. Whitman. Principles and Practices Used in Child Psychiatric Clinics. *Quart. J. Child Behavior,* 4: 57-65, 1952.

8

The Therapeutic Approach of Parents

PRINCIPLES and practices derived from child therapy offer parents an opportunity for understanding the inner world of the child. A therapeutic approach can be significant in the child's growth only when parents feel that the child is a worthy, lovable person whose presence is a source of joy and fulfillment. Parents must convey in a deep, personal sense their faith in the child as a positive, growing person and their respect for his individuality. They must accept him each step of the way and value his unique interests and peculiarities. Through their belief, acceptance, and respect, through their valuing and love, the child has the environmental conditions which enable him to realize his potentialities and develop into a self-consistent personality, a person related to others but with unique patterns that distinguish him from every other individual.

Even in the healthy family, situations arise which temporarily disturb the child and make it necessary for parents to be especially sensitive to his emotional expressions. The arrival of a new baby, movement from one school to another or from one home to another, death of a family member, separation of parents, illness, and tragedies of floods, tornadoes, and other catastrophes deeply upset and frighten children. Lack of adequate sleep, occasional fears, anger and regression, temporary difficulties in social relations, and temporary absence of friends are also upsetting conditions which require special patience and understanding on the part of the parent. Any of these situations can become a basic issue between parent and child and can develop into a serious problem. Disorganization and inconsistency in the child's behavior may result. The child's irritation, anger, and fear can become intense and prolonged unless there is particular regard for and understanding of his feelings.

A situation which creates temporary anxiety is the learning of a new skill. Unless care is taken by the parent to accept and follow the child's direction and reaction, a complex may result which spreads to other areas and makes the child feel incompetent. Learning to ride a bicycle, to swim, to use swings and slides, to play games according to specific rules and similar activities sometimes begin with strong child interest and confidence and end in the child's sense of failure and inadequacy.

The parent whose intent is therapeutic allows the child to set the pace, understands what the experience means to the child from the child's own cues and expressions, and accepts the child's feelings and words no matter how illogical or distorted they may seem. These parents listen to the child, try to understand his thoughts and feelings, and value his views. They give the child their full attention, concentrate on his experience, and empathize with him. Sometimes they convey to the child their understanding of how difficult, complex, or frightening the learning of a new skill can be. They let the child lead the way, allow him to say when he is ready for the next step, and accept his behavior as he approaches the task or problem. Throughout the experience, the parent participates as a person interested in the child's accomplishment.

Learning a new skill is the child's situation, understood and perhaps supported, but not judged or directed. If the child asks for help, the parent participates, not by taking over for the child, but by giving only the requested aid. For example, when the child decides he wants to learn to ride a two-wheel bike, the parent may have to hold the bike and go along with the child until he is ready to ride on his own. Steering, stopping, and starting are all aspects of the skill which he must realize in his own way and in his own time. Nothing can be more destructive to the child than words of criticism and belittlement, or comparison of the child with other children. He must feel the full, unqualified presence of his parents to proceed in accordance with his own readiness. Coaching and giving instructions on how it *should* be done are external to the learning situation and interfere with the child's spontaneous perceptions of his direct experience.

When the child is expressing his feelings, attempts to cut him short, change the subject, or deny their validity will create a tense and false learning atmosphere. The therapeutic approach calls for complete acceptance of the child's expressions. If he becomes frightened, his fears are recognized and accepted with a comment such as, "Sometimes it is scary," or "I know how you feel. You're afraid you may fall and hurt yourself." It may be necessary to give the child information such as, "When you want me to, I'll hold on with only one hand," or "When you're ready I'll just hold the seat," or "If you want to steer by yourself, let me know." Because parents may have to cope with the comments and advice of others, for example, neighbors and relatives, it may be necessary for the parent to support the child with comments such as, "It doesn't matter to me how Bill does it, the only thing that counts is that you learn to ride your way," or "I don't care if Suzy does start by herself. The important thing is that you learn in your own time," or "I like just the way you're doing it."

Only the child knows when he is ready to learn a new task or skill. If the parent will accept this fact and live through the child's trials, failures, fears, and irritations, if the parent listens and accepts the child's way, the child will make independent gains and achievements commensurate with his capacity. As amazing as it may seem, the child learns when he is free to learn in his own way, when he has only the help he requests, when he is listened to and respected, and when he feels he has the capacity to learn. He sometimes needs the parent to *live* with him through his anxiety in learning a complex task—a person who will share his experience and support him when others are advising and belittling.

Some time ago my daughter Wendy climbed the steps to the top of a slide. At the top she wavered, wanting very much to climb down the pole but afraid she would fall. My first response was an offer to help her down the pole. This remark upset her greatly, for it sided with her wish to slide down the pole and ignored her fear and ambivalence. I wanted her to go down because it was what she wanted and I knew she could do it. Momentarily I forgot that she had to set the pace. I had intensified her fear. She became jittery and began to cry. I told her quietly that it did not matter whether she went down the pole or not— but to *her* it mattered a great deal. I tried to minimize the significance of the situation so she would feel better, but my comment made her feel worse. Her body shook. She cried louder. It was the struggle and pain she experienced at the moment that was important, not the making of a decision. I was responding to a goal, not participating in a process. When she became hysterical, I insisted that she go down the slide the regular way hoping to escape any further need to face her struggle. She did not move or speak. At last, I realized that I had failed to accept the situation, to listen to her, to share her experience. My concern was for an immediate solution that would get us out of the dilemma, but Wendy was involved in a process and had to let the decision emerge out of her own experience. For her, the suffering was not something to be avoided but faced. Finally, I climbed to the top of the slide and said, "I know how difficult it is to decide; you want to go down, but you're afraid." Then I realized that all I could do was stand by. There was a long period of silence between us. We stood there together. Wendy crying and I waiting. Then she said, "I feel so much better inside, Daddy." She decided not to go down the pole that day, but a few weeks later when we visited the park again, she slid down the pole without any fear or hesitation.

Sharing the experience with the child and waiting for him to come to terms with it is the major requirement in resolving a disturbance caused by the conflict and stress of a temporary situation. Every parent, through listening to the child's feelings and accepting his views, by living with him in the experience, reflects a mental health attitude. Such an approach is sometimes the only way of preventing the development of a serious complex toward the learning of skills or toward approaching any potentially new experience.

Application of principles of therapy by parents frequently is in terms of temporary situations like those described. There are times, however, when problems of a more severe nature are handled, problems connected with a new baby in the family, toileting, sleeping and eating experiences, a lengthy illness, or impaired social relations.

Some time ago we brought our new baby home from the hospital. Steve who was not quite two years old became greatly upset upon seeing her. His disturbance was reflected particularly during his nap and sleep at night. He suddenly developed extreme fears of the dark, of being alone, and of flies and insects. At first we held him to the formal routine.

We put him to bed at the usual time and insisted he stay there. Each time he would get out of his crib, we would put him back. This sequence continued anywhere from ten to thirty times. We tried to be patient, talked quietly to him, but stated firmly that it was bedtime. His disturbance became more severe. He would scream, cry, pound on his crib, and shout that he would not sleep. He was awake many hours during each night. We attempted logical approaches and tried to prove to him there was nothing to fear. We put a night light in his room, took him special toys and blankets and many glasses of water. Nothing worked until I decided to share this experience with him, to live with him and with his terror and anger. I slept next to his crib for two months, listening to his fears, repeating his words and phrases, reflecting his feelings, accepting his perceptions, and supporting and comforting him. His awaking and screaming during the night gradually lessened and after about four months he was sleeping through the night. Soon he was sleeping without a night light. He rarely expressed any fear of insects. When he realized he was still a central figure in the family, not alone or forgotten but understood and loved even when he regressed, he began to express an interest in the baby and often played with her. He would occasionally express hostility against his sister, but for the most part he accepted her and expressed feelings of affection for her.

Although play itself frequently offers emotional release to the child, it is not automatically accompanied by change in attitude. The presence of the parent who encourages the child to express his feelings openly to accept the child's feelings and to share in the experience is sometimes essential. The adult should not force the child to play, probe into the meaning of the child's play, or question him, but should allow the child to express himself as he wishes and to use the play materials in his own way. Play therapy in the home is essentially a relationship between a child and his mother and father through which the child discovers himself as an important person, sees that he is valued and loved, and recognizes his irreplaceable membership in the family. It is a way through which the child opens himself to emotional expression and in this process releases tensions and repressed feelings. Through his play experiences with his parent, the child is helped to express "bad feelings" and to move toward a healthy orientation to developmental tasks and problem situations. He learns to count on regular meetings with the parent once or twice a week for one-hour periods in which he is the center of the experience. A variety of play materials are made available to him at this time: sand, water, paints, family doll figures, and other toys suitable for his interest and age. These become the media through which he expresses his feelings. The child chooses the play materials and decides how he wants to play, whether he wants to talk or remain silent. The parent does not tell him what to do, but sits nearby watching him closely and showing interest and regard.

In his play, the child expresses painful, frightening, and angry experiences. He reflects his attitudes toward his family, friends, and himself. The parent does not push his child to get started, does not question, suggest, or advise, but permits the child to decide completely, listens carefully to everything he says, and talks only when it will help the child feel that he is accepted and respected in the deepest sense. The parent sets as few rules as are absolutely necessary. For example, usually the child is not permitted to physically attack the parent, but he must be free to verbalize angry feelings against the parent.

The child will fight any attempts or plans to change him. However inadequate his behavior, it is the only way he knows and he will defend it against all pressures. He will battle his parents when they attempt to take his personal world away from him or deny the rightness or appropriateness of his feelings. Strange as it may seem, he may come to modify his attitudes if they are accepted completely and if he is free to express them. He can become more confident when the parent accepts his perception of lacking confidence. He can become less hostile when his angry feelings are accepted and recognized as valid. He can become less afraid when his fears are accepted as real. There must be a complete acceptance of his suffering and a willingness to understand and share his emotional expressions.

The parent conveys to the child a feeling of human empathy and experiences what the child feels as he plays and expresses himself. He does not avoid the child or deny his feelings in any way. Nor does he interpret the child's play but rather accepts the stated meaning.

The parent must relate to the child in the special play situation for as long as the child requires it. It may take but a few weeks or it may take many months, but parents who have tried play therapy and succeeded in sharpening their understanding and improving their relationship have felt the results were well worth the effort and struggle. Some parents have reported that the early experiences are often discouraging. It takes real faith and patience to maintain the special relationship in the light of the early frustrations and pains and the later temporary setbacks.

In the play therapy relationship created in the home, the child finds that his parent really cares, wants to understand, and accepts him as he is. He comes to realize that his parent trusts him and regards his qualities of self of ultimate and immeasurable value. The following principles reflect the essential conditions of play therapy in the home:

1. There should be a particular room, a regular meeting place which the child comes to regard as his special place to play.

2. There should be some provision for selected quantity and variety of play materials, both structured and unstructured. Unstructured items are those without any clear shape or form, such as clay, paints, sand, and water. These enable children to express their feelings without having to make concrete identifications. Frequently used structured items are family dolls, a house and furniture, puppets, blocks, darts, rubber knives, guns, scissors, paper, crayons, balloons, comeback toys, nursing bottles, and games. These are often used in dramatic play, free association and role playing.

3. Children should be permitted to express what they wish and not be obliged to follow a model or product that meets a social or art standard.

4. No attempt should be made to interpret to the child the symbolism involved in his play. Unless the adult makes the correct interpretation

(an interpretation which coincides with the child's experience at the moment), the adult may generate disturbed feelings rather than facilitate their release and resolution. The child's own judgment and expressed feelings provide the best clues to the meaning of his play. These should be accepted exactly as they are expressed.

5. The parent should listen to the child's expressions, take his cues from the child, and convey full acceptance and understanding.

Severe emotional problems and difficulties involving a prolonged history usually cannot be resolved through an application of play therapy in the family. Such problems ordinarily require intensive psychotherapy by an experienced professional worker.

EXPERIENCE OF MRS. FUCHS

Recently Mrs. Fuchs (1) published a report describing her experience, an application of play therapy in the home. I quote from this publication:

There are times when even the happy and healthy child may develop nagging fears or persistent hostilities. At such times we parents do our best by loving, cajoling, rewarding and punishing. Parents do not usually think in terms of therapy for the normal youngster, and if we did, we might not think of ourselves as possible therapists. A recent experience of mine, however, persuades me that reasonably intelligent, sensitive parents can help their children over some of the rough spots of growing up by using the techniques and attitudes of a play therapist.

Mrs. Fuchs goes on to describe the fears that Janet, her daughter, developed in connection with bowel movements and the use of play therapy in resolving this problem. A letter written by Mrs. Fuchs describes some of the significant episodes in the therapeutic relationship.

Dear Dad,

Janet's last few play-therapy sessions will interest you, I think. A week ago she started putting the clay in the toy potty-chair and said she was putting "cakes in the toilet." She put it in the toy bathtub and the little bed she calls Dad's bed. After several days of this she called it "b.m." and wanted me to eat it! I said: "I know you'd like me to eat the b.m., but I can't do that. It would give me a tummy ache. But I can pretend to eat it if you want me to." She accepted this and I munched at it in a make-believe fashion. She was quite preoccupied with the idea that "b.m.'s" come from my tummy.

During this time (about three weeks of play-sessions altogether) she has changed her attitude a lot about the toilet outside of playtime. She asked me to sit on the big toilet, which she does a couple of times a day now, though she never does anything in it. And she has tried out her own potty-chair. Before this she wouldn't go near either and the suggestion to do so was always emphatically turned down. Though I don't think I have been overanxious to toilet-train her at this age, I had originally bought the potty-chair in the hope that she would sit down to eliminate, making it easier for her. This approach didn't succeed. In fact it boomeranged and made the toilet and potty-chair places to dread.

Yesterday she got the clay and dumped it all in her own potty-chair (the real one) and said: "There are b.m.'s." Today she put some of the clay in the toilet and flushed it down, commenting on it.

The amazing thing is that she seems to have really conquered her fears in the past few weeks and it certainly shows in her behavior. She no longer makes any fuss when she does her own bowel movements. She doesn't say "hurt me" or strain while she is doing them. I have stopped giving her mineral oil and she gets along nicely without it. It is hard for me to believe after so many months of trouble with the problem that she has been able to work it out in this fashion, and in so short a time. We hope it lasts!

The final outcome of this experience and Mrs. Fuchs' assistance of a friend are presented to provide additional detail of the value of play therapy in the home.

Janet is now three and a half years old. Several things that have happened make me want to share our experience with other parents. First, Janet's troubles over her bowel movements have vanished permanently. Our results were so startling that my first reaction was, "it won't last." But it has. And there have been several times when I felt Janet might regress to her original fears. She was very upset when I made a middle-of-the-night trip to the hospital for an emergency appendectomy. Also, she might have regressed to her earlier fears when her baby sister arrived on the scene. Instead, Janet has continued to work out anxious feelings about doctors and hospitals, jealous feelings toward baby, etc., through the continued use of the special toys.

Another reason I wish to share my experiences is that I have found friends whose children have similar, if not identical, problems. These children are basically happy, secure individuals who, for some reason or other, have developed very strong emotions or fears in a particular area. Talking to a mother whose child had similar anxieties about having bowel movements and also fears about water and bathing we discussed the use of play therapy. She felt she wanted to try helping her daughter, Ellen, using these techniques and attitudes.

Until the day the mother started therapy, Ellen was cautious about water and insisted that towels, toy fish and other toys be removed far from the tub so that they wouldn't get wet. Six days later, during her special-play Ellen washed the fish for ten minutes, floated him, then submerged him, laughing all the while. Then she took a towel, started by wetting one corner, then dunked the whole thing. She wrung it out and soaked it again and again. At one point, Ellen, eyeing her mother's reaction, filled the sink until it was almost overflowing. She was apparently testing herself and the permissiveness of her mother.

In discussing this with Ellen's mother I realized that these are special problems concerning limits of play during therapy that a mother must face. Play therapy is going on in the home where there is furniture that cannot be harmed, toys that shouldn't be broken and general rules of the household. A mother-therapist does not have a special playroom where the child can do damage or feel free to express his emotions by creating an unusual mess. So the mother must be able to find ways of setting permissive limits within the confining boundaries of the home. Since we are discussing play therapy with normal children (not deeply disturbed ones) the problem is not insurmountable.

The special toys will be the only objects which the child can treat differently than his usual play things. The child quickly senses that this atmosphere is different from the usual mother-child relationship and seems to comprehend that the special toys can be broken, thrown about or mutilated. If the child includes household furnishings in his dramatic play, as Ellen did when she took her special toys to the bathroom and used real water and sink, limits must be established which will be acceptable to the mother's standards of housekeeping. A mother can reflect feelings and at the same time set the limit. To Ellen, the mother might say, "You are wondering whether or not you'd like to let the water go over the top of the sink." Ellen may look to mother, then to the sink, debating whether she dare flood the floor. The mother could interject: "I guess you might like to flood the floor but I can't let you do that. It would ruin our kitchen ceiling." If Ellen does flood the floor, the mother must turn off the water herself, though she can still understand and reflect the child's feelings in wanting to break the limit.

The general thought about limits might be that anything which would cause the mother to be upset or unhappy later should not be allowed. If the mother does get disturbed by her over-permissiveness, the child will undoubtedly sense this and feel guilty. The rule is applicable to a child who would like to hit his mother during special-play. Some mothers might not object to a physical attack by their offspring but I know that I don't like to be hit and in my own play contacts with Janet I didn't allow it. I feel this gives a sense of security to me and my child since neither of us would be happy if things got out of hand.

It is interesting to me that my own child, and Ellen in her play too, immediately felt the special-play hour was different. No lengthy explanations were needed. When a mother eliminates all value judgments, does not praise or condemn, suggest or divert her child's behavior, the child *knows* this is different. For a mother to listen carefully and watch her child's most simple play or complex emotions is probably a new and rewarding experience for her, too. Until one had tried it, it is almost impossible to realize how unusual it is simply to try to understand the child's feelings as they seem to the child without making any judgments about them. It is so unusual that a mother may find that changes have taken place within herself as a result of play therapy. After my experience I found I had greater patience with Janet and was willing to really listen to her before responding in our every day routine. I also found that while I was more capable of accepting her feelings I was also more free to express my own attitudes to her. I felt I was able to establish my own rights as a person without feeling I was neglecting my child.

It is difficult to say how or why children (or adults) respond to the therapy situation as they do. With Ellen, after about two weeks of play-therapy her attitudes about her bowel movements improved greatly (as well as those of fearing water) although she never discussed bowel movements or played out her feelings on the subject. A letter from my father* put it this way: "I can speculate to my heart's content as to what caused Janet's difficulty and what, specifically cured it, and at the end will have to admit I don't know. It confirms my feelings that though we do not know all that might be known about the process, we do know how to establish the conditions which facilitate therapy; warmth, interest, and intent to understand empathically, a willingness for the individual to have his own feelings, and in this way to be a separate person."

*Prof. Carl Rogers, University of Wisconsin.

My experience confirms this statement. I do not entirely understand what went on in Janet's mind, or in Ellen's. I only know that as a mother I was able to provide enough of the conditions of play therapy so that my child responded most constructively. Perhaps this possibility will be a useful one for other mothers to consider.

THE EXPERIENCE OF MRS. A.

The author once gave a talk to a small group of mothers, during which he presented some of the ways of understanding children's feelings and assisting them to grow emotionally. Mrs. A., one of the mothers in the group, later made an appointment with the author. During the interview Mrs. A. stated that she had never clearly understood Betty, her eight-year-old daughter. She said, "I have never really tried to understand her feelings, I guess. Maybe it was because I was afraid of them. But now I want to try and help her express her feelings more easily. I know she keeps so much to herself."

At the end of this conference, Mrs. A. declared that she would make a real attempt to listen to Betty's feelings, to accept her feelings completely, and to indicate to Betty that she understood them. Approximately four months later Mrs. A. reported the following: "You won't believe it, but quite a bit has happened to me. When I left your office I was a very determined person, but I ran into all kinds of stumbling blocks. First of all, Betty wouldn't talk about her feelings. At least, I could not detect or clearly follow her attitudes. Then one day I made a decision. I had been on the verge of carrying it out before and had thought about it a hundred times. I went to my parents' house. I told them I had something to say to them and I wanted to say it privately. I took them into the kitchen and closed all the doors and told them to sit down. I think it was the hardest thing I ever did. They looked at me in a puzzled way and wondered what in the world it was all about. After about two minutes' silence while I was struggling to hold onto myself, I finally said the words: 'I want you to know that there were many times in my life when I hated you both. I couldn't say it then, but you said many things to me and did many things to me which really hurt me, and I hated you for them.'

"Then I poured it all out to them, relating some of the incidents which had particularly affected me. To my amazement they listened, and they listened with understanding. They let me talk it out. You don't know how wonderful that made me feel. Then they told me that there were times when they hated me, too, and for the first time I was aware I was listening to their feelings. When they were through talking, we all cried, and we knew that we really loved each other. For the first time in our lives, I believe, we could be thoroughly honest in expressing our feelings toward each other, and since then we have all been much happier people.

"After this incident I seemed to be a different person. I began to see many attitudes in Betty that I never knew existed before. I had never imagined that she was so compulsive about cleanliness, yet she had been telling me in so many ways for such a long time that she was afraid to get dirty. I wrote down some things that she had said to me each day for a few weeks, and there in my notes were her fears, holding her in, preventing her from being free and warm and friendly with other children. . . .

"So I bought some finger paints and plenty of paper, and I put a large table in the backyard. We sat down together, and I said to Betty, 'Now let's make the messiest picture we possibly can.' At first it was very difficult for her. She was reluctant. She was afraid to even touch the paints, and I didn't force her. It was difficult for me, too. I never imagined it would be so hard to smear paints. In a sense, we learned to do it together, and it released a lot of the feeling inside. . . .

"As time went on, Betty began to express some of her feelings more clearly. I encouraged her to go ahead and talk about them, even though sometimes what she said was somewhat critical of me and her father. It was hard to take, but I continued to accept her feelings nonetheless, and little by little I felt her feelings change. I felt my own feelings change, too.

"It was exciting to watch Betty become freer not only at home but also in the neighborhood. She became friends with some of the children on the block and invited them to the house. She played with her baby brother more and kissed him and showed him more affection. One day she set up a table in the yard, and they finger-painted together. This was the first time she had ever shown him much attention. . . .

"Her paintings changed, too. When the messy painting first started I thought it would last just a short time, and then for a while I wondered if it wouldn't continue forever. But it changed, and she began to make very beautiful designs and wonderful arrangements of form and color.

"Betty has shown improvement in many ways. She is much warmer and affectionate toward me. It's like having a new relationship with someone you've known a long time. We're more secure with each other. I'm not so critical of her any more. I just let her be herself. It's been a wonderful experience for me. We've grown together, and I know we'll continue to grow in this way. . . ."

Here is a mother who was able to utilize the philosophy, concepts, and guides of relationship therapy. She was able in her own way to work out difficult emotional patterns with her parents and with her daughter. The process was not an easy one. It involved a strong emotional struggle and inner motivations which were maintained and strengthened even in the light of many threatening setbacks.

What happened to Mrs. A. and Betty may be considered a normal growth experience which had been temporarily shut off by harbored fears and insecurities. As Mrs. A. renewed her faith in herself as a competent mother, and as she accepted her attitudes toward her parents and respected her own judgments and values, she was able to free herself from inhibiting emotions. She was able to create a different kind of relationship with Betty. And in this warmth and inner peace, mother and daughter achieved understanding and acceptance of each other which enabled them to become happier and more creative in their relationship.

SUMMARY AND CONCLUSIONS

The philosophy, principles, and methods of relationship therapy have potential value for parents, particularly in dealing with specific areas of development in which the child seems to have strong fears or hostilities, in temporary situations such as an illness or the arrival of a new baby, in situations where the child is attempting to establish independence in eating or toileting, or where the child is learning a new skill. The situation and the problems involved determine whether the therapy need be long or short in duration and whether a formal structure or a spontaneous approach is required.

In each situation the relationship between the parent and the child is crucial. It must be a relationship in which the parent really lives with the child and shares the child's emotional experience. The child must feel free to express his feelings and must know that these expressions will be listened to, accepted, and honored. The parent participates step by step in the child's experience, conveys respect and understanding, and shows his concern for the child's pain and struggle. It is a meeting where the resources and potentialities of two persons are brought to bear in some particular area of difficulty so that eventually the tensions and frustrations are alleviated and the child's sense of self and self-consistency is restored.

REFERENCES

1. Fuchs, Natalie P. Play Therapy at Home. *Merrill-Palmer Quart., 3:* 89-95, 1957.
2. Moustakas, Clark E. *Children in Play Therapy.* New York: McGraw-Hill, 1953.

9

The Therapist and the School

RELATIONS between the therapist and the school are an essential aspect of psychotherapy with children. Through school visits the therapist can understand the nature of an experience which represents a major part of the child's life. Contact with the school makes it possible for the therapist to present to the teacher basic themes, dynamics, and underlying attitudes in the child's behavior.

The therapist's attitude in visiting the school need not be that of a consultant or adviser. His basic interest can be to understand the school philosophy and practice and how it affects the child, as well as to give information which may eventuate in positive school experiences for the child.

Many referrals for child therapy are precipitated by the child's failure or disturbance in school. The teacher may have failed to grasp the child's point of view, his personal attitudes and goals, and the conditions which impel him to behave as he does. The teacher may be a critical person, sometimes even expressing hostility and rejection in the relationship with the child. Whatever the nature of the relationship between teacher and child, the therapist must accept the teacher's feelings and encourage him to express them. If the teacher describes the child as lazy and indifferent, this is accepted. If he feels the child must be forced to learn, that he cannot escape his responsibilities, the therapist tries to understand this attitude. If the approach involves belittling, carping, and punishing the child, it is not challenged. Even when the teacher speaks of the child with disgust the therapist listens to understand, not to discredit or disapprove.

Often, the teacher wishes to help the child find his way in the classroom and wants to see him realize his potentialities. The teacher wants to understand but may be baffled or confused and unable to reach him. The therapist must have a regard for the teacher and recognize the reality of the teacher's situation. He listens with a positive feeling as the teacher relates his experience with the child. He waits until the teacher is interested or ready to discuss the child's experience in therapy. The therapist sometimes selects episodes which illustrate the child's major disturbance, how it was expressed in therapy, and the way the therapist

217

responded. From these examples the teacher may see possibilities, approaches, or methods that would be applicable in the classroom situation. The examples may serve as a basis for further discussion and interaction. Sometimes the therapist mentions his interviews with parents to communicate factors in the child's life which intensify and increase his problems or which explain his behavior. The therapist conveys enough personal data to encourage the teacher to view the child with a fresh vision, with renewed confidence, and with a belief in the child as a potentially positive person. Thus through a deepened and extended understanding of the child, teacher and therapist work together to discover ways of facilitating the child's expressions of self and the full development of his potentialities.

Sometimes the nature of the problem requires the presence of the principal and the parents. In these meetings, the therapist may take a definite stand. For example, if his experience with the child leads him to believe that failing the child would further defeat him and aggravate his disturbance, the therapist expresses this view. He makes specific suggestions when a discussion may have far-teaching consequences for the child. For example, if he knows that a particular teacher in the school relates well with disturbed children, he may suggest that the child be placed in this teacher's class.

The therapist maintains continued relations with the school. This means making regular visits during the year. The therapist discusses these visits both with the child and the parents. He meets with parents after the visit to relate his experience and sometimes to make suggestions. For example, on the basis of talks with the teacher he may recommend special tutoring, and help parents locate a qualified person.

Often the child wants the therapist to visit him in the classroom, but occasionally he opposes this. The therapist accepts whatever decision the child makes. In visiting the classroom the therapist usually sits in the back of the room, observing and listening but not participating. In some instances, however—for example, when the child or teacher insists—the therapist may join the group. In the therapy sessions, the therapist speaks of his visits only if the child initiates such a discussion.

Arrangements to visit the school are made in advance with the principal or directly with the teacher. Often the procedure involves meeting the principal first and briefly stating the nature of the visit. Sometimes the principal wishes to participate in the discussion and joins the teacher and therapist. The therapist participates in accordance with the school requirements. He responds to realities of the situation while at the same time maintaining his convictions and views. He approaches the teacher and the principal with respect for their work, acceptance of their feelings and views, and belief in their capacity to effect a healthy relationship with the child.

When there is a continuous relationship between the home, school, and counseling service, many resources become available to help the child release his tensions and frustrations and resolve his problems. When cooperation and mutuality exist among these significant persons, it is rare that the child does not begin to move in a positive direction.

But when there is an absence of positive interaction, progress is often slow and the child sometimes suffers severe setbacks.

The Experience with Dick's Teacher

The therapist called the principal of Dick's school to make arrangements for a school visit. He expressed his interest in learning about Dick's experiences in school. On the basis of the conversation, a conference was scheduled. On the day of the visit, the therapist went directly to the school office. A clerk met him and directed him to a conference room where Mrs. Armstrong was waiting. The teacher began talking immediately, saying, "Dick is the laziest child I have ever known." Then she read from her notes, "He's good-natured but never completes his work. He sits all day looking out the window and daydreaming. I stand right over him and order him to work. He makes some effort to do the assignment. He is yelling more and more and is behind in school. He has no friends and is interested in no one. He is so indifferent and unresponsive nobody cares about him."

Mrs. Armstrong brought out a sheaf of Dick's papers—all were incomplete and all were marked with failing grades. Next, she showed the therapist the grade book. Most marks were low. But the therapist noted two scores, one 91 and the other 99, as he looked down the column of grades. When he asked about these, Mrs. Armstrong minimized their value. They were scores on bi-weekly unit achievement tests covering skills in reading and arithmetic. The therapist wondered whether the grades on the comprehensive examinations did not indicate that Dick listened more than was apparent. Mrs. Armstrong dismissed this possibility. She went on to say that, apart from everything else, Dick was a slow learner. She referred to an intelligence test score which classified Dick as "borderline" mentality. The test had been given three years previous, when Dick was six years of age. Mrs. Armstrong felt strongly that Dick belonged in a lower grade. She asked the therapist if he had learned anything that would explain Dick's "extreme laziness." The therapist gave a brief account of his relationship with Dick, showing that his experience reflected a very different pattern. In the therapy situation, he was beginning to be active and interested. He stated that because Dick had defeating and belittling self-attitudes he needed positive recognition and acceptance. He was rarely indifferent when approached in this way. When he initiated a project in therapy he saw it through to completion. The therapist wondered whether the difference in his behavior in school and in therapy might be understood in terms of his need to be recognized as a worthy individual, to be free to make decisions and to set his own pace. He expressed his belief that if Dick could feel more self-confident in school he would show more interest in his academic work.

Continuing his report to the teacher, the therapist mentioned that Dick's father consistently criticized Dick for being lazy and irresponsible. Dick had come to believe this himself. Gradually he withdrew from most family activities to solitary endeavors and daydreaming. Both parents had only recently come to realize that Dick's perception of himself

as an inadequate, unlovable person resulted from their treatment of
him. They wanted to change their relationship with Dick and both had
become involved in a counseling experience.

Mrs. Armstrong responded to this report by saying that, where the
parents had failed, she could succeed. Her plan was "to make" Dick industrious and responsible. On two occasions, Mrs. Armstrong had so
upset the parents they were unable to eat or sleep. To avoid further suffering, the therapist asked her not to send notes to them or call them.
Mrs. Armstrong agreed to discuss problems with the therapist before
she made reports to the parents. The therapist left the school feeling
somewhat discouraged. He had failed to meet this teacher. Nothing he
had said had touched her or influenced her attitude. She was determined as ever to *force* Dick to give up his "lazy, irresponsible attitude."

The therapist made two more visits to the school during the semester.
The second trip was similar to the first. There had been no change. Mrs.
Armstrong felt that Dick was even more withdrawn, indifferent, lazy,
and irresponsible. The therapist suggested that perhaps pressuring and
criticizing him made the problems more severe, made Dick feel he could
never meet school standards. Mrs. Armstrong discounted this possibility
and indicated that she was now convinced that his attitudes were
caused by a deficient mental capacity. The therapist pointed out that
Dick's vocabulary, sentence structure, and ability to solve problems indicated at least average mental ability. Mrs. Armstrong maintained her
conviction saying that test data in the school records were reliable. The
therapist suggested that another intelligence test be administered. Mrs.
Armstrong agreed that a new rating would be helpful. Although the
teacher finally agreed to a new test of intelligence, the therapist left
with a feeling that he had again failed to share a real experience with
Mrs. Armstrong. The therapist, although philosophically opposed to
testing and evaluation, decided that another rating might convince Mrs.
Armstrong that Dick was not a mentally slow child and might lead her
to view him with a fresh perspective.

The therapist arranged for the administration of the Wechsler Intelligence Scales for children. The following excerpts from the examiners report were presented to Mrs. Armstrong in the final meeting, which took
place near the end of the school semester.

Dick was seen on two occasions to complete the administration of the test.
On the first occasion, he was anxious and easily distracted from the test
items. In many ways he tried to evade what was obviously a trial for him —
by talking, moving about the room, looking out the window, etc. In each
case, however, it was possible to bring him back to the task at hand. On the
second occasion he seemed relaxed and able to concentrate at length on
some tasks.

Because Dick was curious about "what was in the box," the performance
items were administered first— this was perhaps unfortunate as he did less
well on these tests and was in part upset by an awareness that he failed
some items. On the verbal scale he was more successful and seemed to feel
less pressure. He was constantly upset by the pressure of finishing an item
within definite time limits. He frequently needed encouragement and with

this often was able to go ahead and successfully complete an item which he at first felt was too difficult for him.

With the Full Scale IQ, this boy is presently functioning within the average range of intellectual ability. However, there are several indications of a higher potentiality which suggest that under more favorable circumstances in his life situation, he might be able to function more nearly at his capacity which is probably considerably higher. It might be well to point out some of these indicators.

(1) The deviations of subtest scores, which range from a low of 7 to a high of 13. If a score of 10 be taken as average (a score of 10 on each subtest would yield an IQ of 100), it can be seen that his scores vary considerably around this. Such marked variation is usually an indication of anxiety which impedes the free use of the particular function. It should be noted that most of his lower scores are on timed tests, and his reaction to timing and the pressures it seems to exert on him has been noted above.

(2) The high score of 13 was achieved on the Information Test which correlates most highly with general intelligence. This is a test of general information, of knowledge which a person absorbs from daily living. This is an untimed (and hence for him without pressure) test, and it should be noted that Dick's functioning here is at a superior level—and this is with rather strict scoring, as there were several items on which he had the general idea, but not sufficiently adequate to be given credit. From this it can be inferred that he is alert and learning much in his casual day-to-day contacts.

(3) The subtests each begin with easy items then become progressively more difficult. On almost every test, Dick would become momentarily flustered and fail some very easy items, and then go on to achieve success on a much more difficult item. Here again we see some of the effects of fear which would upset the use of his intellectual function.

(4) Besides the factor of time, there seems to be another factor contributing to the discrepancy between Verbal IQ and Performance IQ. The Performance tests are all tasks involving some kind of manipulative skills. Dick is not a child who uses his hands easily—he wastes motions and does not seem to enjoy this kind of activity. This may be an inherent thing with him, or it may simply be a developmental stage of growth which shows itself in some muscular clumsiness.

In view of these comments, the question of the validity of this test might be raised. It is my belief that under the circumstances, Dick did the very best that he could. The test situation undoubtedly represented a similar structural kind of learning situation which he fears in school. Instead of competing with other children, here he competed with time with similar reactions of fear of failure and partial immobility.

It is my opinion that with some discerning help Dick could begin to realize some of his innate capabilities. It would require patience and the relieving of competition as much as possible. He needs acceptance of the successes he does achieve and time to work things out for himself at his own speed. In this kind of milieu, he might even begin to enjoy making things and doing things involving muscular skills. At any rate, it would provide a favorable environment in which he could learn and grow more into his real intellectual capacities.

Mrs. Armstrong read the report but made no comment on either the results or the recommendations. She had already come to a conclusion about Dick and his ability. The test data did not influence her attitude.

She told the therapist she had decided to fail Dick. In spite of the arrangement, she had sent a note to Dick's parents the previous afternoon indicating that Dick would be failed. The therapist told Mrs. Armstrong that the note would greatly disturb the parents. He pointed out that failing Dick would only increase his feelings of inadequacy and worthlessness and compel him to continue to be "lazy" and indifferent to school work. She stated that failing him was the only choice she had. She brought out the evidence in the form of Dick's papers. He had continued to get high grades on the bi-weekly examinations but failed to do the daily assignments. The therapist pointed out that his high scores on the tests indicated he had successfully achieved the required abilities of the grade. This was confirmed by the results of the standardized achievement test given at the end of the semester by the teacher herself. Mrs. Armstrong commented with finality, "It would be unfair to the other children to pass him. It's time he learned that his laziness and irresponsible behavior will not be tolerated."

In spite of his disagreement with her, the therapist believed that she had acted in terms of her own convictions. Since he still felt that failing Dick would be detrimental to him, he suggested further discussions with the principal of the school. Mrs. Armstrong refused to participate in any more discussion. She said, however, that she would change her decision and pass Dick on the principal's recommendation. This shift in attitude troubled the therapist. She was unwilling to pass him on the basis of intelligence and achievement test results, but would do so on the advice of the principal. The therapist talked with the principal again, presenting the available data and recommending that the question be reconsidered. The principal stated firmly that Dick would be failed because in her school children were passed on daily results, not on potentiality or on occasional demonstration of ability. She indicated that Dick had to learn a lesson. The therapist asked about Dick's placement the following semester and was referred to the assistant principal. After further discussion, it was agreed that Dick would not repeat the grade with Mrs. Armstrong but would be placed with a teacher who was concerned not only with subject matter but with the individual child. The assistant principal suggested a person who placed personal growth above achievement of discrete skills.

Dick entered Mrs. Siebert's room the second semester. The therapist decided not to visit the school until teacher and child had ample opportunity to establish a relationship in their own way and on their own terms. The therapist made two visits to the school. On the first visit, Mrs. Siebert said she was surprised that Dick had been failed. There was no question that he could do the work. She said he needed a little encouragement from time to time. He always completed the daily assignments and enjoyed being given special responsibilities. Dick received A grades in handwriting, arithmetic, reading, and spelling during the first marking. He maintained this average throughout the semester. In the playroom, he often spoke of his teacher and always in positive terms. He spoke about his school work with enthusiasm. At the end of the term, Mrs. Siebert indicated that Dick was not only alert and interested in the work but was one of the most active and industrious children in her group. He was in the top reading and arithmetic groups. She was certain he would have no difficulty in the next grade and recommended a teacher who followed a similar philosophy and practice. On her own, Mrs. Siebert had sensed what was required to bring about a change in Dick's attitude and behavior. Whereas his previous teachers had failed, she was able to relate with him in such a way that he could realize his potentialities for superior academic work and for positive social experiences.

THE RELATIONSHIP WITH STEWART'S TEACHER

During the course of Stewart's therapy experience, the therapist established relationships with three of his teachers. The first, Mrs. Johnson, worked with him on an individual tutorial basis three mornings a week, in her home. This work was sponsored and supported by the public school in his community. The therapist visited the public school every two months. The principal always participated in the discussions. The first few meetings were crucial ones, as Mrs. Johnson doubted that she could teach Stewart anything. She felt that Stewart was a hopeless, uneducable child. She was frightened of him because he "growled like an animal" and tried to bite her. She was fearful too that he would destroy the furniture and other items in her home. In the first meeting the therapist presented data to show that Stewart had potentialities for learning. He was a child of peculiar preferences, interests, and ways. He resisted and fought people who tried to force him to participate in activities but was interested and willing to learn if given an opportunity to explore his own wishes and thoughts. In early months, he often expressed hostility toward women and attacked them by kicking and biting. He enjoyed hurting women who were afraid of him. He got more satisfaction in watching them suffer than in hurting them physically. The therapist briefly explained the nature of Stewart's relationship with his mother toward whom he expressed considerable hostility. He suggested to Mrs. Johnson that she refuse to permit his attacks and set limits firmly and consistently. The principal supported the therapist in this view. She had observed Stewart in situations where the firm limit was accepted but the uncertainly stated rule ignored. After this first meeting, Mrs. Johnson had no further difficulty with Stewart's aggressiveness and no fear of working with him in her home. Her belief in his potential for learning wavered from time to time, but in each meeting she presented a considerable number of papers which showed Stewart's progress. Although she occasionally raised questions about his potentiality, when either the principal or therapist raised any doubt she defended Stewart with evidence of his accomplishments. The therapist supported Mrs. Johnson's efforts and expressed his valuing of her work.

In these meetings, the teacher presented her experiences with the child partly to convey his progress and partly to understand more clearly the nature of her relationship. She sometimes asked, "Where do we go from here?" but usually offered several ideas before the therapist or principal could respond. Occasionally, she asked the therapist specific questions about Stewart's behavior which the therapist discussed with examples from his experience in therapy. The meetings offered Mrs. Johnson an opportunity to relate her experience with Stewart, to express her reservations as well as her hopes, and to be encouraged and supported by two persons whom she respected. Mrs. Johnson was helped to understand the basis of Stewart's behavior, to develop methods of presenting learning materials to him, and to use a positive, though firm and consistent, approach in limiting his destructive behavior. She was able to gain support, inspiration, and courage and to face with new vigor the complex and difficult task of helping Stewart learn.

Next, Stewart was enrolled in a private school for exceptional children. The therapist visited this school two times. In the first of these meetings, the teacher doubted that Stewart would be permitted to continue in the school. The same problem had arisen. Mrs. Hines was having difficulty in managing him. Again the therapist explained the background and value of setting definite limits with Stewart. He indicated that none of the adults who had previously worked with him had difficulty as long as he or she adhered to the necessary approach. Stewart at first attempted to violate the limits, but when the adult insisted on maintaining them, he was happy to cooperate. During the next several months, Mrs. Hines had positive experiences both in limiting Stewart and in assigning school tasks and responsibilities. It was possible gradually to increase his school schedule so that after two months he attended school for the full morning and afternoon sessions every day.

Mrs. Hines spoke positively of Stewart's progress. He participated cooperatively in the program which included work with jig-saw puzzles of varying difficulty, singing, games, and writing letters, drawing pictures, and illustrating letters and words. She considered him one of the most cooperative children in the room. Mrs. Hines seemed confident in her relationship with Stewart. When she developed a plan of work which was being successfully achieved, further visits by the therapist were unnecessary.

After one year in the private school, Stewart entered a public school near his home. The therapist had two contacts with his new teacher, Miss Strang. In the first visit (Stewart's second day of school), the therapist explained the importance of establishing firm, clear limits. Three months later the teacher reported that she had had no difficulty with Stewart. He participated in group activities and accepted the rules of the school. Miss Strang kept a journal of notes describing her experience with Stewart. She presented these notes to the therapist and mentioned the many positive changes which had occurred in Stewart's behavior since the beginning of the year. Although Stewart was often a challenge to her, she felt satisfied with his progress. Following this talk the therapist decided there was no further need for regular visits to the school but indicated his availability whenever the teacher wanted a conference.

The Therapeutic Relationship in the Classroom

The teacher is in a position to help individual children to come to be themselves by enabling them to express their feelings openly and freely, by accepting their feelings and showing that they are completely understandable. The teacher can help the individual child by being willing to share and explore with him his crucial emotional experiences. A previous publication (5) of the author gives a detailed account of how teachers recognized and responded to children in significant personal relations in elementary and secondary schools. Sometimes these special classroom relations can be stimulated by the therapist's interaction with the teacher. Through such interaction a teacher was able to evolve a significant personal relationship with a high-school student interested in becoming a teacher. The impact of this personal relationship on an adolescent boy headed for delinquency and school failure is contained in the youth's own story written to his teacher.

I said a juvenile delinquent at sixteen? That was a mild statement. At that time I was so full of hate that my entire self was involved in the expression of it: dislike and revolt against school, parents, friends; hurting the people I liked most—deliberately hurting them to make them "pay" for what hurt me. I stayed out late because it worried my mother. I got poor grades in school because this was the way I felt I could "get at" my dad. I fought teachers because I hated them. I hated them because of my previous experience with two particular teachers. I belonged to nothing; I joined nothing because I was afraid of being rejected. Later I ran around with "the boys," because at least they were socially honest.

Economically I was neither in the poor class or the middle class. My father has worked for Ford Motor Company for 43 years. At the present time he makes eight thousand dollars. Though this is now a fairly decent wage, try stretching it over nine kids. Buy a house, insurance, and pay the doctor bills for a wife who ended up in the hospital twice a year like clockwork.

So I went without new clothes and baseball mitts and spending money. When my friends had money for shows, candy, and comic books every week, I had to satisfy myself with a show once in a while and a box of popcorn. There were other repercussions from these money problems. When my friends had new jackets, I was wearing a hand-me-down; when they were wearing slacks, I was wearing jeans; the first suit I owned, I bought. I was seventeen. To say I wasn't bitter because of those things would be fantasy. Sure I felt sorry for myself. How would you feel going to a school dance wearing your older brother's slacks, that were three sizes too big, a white shirt, the arms of which became caverns for your hands, feeling and looking more like a circus clown than anything else?

What turned me against school and any authority? I think I've been able to narrow it down to two people: the teacher I had in the 1st grade and the teacher I had in the 2A. The first started it; the second clinched it. Of all the unhappy experiences I had in the first grade, one always stands out in my mind. We had reading every day. We read from special story books in special groups. One day I was doing something—I don't remember what it was, but this teacher said before I went on with it I should study the reader. As it was, I had already read the story and was sure I knew it so I told her so. She said when reading time came, I had better know it. Well reading time came and my turn came, and I stumbled on a word—one lousy word! She was infuriated, and said I hadn't studied the lesson. I said I had and she knocked me backwards over two rows of chairs. A real nice experience with teachers!

The second teacher I had in the 2A had a reputation for being rough. When I transferred from the 2B to 2A and found I was to have her for a teacher, I told myself I was going to get along with her. I did for about 6 weeks until she began blaming me for things I didn't do.

I can't remember her name, but I remember her as a small woman with black hair and glaring eyes. I hated her guts. I still hate her guts. As a result of our beautiful teacher-pupil relationship, I was passed on probation into the third grade and six weeks later was promoted to the 3A, which points up the fact that either I was a nasty pupil or she was a lousy school teacher.

I have always wanted one thing above all others, recognition from Dad. Until recently, I never felt that I was receiving this recognition. I say recognition because that is what it is; not attention, or affection, or companionship, but the plain and simple acknowledgment of accomplishments whether good or bad. But the complete passivity with which anything I did was received by Pa nearly drove me nuts! He has never told me that I've done a good job at anything. And believe me, there were times when I would have cut off my right arm to hear those very words.

It was, in my opinion, this eternal frustration of my attempts to be recognized by Dad that was the biggest factor in my maladjustment. In the winter I shoveled the walks and he said nothing. In the summer I mowed the lawn and he said nothing. I cleaned the basement and he said nothing. I was quiet and nothing, I was aggressive and loud and nothing. I got good grades—nothing. I got poor grades—nothing. I started earning my own money so that he wouldn't have to give me any, and there was nothing. I started painting houses when I was 14 and had a small business of my own by 17 and still nothing. No matter what I did he never seemed to care one way or another. All right, now I realize in his own way he was proud of me and what I had accomplished. But try to convince a kid that someone knows you're alive if he never outwardly shows any knowledge of your presence.

The predictability of the outcome of such a relationship is quite plain. I, over a period of time, began to feel that he didn't want me around. At first this was manifested as resentment toward those people in my environment who I felt stood between him and the kind of relationship I so needed. In time, the resentment turned to anger and then to hate and bitterness. And in time I came to conceive of him as being stubborn, cruel, miserly, and unreasonable in the demands he made on others, though now I realize that his rejection of me was unintentional; that his stubbornness was the sum total of his own experiences.

I was jealous of my youngest sister because I could see in her those things I wanted most. She received the recognition from Dad that I wanted and needed. She was automatically given those things I never felt capable of asking for. It was automatic that she should have piano lessons and dancing lessons and flute lessons, etc. I wanted to play the piano so bad that at times I experienced physical pain because I couldn't and still I never asked for piano lessons. It took a long time before I was able to think of her in terms other than anger— to forgive her for existing.

And what of my two brothers? I resented Bill for two reasons. As "Papa's pet," what he did was good, no matter what it may have been. And secondly, because he used his position to "lord" over the rest of us. If he didn't like the radio program that was on, he turned it off disregarding the wishes of the rest of us. And he did this with the complete confidence that there would he no repercussions.

Bob, I disliked for something else. He needed the assurance that Dad needed him, depended on him. This he never received. However as he saw Bill getting the response or attention he so desired he attempted to gain Bill's position by copying him, but in Dad's eyes what he did was wrong. Therefore he was punished for what Bill got away with.

Still needing the same assurance of being needed, Bob began to get into trouble. In this way, he might get recognition. The more trouble he got into, the more he was rejected by Dad—a vicious circle. What troubles me here is that though I held a great deal of bitterness towards Dad, I still became angry about what Bob did. I became angry because, I think, I felt that what he did was hurting Dad. The animosity between us two took a long time to reach a climax, and it is so deeply rooted in our personalities that there exists between us a concrete wall six feet thick; a wall I have been chipping at for a couple of years now and hope eventually to crumble.

At eighteen, I looked upon the world as being rotten. I looked upon people, all people, as being against me. I felt that people disliked me for no reason; that to protect myself I must be continually on guard, and that I must always strike the first blow, before anyone or anything had the chance to hit me.

I refer back to seventeen and eighteen because it was then that a tremendous transition began taking place within me. Though I should like to say it was you who initiated this transition, I can't. It started perhaps eight months before you. However, it was through you that I was able to see myself and my reactions toward the people around me more clearly. It was through you I gained confidence in myself.

Back a few paragraphs I said I had a small painting business of my own by the time I was seventeen. Well, it is here that I first began to change from a juvenile delinquent to what I am now. As I said I was painting. I was painting in hopes that Dad would compliment me on my ability and he never did. But it was while on the ladders that the change first began.

Painting is like any other production job. And when you no longer have to think about what you're doing, you begin to think about your life. My mind wandered around for a bit on my past. I began to analyze what I had done and why, but never seemed to come to any conclusions. I suddenly realized how precious time is. This awakening was perhaps the greatest thing that ever happened to me. I had spent a good deal of time running over the things I had done during my past. I was able to see a relationship with what I was. I had spent three years in high school and was a half grade behind. Though I hated teachers, my attitude towards them was what held me back—not them. It was this admission that began setting my mind to the fact that perhaps it was not everyone else who was wrong, but me.

I went back to school in September not knowing where I was. Not knowing whether I should change or whether I was right about people.

For a long time I had been interested in teaching, but because of my feelings towards school, I never expressed it. Now I did, partly because the Future Teachers Club offered two half days off each month and partly because of my thoughts about teaching. So if I didn't like it, I wouldn't be losing anything. I didn't make a mistake on this decision. In fact I think it was the luckiest thing in my life because through it I met you. For the first time, I found someone who accepted me for myself, who didn't give a damn whether my hair was shaggy or whether my shoes were polished. You listened to me. You were interested in what I said and what I felt. I could talk to you when before I had never been able to talk about myself to anyone. By talking about myself and the people in my environment, I slowly came to see them as human beings. I came to understand and know myself, and see more clearly the problems of others. In a sentence, you opened for me a whole new world where there existed decency, and where there was a place for me.

I've been lucky many times in my life. I was lucky when the scoop of the steam shovel went only part way through me and not all the way. I was lucky when I didn't die of rheumatic fever or when I wrecked the '40 Ford or when Dad wrecked the Victoria. I think about those things now and get the feeling that God was looking over my shoulder. I know damn well I was lucky when I walked into your room at the Washington School. On the other side of that door was, for me, a new meaning to life, a new and brighter understanding of myself and the people around me.

What happened to me in the next few months, as a person, is the most important sequence of events in my history. I'm not perfect now nor was I then, and like most people, I had certain prejudices. You are a Jew. At first I wasn't sure whether to let my feelings about Jews commandeer my intelligence; but, thank God, my better sense won in this battle of ignorance. You destroyed in a short time any animosity I may have had for you because of your race. If nothing else ever comes of our relationship if I slip back to the old plan or if I don't succeed in becoming a teacher, I will never forget one thing that I learned from you—that we are all human beings, whether black, yellow or white, whether Irish, Swedish or Jewish, and as such, we are all equal whether it be in the sight of God or our fellow man.

This I state first although it didn't come until I had known you for some time. But I feel it is the most significant transformation in my life. However, what you did for me in my search for peace of mind should not be lessened. When I met you, I was in the most confused state I had ever been in. I was failing in school, the relationship with my family was negative; towards school, negative; towards people in general, negative. I hated Dad and the rest of the family, because I felt I was being left out and blocked in my attempts at winning Pa's respect and friendship. I hated school for the reasons I stated before, and I hated everyone because I was continually frustrated every time I tried to make friends. To put it in words is a little difficult, but because of the responses I kept getting from the kids, I protected myself by disliking them and eventually my actions toward people became a sort of "revenge." Of course, this came after I tried everything else from supplying them with spending money to acting the clown. How is it then, that this animosity between myself and others no longer exists? This is the result of your influence. I use influence here in a restricted sense. By that I don't mean it was your advice as to what is right or wrong, or to what you thought I should do, but by your presence I came to know what was real and what was right.

The way you led me into coming to the right solutions was beautiful. You never said, "It's this way," or "This is what I'd do, but "How do things stand with you?" or "What do you make of it?" "What do you want to do?" "How did you do it?" You let me talk to you. I'd like to cite an example.

I was flunking Biology. I was flunking it not because I didn't like the subject matter, but simply because I didn't like the teacher. So what did I do?— I did my damndest to make the teacher look like a fool. And brother, I was pretty successful. But, what was happening to me in the process, I was failing a class that should have been a snap.

I told you how much this teacher rubbed against my grain. I felt he was a four flusher and a conceited jerk. There were many talks about this teacher and his teaching methods. What we talked about, I can't remember, but I came out of it with the decision to try to get along with this teacher. One thing about our talks. I said the teacher was picking on me; that he was out to get me; and that he would never call on me in class. You asked me how I would feel toward a student who was an everlasting heckler. I thought about it a while and finally decided that perhaps I wasn't being fair, and that although this particular person wasn't the best biology teacher I'd ever seen, he did have a case against me. It was then I decided to leave him alone and to try to learn something in the class. This is quite important because I also decided that if I succeeded here I would also try it in my other classes. There was more than one class I failed or nearly failed because I didn't like the instructor.

I began by apologizing to him for the way I'd been acting. It was pretty hard to do because it was the first time I'd ever apologized to anyone. I began letting him alone in class; and though I slipped at times, I did fairly well. The change didn't take place over-night. There were times when it was one hell of an effort to keep my mouth shut and ears open, but it paid off. The teacher began calling on me more and more, and when I raised my hand, he no longer shirked with the thought of recognizing me but came to respect my questions and me. The funny thing is, and yet not so funny, that I came to recognize him as a human being and though I still think he is a poor teacher, he turned out to be a pretty nice guy. This, I think, was the first class in which I learned anything in the three years I'd been in high school.

Needless to say, I tried this experiment in other classes after the first success and found that all teachers weren't as rotten as I presupposed. I'm still learning.

I think through my talks with you I came to realize my Dad wasn't the ogre I'd built him up to be. I guess our discussions, and rather one sided discussions, must have run into hours. I told you how he treated everyone else in the family. I told you how he treated Ma, and how I loathed it. We talked about the rest of the family, all of them.

All these things I told you. I don't know when. I don't even know exactly how, but a new idea, a new conception of Dad began to form in my mind. I began to ask myself if I were being fair in my judgments, and if he gave me the impression that he didn't like me, why? Was it something in me, or something in him or his background that made him act towards me the way he did?

Answers came out in my talks with you. That the feeling I have towards him now came about over-night is untrue. It was a slow and painful process. Slow because I had to analyze everything he'd ever done. I had to weigh his past history with what happened in the present. I had to weigh what other people of my family had done with what I wanted to do. Sometimes it took a long time to figure out why this was a particular way and then sometimes the answers came so quickly and suddenly, it was like opening a door that had been sealed shut for years and a great gust of light would burst out which would in turn answer hundreds of other questions. Painful because each time I discovered some new piece of evidence justifying his actions, or each time I had to come to a new decision about him, I had to discard an idea that protected me from what seemed like the unbearable truth. Eventually I saw that I must accept as fact that I could and would never hear a word of praise from my father, that I would never be top man in his eyes, that it was more the way he was than any feeling against me.

It has been only a comparatively short time since I got on the right track, since I've been able to live with myself and the people in my environment. I am learning how to make friends. I'm learning how to live. Dad and I talk to each other now. Not all the time, but enough so that when we do, the talks are enjoyed by both of us. The old bitterness still creeps up now and then but infrequent enough so that I look forward to the time when it will only be a memory.

What did the relationship mean to this person? Through the relationship he came to a new respect, recognition, and awareness of others. He realized a new meaning to life. He came to understand and know himself and to accept all individuals as persons regardless of their color, creed, or national origin. He came to regard himself as a worthwhile person and gained confidence in himself. John had found someone who didn't care whether his hair was shaggy or his shoes polished, someone interested in him, someone who cared about him and his experiences, someone who would listen. By talking about himself with his teacher, he slowly came to see each person in his life as a human being. He came to see his problems more clearly and to recognize the members of his family as they really were.

Through the presence of the teacher, John came to know what was real and what was right. He discovered what he wanted to do. His teacher never advised or urged him, never told him what to do, but rather he asked John to consider his own wishes and his own perceptions in making choices and decisions. And he listened with complete attentiveness. He met John squarely. In short, he recognized him as a person and listened to him with utter respect where others had always looked around him and by him. Others had looked everywhere but in his direction. His teacher directly faced John in a valued personal relationship.

CONCLUDING COMMENT

It is rare that the classroom teacher is not open to the development of a positive relationship with the child. Many teachers have no formal preparation for understanding the disturbed or different child but they want to relate to the child as a person and help him to develop and grow in a positive direction. Some teachers immediately sense the importance of understanding the child's feelings and perceptions, his subjective experience. They want to help the child discover his real self, to see the child come to be a happy person and find a right way of life with other children. They find too that, as they extend their insights in these relationships, their own attitudes change. They come to value the child's difference as a unique attribute, something to be recognized and honored, treated with respect, rather than something to be sublimated, rejected, or changed. A teacher who had suffered greatly in her first meetings with a child wrote:

I tried everything I have heard of in working with him, nothing seemed successful. He had nothing to do with me. There was nothing but a negative relationship between us. He was alone in the group and blamed me for everything that happened. He was sulky and moody. I punished him every day, but it rolled off like water off a duck's back. One day he was hurt. He had bumped into a table and ran off to the closet by himself. I wandered in and talked to him for a while and told him I realized how much he must feel hurt. He stopped crying and for the first time since he came into my room he smiled at me, weakly. He hobbled over and shoved his hurt leg at me. I rubbed it while he sat silently. Then he took my hand and together we left the coat room. Perhaps in those few moments, he discovered there was someone who cared about him and his feelings. It was the beginning of a new relationship, one which not only promoted happiness between us, but affected all the children in the class.

The teacher's experience with the unusual child is an opportunity to realize hidden potentials, for releasing powers in another human being, for stretching unused resources for personal relatedness, and for discovering new value in teaching. The therapist's relationship with the teacher is also an opportunity not only to foster a healthy approach to the child in the classroom but also to gain an understanding of the realities with which the classroom teacher must live and an insight into the child's world in school.

REFERENCES

1. Axline, Virginia M. Morale on the School Front. *J. Educ. Res., 37:* 521-533, 1944.
2. Axline, Virginia M. *Play Therapy.* Boston: Houghton Mifflin, 1947.
3. Baruch, Dorothy W. *New Ways in Discipline.* New York: McGraw-Hill, 1949.
4. Driekurs, Rudolf. *Psychology in the Classroom.* New York: Harper, 1957.
5. Moustakas, Clark E. *The Teacher and the Child.* New York: McGraw-Hill, 1956.
6. Prescott, Daniel A. *The Child in the Educative Process.* New York: McGraw-Hill, 1957.

10

"Supervision" of Students in Child Therapy

To be an alive experience consistent with the philosophy and value of psychotherapy, meetings between the "supervisor" and the student must contain the dimensions of a truly human relationship. This means the supervisor maintains a belief in the student's potential for growth as a therapist with children, respect for the student's perceptions of the nature and meaning of his experiences, and acceptance of his particular way of approaching the child and relating to him.

In a philosophy of self-growth, the student is not trained. He is offered or presented possibilities for growth, i.e., resources for self-development in a particular area of professional endeavor. The student is not supervised. He meets with another person whose background of therapeutic experience may serve as a source of information and knowledge. The only real growth is the student's self-growth as a person and as a professional worker. This the student must do himself. The supervisor participates in the process as a way of presenting a philosophical basis for therapy—not to influence or mold the student, not to direct his behavior or convince him of its validity, but only to point to one basis for understanding the therapeutic process in psychotherapy with children. The manner in which the supervisor presents his philosophy to a significant degree determines whether the student is free to examine his own thinking and experience and to develop a meaningful set of concepts and principles which for him form a responsible basis for child therapy. If the student is interested, he should be encouraged to explore different theories and to examine his own experience as a basis for therapeutic work. It is of utmost significance that the student recognize and be aware of the process of therapy in which he is participating.

Orienting the student to a philosophy of therapy as a way of initiating his self-education is generally a first step in "training" the student for professional responsibility as a child therapist. The philosophy should include principles and concepts of health, growth, and creativity as well as concepts of pathology and psychosocial illness. The student should be given ample opportunity to raise questions, discuss ideas, and examine various theories presented in the literature. When the student fully understands a theory of child therapy, the next step is to provide him with opportunities for observing normal, disturbed, and creative children of different ages and from varied environmental situations. Time should be available to discuss the observations immediately after a therapeutic session is completed. This enables the student spontaneously and openly to discuss his reactions, questions, and interpretations when they are still fresh and alive in his mind.

Another source of experience is the tape recordings of sessions he is observing, as well as recordings of previously completed cases. These may be presented to the student as a way of studying the therapeutic process and seeing the nature and problems of initial, middle, and terminal interviews. The recordings should also be made available to students who wish to listen to them and study them privately. The list of references in child therapy is another possible resource. Although the student may wish to discuss his reading experiences with the supervisor, he should be free to decide what he wishes to read, what is relevant to his own interest and purpose.

Thus the preliminary experiences to direct work as a child therapist include the orientation to and development of a theory; observation in therapy of a number of children of different ages; discussion of the process of child therapy as reflected in completed cases; study of initial, middle, and terminal interviews through tape recordings and observations; and reading experiences of theory, practice, and research in child therapy. During these experiences the "supervisor" should be available to meet with individual students to discuss their ideas, questions, or other reactions.

Having arrived at an initial theory to a point of real understanding and having observed and discussed a number of cases involving distinctly different children, the student is ready to begin the direct experiences. The exact decision as to when he is ready to begin work with children is made by the student. He must be aware of the resources and opportunities but free to decide when he wishes to initiate his own direct experience.

Instruction, caution, and direction inhibit the student, make him uncertain, and contribute to rigid and static preconceptions. The training is not aimed at teaching the student what to say and what to do or how to approach and relate to children in therapy. The preliminary experiences are offered as background to the central purpose which is the evolvement of a significant therapeutic relationship with a child. The actual experience cannot be alive unless the student is free to approach the child in his own way and to develop skill through his own insights and errors.

As a way of helping the student to feel the essence of child therapy and to experience the process of relating with a child in such a setting, the student is given the opportunity of meeting children in individual sessions who are regarded as normal, average, or well adjusted. Sessions with these youngsters enable the student to become comfortable in the therapeutic setting, to develop confidence in his ability and to discover ways of meeting the child and relating to him. The student may wish to record these sessions as a way of studying the process and the nature of his own participation.

Regular weekly meetings are scheduled between the supervisor and student. In these meetings they explore the nature and meaning of the child's behavior. At this time, the student is free to express anything he wishes, related either to the therapeutic session or to his own personal life. The "supervisor" listens in order to understand the student's experience. Sometimes the supervisor points to his own related experience which may contribute to the student's recognition, awareness, or understanding of the emerging patterns or themes in the child's behavior. In such a philosophy, the supervisor does not advise students what to do or what not to do, nor does he probe into the background of the student to analyze his motives or goals. The meetings are mutual explorations, conversations in which two persons work together to understand more fully a particular child in therapy and a particular therapeutic process. Sometimes the exploration is an examination of the case and sometimes it is an effort of the student to recognize experiences in his own background which relate to his current therapeutic work.

The experiences with average children and the supervisory sessions enable the student to develop a feeling of confidence as well as a meaningful understanding of the therapeutic process. The student is then assigned a case involving a disturbed child. It is important in making the assignment that a case be selected which can be terminated during the student's period of training. For students in training for one year it is generally not possible to carry on intensive work with more than one or two children. This usually will not be adequate to enable the student to do independent work. Even two or three years' experience is only a beginning in understanding the various dimensions of child therapy. Every therapist continues to benefit from discussion and mutual exchange with persons having a related background of experience, especially when therapists can bring to such a discussion listening attitudes and a willingness to learn and contribute to new knowledge, ideas, and approaches.

Conferences between supervisor and student continue throughout the student's training. Usually these are weekly meetings, but sometimes they occur more often, depending on the student's interest or need. The student should be free to use the meeting in his own way. He can bring a tape recording of the session and, with his supervisor, listen to it as a way of discussing the significant episodes or themes in the session. He may play back a specific segment of the interview about which he has questions. He may wish to point to some emerging insight which he would like to explore further. He may make a typescript of the interview which his supervisor reads before the meeting as a basis for discussing the significant interactions between the student-therapist and child. He may raise problems or spontaneously comment on the episodes which excited or disturbed him, the incidents he felt satisfied with and those about which he felt confused or worried. It is important in every case that the student structure the meetings, initiate the content of the discussion, and raise the questions. Sometimes the student will not discuss the current interview but will express something from his own personal experience which was evoked in his relationship with the child.

The supervisor maintains a nonjudgmental attitude, allowing the student to make his own decisions and arrive at his own evaluations and conclusions. This enables the student to continue to grow through his own self-conscious explorations and through the support and encouragement of the supervisor. The supervisor is concerned and cares about the student's growth as a child therapist. He participates by sharing the student's experience with him, and by conveying a respect and valuing of the student as a person.

The supervisor is also a learner. Every therapeutic relation is unique. He cannot understand the particular relationship and process unless he is open to the student's experience and willing to arrive at essentially new understandings.

Since most agencies require reports of therapeutic sessions, the supervisor often must request that the student write a summary and discussion of each interview. He does not, however, tell students how to write good reports or what to write but trusts that in time each student will come to express the essential dynamics of the particular case in terms of his own thoughtful examination of the material. If he is open to his experience and free to express it in his own way, he will be able to write about the basic developments of each session. The supervisor may offer suggestions or give information if this is requested by the student, but he respects the student's judgment and knows that the student is interested in developing a meaningful report. Giving the student this freedom not only eventuates in a concise, clear statement for the records but also enables the student to come to relevant self-insights. The student's growth results from a sense of inner responsibility and relatedness, from self knowledge and self experience, rather than from external standards and pressures or stereotyped phrases and forms. His work is fresh and unique because it grows out of real experience .

In summary, the following are major experiences in the training of students for work as a child therapist: (1) discussion, absorption, and integration of a theory of child therapy; (2) reading experiences on the different approaches to theory, practice, and research in child therapy; (3) observations of average, disturbed and creative children in therapy; (4) discussions with students after the observed sessions; (5) assignment of brief short-term cases with average or well-adjusted children to enable the student to evolve a significant relationship and to experience the therapeutic process; (6) assignment of cases of disturbed children which can be concluded during the student's period of "training"; and (7) conferences or supervisory hours which the student uses in his own way to explore and discuss the nature of his experiences as a therapist as well as to arrive at understandings of the dynamics and meanings of the child's play and expressions.

STUDENTS' VIEWS OF THEIR STRAINING EXPERIENCES

THE PHILOSOPHY

"This experience is a visible conscious means of studying and understanding a child through his natural medium of expression, his play. It is an opportunity to observe the child's behavior and development in a situation where he is free to express himself and to initiate a change toward self-growth which is necessary for his continued development. In play therapy, the child is not urged or forced to struggle to grow up nor must he battle with rejecting persons whose attitudes conflict with his own. He discovers ways of expressing himself which help him to realize something of himself. The world for a time belongs to the child, and he is free from the hampering of outside direction and pressure. The important factor here is the feeling and the knowledge that the child has within him one all-encompassing striving, to grow and develop himself, his unique personality. A belief in this potentiality and a deep respect for the individual's dignity, his personality, has to be a basic attitude of the therapist. Without this belief in the child, this love, it would be a highly superficial situation."

SELF-EXAMINATION

"I found that only to the degree that I was able to feel free myself and trust my feelings, only to just such a degree was I able to sense the underlying basis or motivation of a given child's feelings. On the occasions when I did not trust my own feelings and impressions I found that my sensitivity, empathy, and skill were blocked off and unavailable. In 'blocking off' my own self, I was preventing myself from making the errors which result from distorted perception or feeling. In avoiding the expression of a 'blind spot' I fell into a more serious trap. I blinded myself at these moments to the essence of the child's feelings by repressing my own feelings in the situation."

OBSERVATIONS

1. "The first few sessions I observed had little meaning for me. I felt I should be looking for something but didn't know exactly what. I thought I should be feeling in some particular way but all I felt was that I was seeing a child and an adult in a playroom. I was quite disturbed at my failure to realize what was happening, to understand the feelings and actions of the child and to comprehend the therapist's function and responsibility. Because of my own sense of inadequacy I began to criticize other student therapists. The day when I had my first therapy session with a child I stopped being critical of other students and realized that it's so much easier to sit behind the mirror and judge the other person, recognize his mistakes, and think of what he should have done than to be faced with the experience directly and have to function spontaneously as a therapist. Through my own participation I have come to understand

such terms as acceptance, respect, value, sheer being, and empathy. Before they were only concepts that had no living reality. I find that I have a much deeper feeling for the student therapist. I have learned that there is no single 'right' way to act in a given situation. The important thing is to be with the child fully as a human being, and respond to him by accepting him as he is, trying to understand what he really says and means, and allowing yourself to be a free, comfortable person in the situation. I learned also from my observations and my direct experience that limits are necessary not only to provide a definite, consistent structure for the child but also to enable the therapist to feel secure and relaxed knowing there are some matters within the relationship which cannot be violated. The area that still bothers me is how can I be one person, a consistent self in the playroom and outside. In order to be a consistent person the therapeutic philosophy must become a philosophy of life. Yet somehow I don't feel right when I try to relate with children in the nursery school and club programs in the same way that I relate to them in play therapy. How can I practice it in all of my relations when I don't have the same feeling of freedom and responsibility?"

2. "I don't think I shall ever forget the moment I observed Jerry in the play room when he was able to show his first timid gesture of aggressiveness—the frightened look in his eyes, the disbelief in his face, his searching of the therapist's face for a response. It was my feeling that in this moment, Jerry was ready to discover a real self behind the mask of timidity and gentleness, that he was not ready to face his inner aggressions openly."

3. "During the first session I observed I did not understand what was going on. I left with a feeling that I did not understand play therapy though I entered it with a clear concept of the theory and process based on our class discussions. All I saw was a child doing what he wanted, a therapist sitting nearby watching and listening, the child always speaking first and the therapist responding verbally only to the child's comments. But the second session surprised me. There was a considerable amount of hostility expressed by the child. The therapist made some interpretations that seemed to arouse the child to further expressions of his hostile feelings. I realized that every account of the child's does not have deep, hidden meaning, that much of his behavior can be accepted as meaning exactly what it appears to mean. The help comes for the child when he expresses his feelings and is accepted no matter how severe these feelings may be. The next session I observed the little girl was very dependent on the therapist to do things for her. The question arose in my mind as to just when you help the child and how much help you give. I noticed that the therapist never helped immediately but encouraged the child to do it on her own. It was interesting to see how at a certain point the therapist directly assisted the child when it appeared that she could not go on alone. My fourth observation was entirely different, the therapist actively played with the child during the entire time. It seemed more like a good friendship than a child-therapist relationship. She did a good job and was

very much at ease. Her interpretations seemed to get right at the heart of what the child was saying. She must have been encouraged after this session and she had a right to be. I thought she made a great deal of progress in understanding the child and in being comfortable herself."

4. "Because I had never observed a play therapy session before I was fascinated with the proceedings. The therapist seemed a bit stiff as she entered the room with the children. I thought she got off to a disadvantage by not having the boys leave their coats upstairs, for there was quite a struggle to get them to remove them. After this the session went smoothly. Philip was anxious and tense. He was constantly hitting Bobo and stabbing the family dolls with a dagger. At one point Tommy picked up the daddy puppet and, saying, "Daddy," threw it on the floor. At the end of the session, the therapist made her big mistake of the morning. She was trying to get the boys to put on their wraps and leave. Finally, Tommy put on his coat. The therapist turned to Philip and said, 'Tommy's a good boy. He put on his coat and hat.' Immediately Philip ran to the cupboard, got the baby bottle, and started sucking it violently. Then he ran around the room, hitting and throwing things. The therapist's inadvertent remark really set him off. He resented the implication that he was a bad boy. Philip reacted both with regression and hostility. The therapist became quite distressed after this and showed it. She had a great deal of difficulty in getting the boys to leave. It was good to see the therapist later and to realize how much she has learned from her earlier mistakes."

PRACTICE

1. "I finished my session with Gary with a queasy, empty feeling in the pit of my stomach. I found it difficult to put his deeper, underlying feelings into words even when I understood. In this session, he came out with more emotionally significant statements, such as his mother scolding him whenever he got his hands or clothes dirty and the fact that no one liked him, that he has no friends. This last statement hit me hard. It hurt to hear him say that no one really cared about him. Now I feel I must reach him, show that I care, that I understand how it is and how he feels."

2. "I was shaken when Tommy accidentally hit himself in the face with a truck. I wanted to take him in my arms and comfort him. I realized, fortunately, that these were his feelings, that this was his hurt and I could not take that away from him without depriving him of this self-experience. But the feeling was there inside me. I thought I wanted to comfort him but I saw that this was more a comfort for myself. So I said, 'Now calm down, control yourself, let him manage this thing!' I felt too that I talked too much, tried to comment every time he said something. There were times when I really missed the central feeling, but he seemed to understand that I really wanted to be with him and he overlooked my mistakes."

3. "During the time of my direct work with children I found it exceedingly difficult. Various factors in my own personality plus factors in the situation contributed to this. Right now I can say I would like to go on to further experience and training as a child therapist but several months ago I never thought that I would feel this way. The responsibility for the child and seeing some results for my work helped me to grow in confidence. This continued as I felt my relationship with the child slowly develop. My spontaneity is not what I would like it to be. I still ponder over what I should say and how. Perhaps this will come with further experience. At least, now I know that I want to go on. I think I can become a good therapist."

DISCUSSION OF SESSIONS

"Outside of the observation booth, in the discussion periods of the therapy sessions is where the real learning took place for me. The atmosphere of these discussions allowed me to express my criticisms of the way the therapist responded to the child. The freedom and the acceptance I felt even when I was critical helped me to accept the student-therapist as a learner. This freedom and acceptance I have never experienced in a classroom before and it has left a deep feeling with me. These two elements which are also the primary elements of the therapy situation have enabled me to see the important ingredients of a classroom atmosphere. And I must not stop with the classroom. They are important in all of life. At first I confused philosophy and technique. I found in some personal experiences when I tried the techniques or when they were tried on me they irritated and angered others and myself. I was ready to discard both philosophy and technique. Now I have come to reject the techniques in important personal relations but to embrace the philosophy even more wholeheartedly. It takes great faith to have faith in every individual, to sincerely respect each individual as a worthwhile person, and to accept even the obnoxious feelings and allow people freedom to express them."

THE "SUPERVISORY" CONFERENCES

"It is difficult for me to put on paper what has happened to me recently—since I have been doing my work in child therapy. While many changes taking place inside of me seem to be due to my experience in play therapy, I have had other important experiences and it is difficult to know just what has helped me most. I guess it doesn't matter whether it is the sunshine or the rain that finally provides the stimulus for growth.

"Here is my picture as I was at the beginning of the year:

"(1) I didn't know who I was: Wife? Mother? Teacher? Therapist? Administrator?

"(2) I didn't like to express my feelings. I laughed at my own sincere feelings because I was afraid someone else would laugh first.

"(3) I was afraid to express my ideas. I covered up real thought with aggressive behavior forcing people to listen to my surface thinking.

"(4) I was afraid of authority figures, withdrew into a shell with them, and never took a stand even when I knew I was right.

"(5) My first reaction to adults was one of dislike and distrust and this persisted until they proved to be otherwise.

"Yes, I realize that's pretty adolescent, but it was me. Do you want to know how I see myself now? Well, I feel I have grown up a little. I never realized that I was emotionally blocked at an adolescent level. My adolescent years were extremely stormy and difficult. I know now how certain events filled me with antagonism, suspicion, and hatred. I never really knew what being emotionally blocked meant—until now. It's like a dam holding back a mighty river. The dam finally gives way and there's nothing any more to hold back the powerful rush of water. The tumult, the outpouring of thought and feeling leaves such a fresh perspective and freedom, where before there was only restraint. Maybe it's natural that I've been carried away and perhaps gone to extremes. But there was so much I've wanted to say for such a long time and to so many people. There were so many feelings I've wanted to express and such a yearning to take a stand based on my own convictions and values.

"Having done so already I feel a leveling off. I know now that I was partly right. All adults aren't nice, friendly, honest people, but I've learned that they all aren't competitive and dishonest either. I know they often become friendly and interested when I'm friendly and interested in them. I know that I have some good ideas and that people will listen—a good many people. It isn't necessary either to take a stand 'against' people in authority. There are different points of view and these can be exchanged and discussed among adults. I know it's quite all right to have feelings and to express them without shame or explanation and without feeling sloppy or sentimental. It is surprising to find how many people will listen and try to understand. I now understand myself. I know who I am. I can distinguish my functions and roles. I am sure that my talks with you helped me to think all this through and helped me to relate in a real way with the children I am now seeing in therapy."

CONCLUDING COMMENT

In some training programs, only advanced doctoral candidates are permitted to take courses in child therapy. I believe that this is a mistake. It is my experience that the philosophy, concepts, principles, and methods of child therapy have a potential significance for students in many professional areas. Application of play therapy is possible for teachers, parents, marriage counselors, social workers, visiting teachers, and others who wish to integrate relevant principles in their working and living with children. It happens often that formal training, externally perceived and received, inhibits humanness, warmth, and spontaneity and makes it difficult for the student to relate in a personally significant way with a child. With an adult it is sometimes possible to play the therapeutic role, but children usually insist that the adult be a real person. They react negatively to techniques, skills, and the rules and procedures of a book. It takes a long time for a person with concentrated, formal training to stop trying to act like the professor in the classroom or clinic, to stop repeating the abstract concepts in the book and the dictates of a preconceived expert, and to start living the fresh, unique experience of a relationship in child therapy. It is sometimes a difficult, painful process for the "trained" student to come to see that even in a professional capacity the most significant dimension is his own spontaneous self.

The available resources to some extent determine which students will be admitted to the "training" program. It is understandable that individuals who will go on to further training and experience and eventually make child therapy their life's work should have priority. Perhaps an introductory course should then be made available to other students who wish to understand the philosophy and principles and to apply the methods in their own situations. At The Merrill-Palmer School, both doctoral and postdoctoral students in psychology and students from other professions have participated in practicum and clinical experience in child therapy. There seems to be no difference in the effectiveness of these students and their growth as therapists. The crucial requirement is their ability to enter into a significant relationship with a child and to bring to the therapy meetings a blend of personal and professional talent and skills, a natural integration of knowledge, understanding, and experience. It demands of the individual immediacy, presence, and responsibility within a concrete relationship. It requires a willingness to participate spontaneously and share with another person a vital, unique, emerging process of life and growth, offering one's self as a human being but waiting for the child to come to his own fulfillment in his own time and way.

Index